Unclaimed Property
Laws, Compliance, and Enforcement

Anthony L. Andreoli, CPA
J. Brooke Spotswood

CCH INCORPORATED
Chicago

Editorial Staff

Book Production . . . . Holly J. Porter

Index . . . . Lynn Brown

ISBN 0-8080-0777-7

4025 W. Peterson Ave.
Chicago, IL 60646-6085
1 800 248 3248
http://tax.cchgroup.com

To my wife, Margaret, who has been an inspiration to me and has provided invaluable assistance in my development of this work. I also must acknowledge my close friends and associates in the unclaimed property world who have been my inspiration over the 30 years I have been involved in this arcane field including Valerie Jundt, Vivian Herbert, Robert Shuman, and others too numerous to mention. Thank you all.

Anthony L. Andreoli

And to Lu, Taylor, and Joanna.

J. Brooke Spotswood

About the Authors

Anthony L. Andreoli, CPA. Anthony L. Andreoli is a Certified Public Accountant who has devoted his professional career to the field of unclaimed property for 30 years. Mr. Andreoli regularly consults with companies on unclaimed property compliance issues and on providing audit defense and settlement. In the past he has consulted with over 39 states in the development of their unclaimed property compliance and auditing programs. Mr. Andreoli is currently the National Director of Unclaimed Property Services for Deloitte & Touche LLP. Mr. Andreoli is a graduate of the University of Southern California in accounting and finance and is a graduate of Pepperdine University—School of Law.

J. Brooke Spotswood. J. Brooke Spotswood is a practicing attorney in the Commonwealth of Virginia and has spent 19 years in the field of unclaimed property law. He was formerly Assistant Attorney General for the Commonwealth of Virginia and represented the State Treasurer of Virginia in lawsuits for the recovery of unclaimed property. Mr. Spotswood consults with companies on unclaimed property compliance matters and lectures on the topic frequently. Mr. Spotswood is a graduate of the University of Virginia and the University of Richmond—School of Law.

Preface

The field of unclaimed property has grown dramatically over the past few years. States have become much more aggressive in enforcing their unclaimed property laws and have changed them substantially nearly every year. This has created a compliance issue that is complex and at times confusing to companies who generate and hold unclaimed money. A whole industry of unclaimed property service providers has grown up in the past ten years to address the issues of compliance with these complex and ever-changing laws.

Owners of unclaimed property can now access this information on the Internet through several web sites, including sites provided by the states themselves. The public policy goal of the unclaimed property laws has been achieved by putting into the public's hands online access to the vast databases of unclaimed money owed to individuals and corporations by the states. This has substantially raised the consciousness of unclaimed property laws, the responsibility to report unclaimed property by corporations, and the operational issues that such compliance raises.

This book is an attempt to put the entire body of unclaimed property law in one concise work that gives not only the statutory law, but also carefully analyzes the rich body of case law that has developed in the field over the past century. Many major concepts in the law of unclaimed property have come from the courts in countless decisions on what rights and obligations holders of unclaimed property have and how these laws serve to protect the interests of owners who have lost or forgotten certain of their assets. The authors have summarized the duties imposed by the statutes upon holders, have carefully analyzed the case law, and have interwoven the state administrative aspects that make unclaimed property compliance perplexing to many.

As the states step up their enforcement of their unclaimed property laws by hiring more auditors, including contingent-fee private contract auditors, holders of unclaimed property will be compelled to address the issues raised in this field. Readers should find this book a complete, self-contained reference source for most of their questions on the law, compliance with the law, and how states enforce the law.

Anthony L. Andreoli

J. Brooke Spotswood

February 2002

TABLE OF CONTENTS

Chapter 1

OVERVIEW, SCOPE, DEFINITIONS, AND HISTORICAL DEVELOPMENT OF THE LAW

¶ 101 Overview

In general, unclaimed property is property to which the owner has not, during a certain length of time specified by law, taken some action to indicate his ownership, interest, or awareness. When this non-interest or "abandonment" of the property occurs, it then becomes the obligation of the party "holding" the property to report that fact to the proper state and, concurrently or subsequently, turn the property over to the state.

The modern rationale for such laws is that the state can best preserve and protect the interest of the rightful owner and possibly reunite the owner with his forgotten property. If that objective cannot be accomplished, the state, rather than the holder, should be allowed the use of the property while it remains unclaimed by the owner. Thus, these laws reverse the principle of "finders keepers; losers weepers."

The terms "unclaimed property," "abandoned property" or "escheated property" are generally interchangeable, but different state laws may call for the use of a particular terminology. Definitions of these and other terms are discussed at ¶ 105.

Lost and found property is discussed in Chapter 6. Although such property may be "unclaimed" in the general sense, it is not generally the type of property that is covered by the unclaimed or abandoned property laws with which this discussion is primarily concerned. Disposition of lost and found property is usually covered by separate state laws that provide a mechanism for returning the property to the owner or, failing that, vesting title in the finder. However, a state may be able to take custody of such property under the common law concept of "*bona vacantia*" which is discussed at ¶ 110.02.

.01 What Is Not Covered

Because the unclaimed property laws generally do not apply to real property (i.e., land and things affixed to land), only the escheat of personal property, tangible or intangible will be discussed. The escheat of decedents' estates is not covered because that subject is primarily separate from the body of law relating to abandoned property. However, concepts pertaining to the escheat of decedents' estates occasionally overlap into the abandoned property field.

¶ 105 Definitions

Administrator—The state official (state treasurer) or department (department of revenue) charged with the administration and enforcement of the unclaimed property law.

Apparent owner—The person whose name appears on the records of the holder as the person entitled to property held issued or owing by the holder.[1]

Banking association—A bank, trust company, savings bank, industrial bank, land bank, safe deposit company, private banker, or any organization defined by other law as a bank or banking organization.[2]

Business association—A nonpublic corporation, joint stock company, investment company, business trust, partnership, or association for business purposes of two or more individuals, whether or not for profit, including a banking organization, insurance company, or utility.[3]

Cut-off date—The date prescribed in the unclaimed property law for the determination of what items of property have met the escheat period.

Domicile—The state of incorporation of a corporation and the state of the principal place of business of an unincorporated person.[4]

Escheat—At common law, the term referred to the return of tenurial land to the lord from whom the tenure was derived because of the death of the tenant without an heir eligible to inherit, or the occurrence of some other event that interrupted the normal course of descent. In some states, "escheat" is used only with respect to property that has absolutely vested in the state. Other states may use the term in a broader sense to include property that the state holds as custodian

[1] Act Sec. 1(2) of the Uniform Unclaimed Property Act (UUPA 1981).

[2] Act Sec. 1(4) of UUPA 1981.

[3] Act Sec.1(5) of UUPA 1981.

[4] Act Sec. 1(6) of UUPA 1981.

to claim by the rightful owner. As used in this discussion, "escheat" means the transfer of title or possession of property to the state, whether or not it may be reclaimed by the owner.

Escheat period—The period of time required by the applicable state law that must elapse before the property escheats or is presumed to be abandoned to the state. For example, the "escheat period" for miscellaneous intangible personal property is usually five years after it became payable or distributable.[5] The "escheat period" is also referred to as the "holding period" or "dormancy period."

Financial organization—Any savings and loan association, building and loan association, credit union (cooperative bank), or investment company.

Holder—A person, wherever organized or domiciled, who is:

- In possession of property belonging to another,
- A trustee, or
- Indebted to another on an obligation.[6]

Insurance company—An association, corporation, fraternal or mutual benefit organization, whether or not for profit, that is engaged in providing insurance coverage, including accident, burial, casualty, credit life, contract performance, dental, fidelity, fire, health, hospitalization, illness, life (including endowments and annuities), malpractice, marine, mortgage, surety, and wage protection insurance.[7]

Intangible property—Includes:

- Monies, checks, drafts, deposits, interest, dividends, and income;
- Credit balances, customer overpayments, gift certificates,
- Security deposits, refunds, credit memos, unpaid wages, unused airline tickets, and unidentified remittances;
- Stocks and other intangible ownership interests in business associations;
- Monies deposited to redeem stocks, bonds, coupons, and other securities, or to make distributions;
- Amounts due and payable under the terms of insurance policies; and
- Amounts distributable from a trust or custodial fund established under a plan to provide health, welfare, pension, vacation, severance, retirement, death, stock purchase, profit

[5] Act Sec. 2 of UUPA 1981.

[6] Act Sec. 1(8) of UUPA 1981.

[7] Act Sec. 1(9) of UUPA 1981.

sharing, employee savings, supplemental unemployment insurance, or similar benefits.[8]

Last known address—A description of the location of the apparent owner sufficient for the purpose of the delivery of mail.[9] This is usually defined as a three-line address containing a name, street address, city, state and zip code.

Lawful charges—Charges imposed by a holder against property in the holder's possession that are specifically authorized either by statute, other than the state's unclaimed property law, or by a valid, enforceable contract.

National Association of Unclaimed Property Administrators (NAUPA)—The national membership organization of state unclaimed property administrators. NAUPA is now affiliated with the National Association of State Treasurers (NAST).

Owner—A depositor in case of a deposit, a beneficiary in case of a trust, other than a deposit in trust, a creditor, claimant or payee in case of other choses in action, or any person having a legal or equitable interest in property subject to the 1981 Uniform Unclaimed Property Act (UUPA 1981), or his or her legal representative.[10]

Person—An individual, business association, state or other government, governmental subdivision or agency, public corporation, public authority, estate, trust, two or more persons having a joint or common interest, or any other legal or commercial entity.[11]

Reinstatable property—Property that has been written off, service-charged, or otherwise deleted from the accounting records of a holder but which has not been held for the statutory escheat period. Although such property is not reportable or payable to the state, it represents a future obligation of the holder, either to the rightful owner if claimed or to the state when the escheat period has elapsed.

Report—(Noun): The forms or documents filed by the holder with the state, listing the items of escheated property and applicable owner information as required by the state's unclaimed property statutes; (Verb): The act of furnishing the required unclaimed property "report" to the state.

Uniform Unclaimed Property Act—The 1981 Uniform Unclaimed Property Act (UUPA 1981) serves as the basis for most states' legislation. Some states, however, use either the 1954 Uniform Disposition of Unclaimed Property Act, the 1966 Revised Uniform Disposition

---

[8] Act Sec. 1(10) of UUPA 1981.
[9] Act Sec. 1(11) of UUPA 1981.
[10] Act Sec. 1(12) of UUPA 1981.
[11] Act Sec. 1(13) of UUPA 1981.

of Unclaimed Property Act, or the 1995 Uniform Unclaimed Property Act.

Utility—Any person who owns or operates for public use any plant equipment, property, franchise, or license for the transmission of communications or the production, storage, transmission, sale, delivery, or furnishing of electricity, water, steam, or gas.[12]

¶ 110 Historical Development of the Law

In this chapter, the history, development, general scheme, and significant features of escheat and unclaimed property laws will be discussed.

.01 Escheat

At common law, escheat was the concept under which land held by tenure was returned to the lord from whom the tenure was derived upon the occurrence of some event which interrupted the normal course of descent, such as death of the tenant without heirs (see definition at ¶ 105). The modern concept of escheat refers to a process by which the state acquires title and/or custody of real or personal property that is unclaimed by, undistributed to, or presumed abandoned by the rightful owner.

.02 Bona Vacantia

While escheat in the common law related only to land, a similar concept, bona vacantia, applied to personal property. Bona vacantia (literally, "vacant goods") were subject to claim only by the crown on the basis of the "royal prerogative."[13]

The crown's entitlement to bona vacantia was premised on the absence of any other owner as opposed to the escheat rationale that the crown was ultimate heir or was the assignee of the last tenant. The hypothesis was that possession by the crown was more equitable than that of a stranger and that the crown's ownership would remove the potential for conflicting claims by private parties.[14] This rationale of bona vacantia can be found in modern statutory law, which provides that the state is the owner of all property of which there is no other owner.

Bona vacantia covered relatively narrow categories of property such as property of persons dying without heirs, property held in failed

[12] Act Sec. 1(15) of UUPA 1981.

[13] Blackstone, Sir William, *Commentaries of the Laws of England,* 1783 ed. Reprint, recent U.S. ed. Garland Publishing, Inc., 1978.

[14] Garrison, *Escheats, Abandoned Property and Their Revenue Aspects,* 35 Ky.L.J. 302 (1947).

trusts, property held by dissolved corporations, and lost or abandoned property such as shipwrecks, treasure troves, waifs, and estrays.

Where bona vacantia occurred because of death without heirs, the deceased's personalty passed to the crown subject to certain rights of the widow to distribution of a portion of the personal property.[15]

.03 Modern Statutory Development

As the common law of England (the foundation of American jurisprudence) began to be supplanted by the statutory law of various states of the American Republic, abandoned property laws were gradually established in the statutes. Early abandoned property statutes were of limited application and more closely resembled true escheat laws. In 1908, Massachusetts enacted a statute covering unclaimed bank deposits. In 1915, California adopted a statute providing for the escheat of money deposited with a bank.[16] This early statute applied only to bank deposits and required a judicial proceeding to be filed by the state attorney general to have the particular deposits declared abandoned and ordered turned over to the state, thereby terminating the rights of owners to recover their funds. Many eastern states had similar laws, some of which encompassed a broader range of property.

¶ 115 The 1954 Uniform Disposition of Unclaimed Property Act

Although several states such as New York, Massachusetts, and Michigan had relatively comprehensive abandoned property laws, it was not until 1954 that the National Conference of Commissioners on Uniform State Laws proposed to the states the Uniform Disposition of Unclaimed Property Act (the 1954 Uniform Act). The 1954 Uniform Act had certain primary characteristics:

- It was custodial in nature, i.e., the state was to act as custodian of the property until claimed by the rightful owner;
- It was comprehensive in scope because it applied to any type of unclaimed intangible property;
- It was theoretically a consumer protection law because it served to safeguard the owner's property and provide a mechanism for reuniting the owner with his property; and
- It was a revenue measure for the enacting states.

---

[15] Statute of Distributions, 1670, 22 & 23 Can. 2, c. 10, § 23.

[16] 1915 Cal. Stat., Ch. 84, II1.

.01 The Purposes of the 1954 Uniform Act

The purposes of the 1954 Uniform Act were summarized by the National Conference of Commissioners on Uniform State Laws as follows:

> The Uniform Disposition of Unclaimed Property Act, if adopted by the states, will serve to protect the interests of owners, to relieve the holders from annoyance, expense, and liability, to preclude multiple liability, and to give the adopting state the use of some considerable sums of money that otherwise would, in effect become a windfall to the holders thereof.[17]

Although this model legislation has been amended, slightly in 1966, much more comprehensively in 1981, and most recently in 1995, the rationale of the Act remains unchanged (see ¶ 305).

.02 General Scheme of Unclaimed Property Laws

Broadly stated, unclaimed property laws in the United States (particularly those based on the Uniform Disposition of Unclaimed Property Act) contain the following provisions:

- Intangible personal property such as bank deposits, dividends, insurance benefits, trust fund distributions, sums owing on money orders or traveler's checks or other debts (wages, credit balances, etc.) that have not been collected or received by the person entitled thereto, or with respect to which the "holder" has had no contact with the "owner" for a period of time specified by law, must be reported to the appropriate state administrator by the holder;
- The report must contain certain information required by law such as the owner's name and address, if known, the type and amount of the property, and any other information specified by law;
- The state administrator will then attempt to notify the owner as to the existence of the property so that the owner can claim the property from the holder. The type of notification attempted by the state varies according to the particular law. If the owner is not located within a certain time, the holder must pay or deliver the property to the state.
- The state then has the use of the property until claimed by the owner or the owner's successor. The state maintains this liability in perpetuity. Upon payment or delivery of the property made in good faith to the state, the holder is discharged from any further liability with respect to the property. Some state

[17] Uniform Laws Annotated 73.

laws make similar provision for tangible personal property, such as contents of safe deposit boxes or miscellaneous types of tangible property which may be unclaimed by the owner at the requisite time period.

.03 Derivative Rights

Generally, the rights of the state to unclaimed property are derived from the owners. Although there are exceptions, the state succeeds to whatever rights the owner of the property may have. The U.S. Supreme Court analogized the state administrator as "conservator" in *Connecticut Mutual Life Insurance Co. v. Moore.*[18] This case, which is discussed in further detail at ¶ 205.06, demonstrates that the determination of what rights the owner possessed frequently becomes the focal point for disputes between states and holders.

States may also insist that the holder afford at least as favorable treatment as owners would receive when dealing with the holder, even though the holder may not be under a legal obligation to provide such treatment to owners but does so as a matter of goodwill or for public relations purposes. Forfeiture agreements between holders and owners may not be a bar to escheat if they are found to be "private escheat laws."

.04 Constitutionality

Custodial-type escheat laws, such as UUPA 1981 or its predecessor the 1954 Uniform Act, have been held by the U.S. Supreme Court to be a constitutional exercise of state power. Such laws have withstood attack based on contentions of violation of due process and impairment of contract, even though certain laws may dispense with contractual conditions that may be proper between the contracting parties.[19] Constitutionality of unclaimed property laws is discussed in further detail at ¶ 205.

.05 Jurisdiction to Escheat

The right of a state to escheat property is well settled by the courts. The U.S. Supreme Court in *Texas v. New Jersey*[20] held that the primary right to escheat intangible personal property belongs to the state of the owner's last known address, as shown on the records of the holder. Therefore, the primary rule of jurisdiction established in *Texas v. New Jersey* is based on the last known address of the owner as evidenced in the holder's records. A Delaware case held that even though the last known address of an owner was known to be incorrect,

[18] SCt, 333 US 541, 68 SCt 682 (1948).
[19] *Id.*
[20] SCt, 379 US 674, 85 SCt 626 (1965).

the test established in *Texas v. New Jersey* did not require a "correct" last known address, but rather only a "last known address."[21]

If no last known address is shown on the holder's records, the property is escheatable by the state of the holder's domicile, e.g., the state of the holder's incorporation. If the state of the last known address does not provide, by law, for the escheat of the property, the state of the holder's domicile has the power to escheat, subject to the right of the state of last known address to recover the property if and when its law makes provision for escheat of such property. This rule is referred to as the "backup rule."

> ***CAUTION:*** A common misconception exists that the lack of an address relieves a holder from the obligation to report and pay unclaimed property. This misconception is incorrect and places the property in the backup rule category and such property is reportable to the state of the holder's incorporation. Property that is calculated as a result of an estimate is by its very nature "no-address" property subject to reporting under the backup rule.

With respect to tangible property, real or personal, the Court in *Texas v. New Jersey* noted that the rule has always been that the state in which the property is located (its situs) has jurisdiction to escheat. This jurisdictional scheme was later upheld by the U.S. Supreme Court in *Pennsylvania v. New York* [22] and more recently in *Delaware v. New York*.[23]

.06 Private Escheat Laws

In an effort to avoid turning property over to the states, some holders have adopted bylaws or utilized contractual provisions to cause a loss of the owners' property rights prior to the time the property would escheat. In *New Jersey v. Jefferson Lake Sulphur Co.*,[24] a corporation amended its charter to provide that dividends not claimed by the owner within three years of the date of issuance would be forfeited to the corporation. Because unclaimed dividends became the property of the corporation prior to the running of the escheat period, the corporation argued that there was no unclaimed property to escheat. The Court rejected this argument, stating that the company had attempted to establish a private escheat law and that such a law cannot circumvent the operation of a public one.

Similarly, in *Screen Actors Guild, Inc. v. Cory*,[25] a bylaw of the corporation that provided that "residuals" paid to the Guild for transmittal to its members would be forfeited to the Guild if unclaimed for

[21] *Nellius v. Tampax Inc.*, 394 A2d 233 (1978).

[22] SCt, 407 US 206, 92 SCt 2075 (1972).

[23] SCt, 507 US 490, 113 SCt 1550 (1993).

[24] 36 N.J. 577, 178 A2d 329 (1962).

[25] 91 Cal. App. 3d 111, 154 Cal. Rptr. 77 (Cal. App. 2d Dist. 1979).

six years was held invalid as against the state's Unclaimed Property Law. The Court, citing *Jefferson Lake Sulphur Co.* for the proposition that a private escheat law cannot circumvent a public one, stated that the Unclaimed Property Law, "as a law established for a private reason, cannot be contravened by a private agreement, which is what plaintiff's bylaw is."

This principle was again enunciated in *Blue Cross of Northern California v. Cory,*[26] in which the court invalidated a provision inserted by Blue Cross in its insurance contracts that stated that the failure of a subscriber to negotiate a check issued by Blue Cross in payment of a claim within six months would result in the claim being withdrawn. Citing *Screen Actors Guild and Jefferson Lake Sulphur Co.,* the court held the provision to be invalid as a matter of law because it constituted an attempt to establish a private escheat law in contravention of the state Unclaimed Property Law.

.07 Sources of States' Laws

The National Association of Unclaimed Property Administrators (NAUPA) maintains a web site that contains the unclaimed property laws of all of the states as well as links to individual state unclaimed property administrators at www.unclaimed.org.

Copies of most states' laws and their reporting forms and instructions are available on their web sites. Some states require electronic reporting of unclaimed property if there are 50 or more unclaimed accounts to report. The software to report electronically is also available on many states' sites.

A complete matrix of property types, holding periods, and reporting due dates is available for a nominal charge on the NAUPA web site at www.unclaimed.org.

[26] 120 Cal. App. 3d 723, 174 Cal. Rptr. 901 (1981).

Chapter 2

FOUNDATION OF THE LAW OF UNCLAIMED PROPERTY

¶ 201 Overview

In this chapter, the constitutionality of unclaimed property law is discussed at ¶ 205. The Derivative Rights Doctrine is explained at ¶ 210. Statute of limitations issues are discussed at ¶ 215.

¶ 205 Constitutionality of Unclaimed Property Law

Today, little doubt remains as to the constitutionality of state unclaimed property statutes, at least those patterned after UUPA 1981. This paragraph will review the principal cases decided by the U.S. Supreme Court dealing with the constitutionality of such laws.

.01 *Provident Institution for Savings v. Malone*

Although the Supreme Court previously had numerous opportunities to decide constitutional questions relating to escheat of lands or decedents' estates, it was not until 1911 that the Court had occasion to deal with a pure abandoned property statute in *Provident Institution for Savings v. Malone*.[1] In that case, a Massachusetts savings bank claimed that a state statute was unconstitutional because it allowed the state to petition the probate court for an order of payment for deposits held by savings institutions where no deposit had been made, no interest had been added to the passbook, no check had been drawn against the account for 30 years, and no claimant or depositor could be found. A copy of the petition had been served on the bank, and notice to depositors had been published in newspapers. The statute also provided that the accounts turned over to the treasurer would be held subject to claim by the true owners and would accrue interest while held.

In upholding the constitutionality of the statute, the Court approached the statute from the standpoint that it was for the sole

[1] SCt, 221 US 660, 31 SCt 661 (1911).

benefit of the true owners. Citing *Cunnius v. Reading School District,*[2] the Court stated that "[t]he right and power so to legislate, is undoubted." Discussing the point that the Massachusetts provision was not an escheat law but a custodial statute, the Court noted that the charter and bylaws of the bank, upon its dissolution, did not prevent payment of unlocated depositors' funds to their legal representatives. Thus, it seemed logical that the state could exercise the power of a legal representative prior to dissolution. In response to the bank's argument that the statute only applied to abandoned deposits in savings banks, the Court found the classification to be reasonable.

.02 *First National Bank v. California*

In 1923, the Court considered a state statute relating to unclaimed bank deposits. In *First National Bank v. California,*[3] the California statute provided for the attorney general to bring an action to escheat bank deposits where for more than twenty years, there had been no deposit, withdrawal, or notice to the bank of the owner's current address. The Court held that the statute could not be applied to deposits in national banks. Viewed as instrumentalities of the federal government, national banks were created by laws whose purpose was to construct a banking system extending throughout the country. Such a purpose, the Court reasoned, could not be frustrated by state laws. The California law would cause such frustration by attempting "to qualify in an unusual way agreements between national banks and their customers long understood to arise when the former received deposits under their plainly granted powers."

The Court further reasoned that "the depositors of a national bank often live in many different states and countries; and certainly it would not be an immaterial thing if the deposits of all were subject to seizure by the state where the bank happened to be located."

.03 *Security Savings Bank v. California*

Shortly after its decision in *First National Bank,* the Court decided another case, *Security Savings Bank v. California,*[4] upholding the constitutionality of the state's escheat statute. Rejecting the bank's argument that the law's provisions for service of notice were inadequate to bind all depositors and that the bank would still be liable to them, the Court held that the seizure of the property was affected by personal service upon the bank. The service provisions were sufficient to bind all interested persons. As to the objection that the statute allowed service by publication without requiring an affidavit that personal service was not possible, the Court held that this determina-

[2] SCt, 198 US 458, 25 SCt 721 (1905).
[3] SCt, 262 US 366, 43 SCt 602 (1923).
[4] SCt, 263 US 282, 44 SCt 108 (1923).

tion by the state legislature did not constitute a denial of due process. In response to the contention that the statute improperly provided for publication of notice in the county of the state capitol rather than in the county in which the particular bank was located, Justice Brandeis, writing for the Court, said "the question 'is one of local experience on which the court ought to be very slow to declare that the state legislature was wrong in its facts' or abused its discretion."

> ***COMMENT:*** It should be noted at this point that the Supreme Court did not seem to have a clear idea of where it was going on the escheat issue. In *Provident Institution,* the Court upheld a type of custodial law and implied that it may have ruled differently on a true escheat type statute. In *Security Savings Bank,* the Court expressly stated that it was immaterial which type of statute was involved; while, in *First National Bank,* it held that an escheat type statute was not applicable to a national bank. It seemed to rely mainly upon the factor of state interference with the national banking system rather that the fact that the statute was in the nature of a true escheat law.

.04 *United States v. Klein*

The next significant unclaimed property case to be decided by the Supreme Court was *United States v. Klein,*[5] in which the United States challenged the validity of a Pennsylvania statute authorizing the escheat of money paid into federal courts in the state where the funds had remained unclaimed for a period of seven years. The funds involved had been paid into the registry of a federal district court in Pennsylvania and, not having been claimed for at least five years, were deposited in the U.S. Treasury as required by federal laws. The United States did not assert title to the money, but argued that the state court's escheat judgment was an unconstitutional interference with a court of the United States, an invasion of its sovereignty, and an attempt to exercise jurisdiction over absent owners and moneys, neither of which were shown to be present in the state.

In upholding the validity of the state statute's applicability to the funds, the Court held that the possession of property by a federal court does not affect the validity of state court judgments concerning the property that are not "in conflict and to make effective such decisions by its control of the property." According to the Supreme Court, the federal court's only other function regarding the money was to pay it to its owner:

> [n]either the nature of the suit in the District Court nor the federal statutes preclude transfer of or change in the interest of the un-

[5] SCt, 303 US 276, 58 SCt 536 (1938).

known claimants, either by judicial proceeding in the state court or otherwise, pending final disposition of the fund by the federal court.

.05 *Anderson National Bank v. Luckett*

In a landmark case, *Anderson National Bank v. Luckett*,[6] the Court dealt with a Kentucky statute, which it described as "a comprehensive scheme for the administration of abandoned bank deposits." Similar to the 1981 Uniform Unclaimed Property Act (UUPA 1981), the statute declared the following presumptively abandoned: deposits held by all banks in the state concerning which the owner had not negotiated in writing, changed the amount, requested interest on his passbook, or notified the bank of some other transaction, within a period of 10 years in the case of demand deposits, or 25 years in the case of non-demand deposits. Banks holding such deposits were required to report them annually to the state, and a copy of the report was to be posted on the courthouse door in the county where the bank was located. After a specified time, the bank was then instructed to turn the deposits over to the state where they would remain subject to claim by the owners, unless the state pursued judicial proceedings to establish conclusively that the deposits were abandoned, in which case a claim could be made within five years after such determination.

The bank contended that the statute violated the Constitution for two reasons:

1. The requirement that the deposits be surrendered without prior judicial proceedings violated due process, and
2. The statute infringed upon the national banking laws and represented an unconstitutional interference with instrumentalities of the federal government.

In rejecting the due process argument, the Court noted that the power of the state to compel, through proper procedures, surrender of abandoned bank deposits is "no longer open to doubt." It was the Court's opinion that the posting of notice was as effective as newspaper publication, especially when accompanied by seizure of the property by the state. Strict judicial proceedings, held the Court, were not an indispensable requirement of due process because the statute afforded the depositors an adequate opportunity to be heard.

As to the contention that the statute infringed upon national banks, the Court refused to apply or overrule its decision in *First National Bank v. California* but instead chose to distinguish the cases. The Court explained that the California statute condemned in *First National Bank* provided for the "escheat of depositors' accounts merely

[6] SCt, 321 US 233, 64 SCt 599 (1944).

because of their dormancy for the specified period without any determination of abandonment in fact." Under the Kentucky statute, however, "dormancy without more is made the statutory ground for the state's taking inactive bank accounts into its custody, the state assuming the bank's obligation to the depositors . . . Escheat or forfeiture to the state may follow, but only on proof of abandonment in fact."

The Court concluded by stating that "we cannot say that the protective custody of long inactive bank accounts, for which the Kentucky statute provides, and which in many circumstances may operate for the benefit of depositors, will deter them from placing their funds in national banks in that state."

> ***COMMENT:*** While the *Anderson* case appeared to settle the question of the state's power to take custody of abandoned deposits, it was curious that the Court did not simply overrule the *First National Bank* decision. Perhaps the Court felt that circumstances may someday arise which may call for resurrection of the *First National Bank* case.

.06 *Connecticut Mutual Life Insurance Co. v. Moore*

In the cases decided after *Anderson,* the Court's decision shifted to narrower, but equally thorny, issues concerning constitutionality and conflicting claims between states. *Connecticut Mutual Life Insurance Co. v. Moore*[7] was a transitional case marking this shift.

In *Connecticut Mutual,* nine insurance companies incorporated outside of the state of New York brought suit seeking a declaration that New York's abandoned property law was unconstitutional in its application to proceeds of life insurance policies issued for delivery in New York on the lives of residents of New York. The New York statute provided for the presumption of abandonment of sums owing on life or endowment policies that remained unclaimed for seven years.

The first contention of unconstitutionality was that the state impaired the obligation of contract within the meaning of Article I, Section 10 of the U.S. Constitution, in that the "statute transforms into a liquidated obligation an obligation which was previously only conditional." This claim was based on a provision of the statute that deemed abandoned moneys that would be owed on any life insurance policy where the insured, if living, would have attained the limiting age under the mortality table on which the reserve was based. The insurance companies also argued that the statute unconstitutionally dispensed with the policy requirement that the policy be surrendered as a condition to liability arising under the policy.

---

[7] SCt, 333 US 541, 68 SCt 682 (1948).

The Court soundly rejected the impairment of contract argument as follows:

> We think that the classification of abandoned property established by the statute describes property that may fairly be said to be abandoned property and subject to the care and custody of the state and ultimately to escheat. The fact that claimants against the companies would, under the policies, be required to comply with certain policy conditions does not affect our conclusion. The state may more properly be custodian and beneficiary of abandoned property than any person.

The Court did not stop at this point, however, but went on to expound upon its reasoning:

> We see no constitutional reason why a state may not proceed administratively, as here, to take over the care of abandoned property rather than adopt a plan through judicial process as in *Security Bank v. California, supra.* There is ample provision for notice to beneficiaries and for administrative and judicial hearing of their claims and payment of same. There is no possible injury to any beneficiary. The right of appropriation by the state of abandoned property has existed for centuries in the common law.

Having disposed of the Contract Clause issue, the Court proceeded to deal with the insurance companies' primary contention that, under the Due Process Clause of the Fourteenth Amendment, New York had no power to take custody of the unclaimed funds. This issue and the general question of the power or jurisdiction of the states to escheat abandoned or unclaimed property is discussed at ¶ 510.

¶ 210 Derivative Rights Doctrine

One of the most important concepts concerning the 1954 Uniform Disposition of Unclaimed Property Act and its progeny is the derivative nature of the rights passing to the state under the Act. Although there are certain exceptions to the rule, the property rights that escheat to the state are generally only those rights that the owner of the property possessed.

The nature and extent of the owner's rights in the property often become the critical issues in determining whether the property passes to the state or under what conditions the property will escheat.

Courts have frequently enunciated the derivative rights doctrine and have often grappled with issues concerning the nature of the owner's rights. In *Bank of America v. Cranston,*[8] the Court succinctly stated the doctrine as follows:

[8] 252 Cal. App. 2d 208, 60 Cal. Rptr. 336 (1967).

> The Controller's rights under the act are derivative. He succeeds, subject to the act's provisions, to whatever rights the owners of the abandoned property may have. In State, by *Parsons v. Standard Oil Co.,* (1950), 5 N.J. 281, 74 A.2d 565 . . . where a similar statute was concerned, it is stated: "The State's right is purely derivative; it takes only the interest of the unknown or absentee owner."

.01 Application of Derivative Rights Doctrine

A classic application of the derivative rights doctrine occurred in *Murdock v. Stetson.*[9] The court concluded that gift certificates entitling the owner to obtain Stetson hats did not escheat under the state's custodial escheat law because the certificates contained a provision that they must be redeemed within one year from issuance. The court also held that the certificate itself must be presented for any liability to honor it to arise. Because the state could not produce the certificates and because more than one year had elapsed since issuance of the certificates in question, there was no liability on the part of the company and, thus, no property to escheat. The issue of whether gift certificates were actually honored after one year was not discussed in *Murdock.*

> ***CAUTION:*** Certain types of property present difficult questions in determining what rights, if any, the state derives. Gift certificates are a good example of this difficulty. Does a gift certificate represent tangible or intangible property? If tangible, what specific items of property escheat? If intangible, does cash escheat if the issuer will only honor the certificate in goods or services? Does the full face value escheat in such a case or some lesser amount?

Insurance policies. Insurance policies often contain various conditions to payment by the issuer. Aside from occurrence of the basic contingency that gives rise to the insurer's liability (such as death, illness, or injury), policies may include requirements that the policy be surrendered, a release executed, or proof of death be furnished before the insurer will be liable to pay. In *Connecticut Mutual Life Insurance Co. v. Moore,*[10] the U.S. Supreme Court held that a state abandoned property statue could validly dispense with certain procedural prerequisites that might normally apply to claimants under life insurance policies. The Court concluded that no unconstitutional impairment of the obligation of contracts would occur by allowing the state abandoned property law to apply to life insurance proceeds, even though the statute dispensed with the requirements of proof of death and surrender of the policy.

Thus, *Connecticut Mutual* recognized that while the state's rights are basically derivative, state law might dispense with certain require-

[9] 32 Pa.D. & C. 2d 300 (1963).

[10] SCt, 333 US 541, 68 SCt 682 (1948).

ments that might apply against the owner. The result appeared to be based on the state's overriding interest in collecting abandoned property and also on the fact that the dispensed-with requirements were merely procedural prerequisites to the liability for payment that the company would normally incur.

Unliquidated claims. A line of recent cases have dealt with the question of whether Alabama's version of UUPA 1981 applies to unliquidated claims, i.e., alleged debts, the validity of which is not conceded by the holder or established judicially. In *Allstate Ins. Co. v. Eagerton,*[11] the dispute centered on amounts allegedly owing on unpresented drafts issued by Allstate for the purpose of settling claims. The court found that the drafts were offered in settling unliquidated and unconceded claims and, thus, did not represent monies due and owing the payees of the unpresented drafts. The amounts, therefore, reflected by the drafts were not subject to the unclaimed property act.

This decision was followed in *Aetna Casualty and Surety Ins. Co. v. State of Alabama,*[12] which involved facts similar to the *Allstate* case. *Mason and Dixon Lines v. Eagerton,*[13] another Alabama case, involved certain "credits" for shipping bills of a motor common carrier licensed by the Interstate Commerce Commission. The court, citing the *Allstate* and *Aetna* cases, found that the "credits" were not unqualifiedly due anyone and did not represent monies necessarily due and owing to residents of Alabama. Thus, the state was not entitled under Alabama's unclaimed property act to recover the amounts represented by the credits.

In these Alabama cases, the decisions seem to turn on the issue of whether, in fact, the property in question was admitted to be due someone, or in other words, whether the property constituted liquidated claims. In each case, the court held that there was insufficient proof to support the contention that the property represented actual, admitted, or established debts owing by the alleged holders.

Pari-mutuel and concert tickets. The derivative doctrine has also been the implied basis for decisions relating to redemption or refund of pari-mutuel and concert tickets. In *Oregon Racing Commission v. Multnomah Kennel Club,*[14] the court held that funds representing unredeemed pari-mutuel wagering tickets were not subject to the Oregon unclaimed property act because there was no liability to pay unless and until the winning tickets were presented for encashment.

The Nebraska Supreme Court reached a somewhat contrary result when it held that unclaimed pari-mutuel wagers were subject to Ne-

---

[11] 403 So. 2d 172 (1981).

[12] 414 So. 2d 455 (1982).

[13] 555 F. Supp. 434 (1982).

[14] 242 Or. 572, 411 P.2d 63 (1966).

braska's unclaimed property statutes because persons wagering in pari-mutuel transactions acquire an interest in the total money so wagered.[15]

A North Carolina court of appeals found that the unclaimed proceeds of tickets to Elvis Presley concerts that were canceled because of the singer's death were not claimable by the state because a refund was only required when a ticket holder presented the ticket and requested a refund of the ticket price.[16]

.02 Derivative Rights and Statutes of Limitations

The principal exception to the rule that the state succeeds only to the rights of the owner appears in relation to the statute of limitations. Ordinarily, a holder of unclaimed property, such as unclaimed wages, could assert the bar of the statute of limitations against an owner who appeared to claim his forgotten wages after the applicable period had run. However, under Act Sec. 16 of UUPA 1981, such a statute of limitations is expressly declared not to prevent the property from being deemed abandoned or escheated nor to otherwise affect any duty regarding the reporting or payment of such property to the state.

The State of Washington initially omitted Act Sec. 16 from its version of UUPA 1981, and in *Pacific Northwest Bell v. Dept. of Revenue,*[17] the Court held that the state was subject to the same statute of limitations defense the company could assert if the owner appeared to claim the property. Hence, by the time that the period had run for the property to be deemed abandoned, the statute of limitations has also run, thereby effectively eliminating the company's obligation both to the owner and to the state.

Another application of the derivative principle in a statute of limitations context appeared in *Bank of America v. Cory,*[18] where the court held that the Bank of America could not assert that the statute of limitations barred the state controller from suing to recover service charges and interest withheld from dormant deposits. The court reasoned that because there was no period of limitations under California law for depositors to bring actions against banks with respect to deposits, the State Controller, standing in the shoes of the depositors, was likewise not barred from prosecuting an action regarding such deposits.

See ¶ 215 for other statute of limitations issues.

---

[15] *Marsh v. Nebraska State Board of Agriculture,* 217 Neb. 622, 350 N.W. 2d 535 (1984).

[16] *North Carolina State Treasurer v. City of Asheville,* 61 N.C. App. 140, 300 SE2d 283 (1983).

[17] 78 Wash. 2d 961 (1971).

[18] 164 Cal. App. 3d 66 (1985).

.03 Waiver Doctrine—The State Benefits from Waivers to Owners

Under the Derivative Rights Doctrine, the state may insist that it receive at least as favorable treatment from the holder as the owner would enjoy. The notion that the holder may not waive rights that it may have when dealing with owners and then seek to impose those same rights against the state to eliminate or reduce its escheat liability was first articulated in *Bank of America v. Cranston.*[19] In that case, the bank argued that travelers checks outstanding more than four years should be presumed lost or stolen. The bank argued that because the application signed by the purchaser contained a provision requiring notification to the bank in the event of loss or theft, the customers should be deemed to have breached their agreement with the bank, thereby relieving it from liability on the traveler's checks. The Court rejected this argument, stating:

> Here the Bank represents to prospective purchasers that there is no time limit within which its traveler's checks must be presented, and then urges the court to apply the sought for presumptions and to hold, the purchaser having failed to give prompt notice of the presumed loss or theft, that the Bank is no longer required to respect and redeem its obligation.
>
> We believe the Bank's representation to purchasers of traveler's checks had the effect of a waiver of any right to repudiate the obligation thereunder for non-timely presentation.
>
> It is probable that the Bank would never attempt such a forfeiture against a traveler's check purchaser, and that the point is now raised only as against the controller. If this is so, the derivative nature of the controller's rights under the act must be borne in mind. If the owner of presumed abandoned property has any rights, those rights accrue in their entirety of the Controller.
>
> The Bank may not waive its contractual rights as to a purchaser of traveler's checks, and then enforce those same rights as against the state and the Controller.

Similarly, the Supreme Court of South Carolina applied the waiver doctrine against an insurance company's argument that the six-year statute of limitations has run on certain life insurance policies prior to the 1971 enactment of the state's unclaimed property act; it was not liable to report or pay the policy proceeds to the state.[20] The company, however, conceded that it would not refuse to pay the policyholders and beneficiaries of the policies in question because of the lapse of time. Ruling in favor of the Tax Commission, the court held as follows:

> The commissioner's rights under the act are derivative. It succeeds, subject to the act, to the rights of the abandoned property owners. It takes only the interest of the absent or unknown owner.

---

[19] 252 Cal. App. 2d 208 (1967).

[20] *South Carolina Tax Commission v. Metropolitan Life Insurance Co.*, 266 S.C. 34, 221 SE2d 522 (1975).

> It is clear from the record that the respondent would never attempt a forfeiture against a policyholder, and that the point is now raised only as against the Tax Commission. The derivative nature of the Commission's rights under the act must be considered. If the owner of presumed abandoned property has any rights, which are conceded by Metropolitan, these rights accrue in their entirety to the Commission. Metropolitan may not waive its contractual rights to these policies against the policy holders, and then enforce those same rights against the Tax Commission.

PLANNING NOTE: Because the state, in effect, "stands in the shoes" of the owner with respect to unclaimed property, it is necessary to examine the rights of the owner in order to determine whether and to what extent the property will escheat to the state. Although holders may argue that their obligations to report or pay such property to the state is limited to the extent of their obligations to owners, the state may insist that it be afforded the same treatment the owners would receive from the holders.

Unclaimed property examiners apply this test when reviewing a holder's records to determine compliance with the unclaimed property law.

¶ 215 Statute of Limitations Issues

As with virtually any law, statute of limitations issues frequently arise in connection with enforcement of unclaimed property laws. These issues, however, appear in different contexts, which will be discussed separately below. The principal questions involving the application of statutes of limitation to unclaimed property matters are:

- Where enforcement of the owner's rights against the holder with respect to the unclaimed property are barred by a statute of limitations, what effect does that have on the holder's obligation to report and pay such property to the state?
- Where the owner's claim against the holder became barred by the running of a period of limitations prior to the effective date of a state's unclaimed property law, is the holder obligated to report and pay such property to the state?
- Where the holder has failed to report or pay unclaimed property to the state, as required by law, must the state bring an enforcement action against the holder within a certain period of time?

.01 Abrogation of Limitations—UUPA 1981

Because the rights of the states to unclaimed property are basically only such rights as the owner possessed, the defense of the statute of limitations posed a serious obstacle to enforcement of the escheat laws. Under the derivative rights principle (see ¶ 210), if the owner's rights against the holder were barred by the running of period of limitations, the state would likewise be prevented from escheating the property. The drafters of the Uniform Disposition of Unclaimed Property Act, cognizant of this problem, which was an issue in the 1950 case of *New Jersey v. Standard Oil,*[21] included Act Sec. 29 in UUPA 1981 in order to eliminate of statute of limitations (between the owner and the holder) as a defense against state escheat actions. In that case, the New Jersey Supreme Court held that the derivative nature of the state's rights allowed for assertion of the defense of the statute of limitations as to certain types of property.

After the state supreme court's decision in *Standard Oil,* the New Jersey Legislature addressed the problem by shortening the escheat period on cash, wages, and other property to which the statute of limitations applied so as to escheat the property before the period of limitations could run. Most states, however, have simply adopted Act Sec. 29 of UUPA 1981 or its equivalent.

Although courts and commentators have frequently discussed the derivative nature of the states' rights under UUPA 1981, the abrogation of statutes of limitation by Act Sec. 29 is one area in which the state has greater rights than those of the owners of unclaimed property.

Non-retroactivity of Act Sec. 29. Much of the unclaimed property litigation involving statute of limitations issues has thus far centered on the retroactivity of Act Sec. 29 of UUPA 1981, i.e., whether Act Sec. 29 revives claims, causes of action, or other liabilities which were barred by a statute of limitations prior to the effective date of Act Sec. 29 (or its equivalent).

The earliest of these cases was *Douglas Aircraft Company, Inc. v. Cranston.*[22] In that case, Douglas Aircraft brought an action for declaratory relief against the Controller of the State of California, contending that California's version of UUPA 1981 could not apply to unclaimed wages on which the statute of limitations had run, as between the holder and the owner, prior to the effective date of the Act. The California Supreme Court did not reach the constitutional issue as to whether retroactive abrogation of the statute of limitations would deny Douglas due process of law. Instead, it relied on the general rule that statutes are to be given prospective effect only, unless it clearly appears that the legislature intended the statute to apply retroactively. Thus, the court held that the California Uniform Act did not apply to

[21] 5 N.J. 281, 74 A2d 565 (1950). Affirmed, 341 US 428, 71 SCt 822 (1951).

[22] 58 Cal. 2d 462, 374 P2d 819, 24 Cal. Rptr. 851 (1962).

property with respect to which claims by the owners were barred prior to the effective date of the Act.

However, the Court stated:

> It is true that the draftsmen of the uniform act indicated that they believed the provision on which section 1515 [Act Sec. 29 of UUPA 1981] is based would apply retroactively. (9A Uniform Laws Annotated pp. 267-269) and that similar provisions of other statutes have been so interpreted. *(Evans Products Co. v. Fry,* 307 Mich. 506, 12 N.W.2d 448 (1943); *In re Philadelphia Electric Co.,* 352 Pa. 457, 43 A.2d 116 (1945); *Connecticut Mut. Life Ins. Co. v. Moore,* 333 U.S. 541; 68 S.Ct. 682 (1948). The draftsmen, however, appear to have been preoccupied with the problem of whether the statute of limitations applicable between the holder and owner could be made inapplicable to the duty to report and pay to the state even as to claims not barred when the act took effect.

Other state court decisions have followed the rationale of Douglas in interpreting their versions of Act Sec. 29. However, an Illinois court not only found that Act Sec. 29 was not intended to apply retroactively to claims barred prior to the Act's effective date but also held that because, under Illinois law, the bar of the statute of limitations constituted a "vested right," the Act could not constitutionally apply so as to take away that vested right.[23]

.02 State Enforcement Actions: Period of Limitations

Even though statutes such as Act Sec. 29 may remove the defense of the running of a period of limitations between the holder and the owner in escheat cases, holders have argued that the state must bring an action against the holder to collect escheated property within a certain time, or the state's action is barred. The theory underlying the argument is that the state's right to receive the escheatable property arises on a certain date, as prescribed by its unclaimed property law, and that the state must commence an action within the period of time specified by general statutes of limitation for bringing actions based on a liability created by statute. In California, for example, an action based on a liability created by statute must be commenced within three years of the date the cause of action accrues.

This argument was considered by a California court of appeal in *Blue Cross of Northern California v. Cory.*[24] In that case, the Controller of the State of California had demanded payment from Blue Cross of sums payable on checks written to satisfy health insurance claims and general obligations of Blue Cross to vendors, which checks had remained outstanding and uncashed for more than seven years. Blue

[23] *Country Mutual Insurance Co. v. Knight,* 40 Ill. 2d 423, 240 NE2d 612 (1968). Also, see *Boswell v. South Cent. Bell Tel. Co.,* 301 So. 2d 65 (1974); *Occidental Life Ins. Co. v. Cranston,* 237 Cal. App. 2d 482, 47 Cal. Rptr. 37 (1965).

[24] 120 Cal. App. 3d 723, 174 Cal. Rptr. 901 (1991).

Cross contended, among other things, that the Controller's claim was barred in part by the three-year period of limitations prescribed in Cal. Code of Civ. Proc. § 338(1) for bringing an action on a liability created by statute (the Unclaimed Property Law). The court rejected the Controller's argument that Cal. Code of Civ. Proc. § 1570 (California's version of Act Sec. 29 of UUPA 1981) abrogates the defense of the statute of limitations in an action brought by him to recover unclaimed property from the holder. In this regard, the court stated that the legislative history of § 1570 did not support the Controller's argument and that § 338 was indeed applicable to an enforcement action brought by the controller because it was one based on a liability created by statute. The court, however, did not apply the statute of limitations against the controller in this instance because of the facts present in the case.

The court noted that Blue Cross had never filed the unclaimed property reports required by statute. Because the law requires payment of escheated property to be made to the state six months after the property is required to be reported to the state, the statute of limitations did not commence to run, because the Controller's cause of action did not accrue until the report had been filed and six months had passed. Thus, the court concluded:

> The three-year period of section 338, subdivision 1, did not commence to run here because Blue Cross did not at any time report to the Controller the unclaimed money it was holding in the amounts of its outstanding checks which had not been negotiated for more than seven years. The statute does not bar the controller's recovery of the money as claimed.

The court in *Blue Cross* also rejected the argument that the Controller's claim was barred by the doctrine of laches, because he had unreasonably delayed enforcement of the unclaimed property statute against Blue Cross. The first basis for this holding was that the controller's action was one at law and not in equity, and laches could only be asserted in equitable actions. Secondly, the court upheld the trial court's factual determination that the Controller did not unreasonably delay seeking compliance, did not acquiesce in Blue Cross' contention that the funds were not escheatable, and, further, that there was no prejudice to Blue Cross resulting from the delay. The elements of laches were not present as a matter of fact.

The *Blue Cross* decision was followed in *Travelers Express Co., Inc. v. Cory,*[25] wherein the Court of Appeals stated:

> It follows that no statute of limitations will commence to run against the Controller's recovery of unclaimed money, pursuant to the UPL,

[25] 664 F2d 763 (1981).

> unless—and until six months after—the holder has reported it in compliance with section 1530 . . . If the money is never properly reported, Blue Cross holds that the present duty to pay does not arise and the Controller's cause of action does not accrue for purposes of the statute of limitations. The controller's cause of action against Travelers in this case, therefore is not barred by the statute of limitations.

This is a just result. Under *Blue Cross,* a bank, insurance company, or money order company will not be able to claim the statute of limitations as a defense unless it has specifically reported the unclaimed property pursuant to Cal. Code of Civ. Proc. § 1530 and thus clearly put the property's legal status in issue. Cal. Code of Civ. Proc. § 1532(b) is available to such holders of unclaimed property as a means of avoiding the present duty to pay with respect to property that is for some reason thought not to be subject to escheat. To facilitate the enforcement by the Controller of unclaimed property law, it is necessary that claims such as Travelers' be stated explicitly to commence the running of the limitation period.

Another case involving the application of the statute of limitations against a state enforcement action is *Treasurer of Massachusetts v. John Hancock Mutual Life Insurance Co.*[26] In that case, the insurance company had failed to report funds represented by uncashed checks for such items as accident and health insurance payments, life insurance proceeds, agent commissions, salaries, and vendor payments. John Hancock argued that the state's complaint was similar to one in tort for conversion and was, therefore, subject to the two- or three-year statute of limitations. Citing the cases of *Travelers Express Co., Inc. v. Cory, Blue Cross v. Cory,* and *Sennett v. Insurance Co. of North America* as precedent, the Supreme Judicial Court of Massachusetts held that John Hancock's decision not to report the presumed abandoned property to the state prevented it from using the statute of limitations as a defense. The court stated that under the state law, the property does not become due the state until the report is filed, and until the property is owed to the state or Commonwealth, the statute of limitations does not begin to run. The court also noted that the concept of a statute of limitations is antithetical to the purpose of the abandoned property act.

In a case subsequent to *Blue Cross* but decided by a different California appellate court, the court departed from the *Blue Cross* rationale and held that the statute of limitations was not at all applicable to an enforcement action by the controller. The court held that an action by the state controller to collect service charges and

[26] 446 NE2d 1376, 388 Mass. 410 (1983).

interest illegally withheld by the bank from escheatable deposits was not barred by any statute of limitations for two reasons.[27]

First, under California law, there is no time limit for depositors to bring actions against banks with respect to their deposits. Thus, under the derivative rights principle (see ¶ 210), the state controller would also not be barred because he stands in the shoes of the depositors as to property subject to the unclaimed property act. Second, the California Unclaimed Property Law contains a provision similar to Act Sec. 29 of UUPA 1981 which abrogates the statute of limitations.

Therefore, it was the intent of the legislature that no statute of limitations could be applied against an enforcement action by the state controller. Act Sec. 29(b) does provide, for those states that adopted the second paragraph, a requirement that state administrators act promptly. This provides holders which report to those states a reliable "cut off" date.

.03 Waiver of Statute of Limitations

It should be noted that even where a state escheat law does not contain a provision abrogating the statute of limitations between the owner and the holder, such as Act Sec. 29 of UUPA 1981, the holder may not be able to assert the defense against the state if its policy or practice is not to raise the bar of the statute of limitations against owners. For example, an insurance company, for public relations or other reasons, may have adopted a policy of honoring claims by policyholders or paying stale-dated checks against which it could refuse payment on the basis that they are unenforceable because of the statute of limitations having run.

There is substantial authority to support an argument by the state that the holder has waived the statute of limitations defense by its conduct and, therefore, is precluded from asserting the defense against the state's escheat action. Similarly, where a state escheat law may contain a provision such as Act Sec. 29, but the statute of limitations had run prior to its effective date, the property may nevertheless be escheatable if the policy or practice of the holder was to waive the defense as against the owners. The holder may also be held to have waived the statute of limitations by paying the unclaimed amounts to the state.

> ***COMMENT:*** Unclaimed property statutes necessarily are directed to property that has not been paid or distributed to its rightful owner for a substantial period of time. Without provisions in the law such as Act Sec. 29 of UUPA 1981, states would be faced

[27] *Bank of America v. Cory,* 164 Cal. App. 3d 66, 210 Cal. Rptr. 351 (1985).

with the alternative of adopting shorter escheat periods so as to escheat the property before the period of limitations could run as between the owner and the holder. This alternative has the disadvantage of escheating property which is less likely to be truly unclaimed or forgotten by its owner and, in such event, putting both the owner and the state through the inconvenience and expense of processing claims to recover the property.

PLANNING NOTE: In light of cases such as *Blue Cross v. Cory, Massachusetts v. John Hancock,* and *Bank of America v. Cory,* it appears that holders are indefinitely liable to turn over escheated property to the state. The only apparent hope for holders to be discharged from accountability for the escheated property is to conscientiously report the property to the state and, if the holder disputes that the property is payable or deliverable to the state, file a written explanation of the reason the property will not be paid or delivered to the state. However, under the *Bank of America* decision even the act of reporting the property would not cause the statute of limitations to run on a state enforcement action.

Chapter 3

THE UNIFORM UNCLAIMED PROPERTY ACT—AN ANALYSIS

¶ 301 Overview

In this chapter, the Uniform Unclaimed Property Acts of 1954, 1966, 1981, and 1995 are discussed at ¶ 305. The requirements of reporting to the state are discussed at ¶ 310. Payment to the state is explained at ¶ 315. ¶ 320 discusses specific property covered by the 1981 Act. Finally, ¶ 325 discusses burden of proof issues.

¶ 305 The Uniform Unclaimed Property Acts of 1954, 1966, 1981, and 1995

At this writing, most states have adopted one of the versions of a model act proposed by the National Conference of Commissioners on Uniform State Laws. Several other states have enacted unclaimed property laws patterned after the 1981 Uniform Unclaimed Property Act (UUPA 1981) but with substantial modifications. Additionally, a few other states have unclaimed property laws which, though not modeled after UUPA 1981, contain various provisions similar to it. Thus, it is essential to study the provisions of UUPA 1981 in order to understand the basis of most unclaimed property laws in the United States.

The National Conference of Commissioners on Uniform State Laws proposed the original Uniform Disposition of Unclaimed Property Act to the states in 1954. In 1966, the Commissioners made some minor modifications to the 1954 Act and thereby promulgated the Revised Uniform Disposition of Unclaimed Property Act. At their July 1981 conference, the Commissioners once again revised the model act and proposed the Uniform Unclaimed Property Act. This version is most prevalent.

After defining various terms used, UUPA 1981 proceeds to classify certain types of property (such as deposits with banks and financial institutions, sums payable on written instruments, funds payable on insurance policies, etc.) as "presumed abandoned," when specified events have occurred or failed to occur for a period of time, usually three to five years. Instead of using the terminology "presumed abandoned," some states, such as California, provide that the property "escheats." Specific types of property covered by UUPA 1981 and the criteria for presumption of abandonment of such property are discussed in more detail at ¶ 320.

By August 1995, the vast majority of the states had incorporated UUPA 1981 into their legislation, either by amending and updating the particular state's version of either the 1954 or 1966 Act or by repealing the older version in its entirety and replacing it with the new Act. However, a number of state administrators and their advisors felt that UUPA 1981 needed further modification. The National Association of Unclaimed Property Administrators (NAUPA) formed a study committee in 1989 to consider possible amendments. The committee, consisting of state counsel who regularly represent their respective state unclaimed property programs, considered changes to both substantive provisions and the administrative procedures.

The committee sought input from the business community and unclaimed property commentators as well as the members of NAUPA. A series of discussion drafts with recommendations were presented to NAUPA at its annual meeting in the years 1990 through 1993. After final approval by NAUPA in 1993, the recommendations were sent to the National Conference of Commissioners on Uniform State Laws. The Commissioners approved the final version in August of 1995. This latest version, cited as the Uniform Unclaimed Property Act (1995), has been adopted by less than a dozen states. Although the 1995 Act contains certain changes, UUPA 1981 is still the legislative basis for most states' laws. Therefore, the following analysis will focus on UUPA 1981 with any changes occasioned by the 1995 Act appropriately noted.

The complete text of the 1981 and 1995 Uniform Unclaimed Property Acts may be found in Appendix C.

¶ 310 Report to the State

When the presumption of abandonment or escheat has occurred (for example, because the owner has not claimed a dividend or corresponded with the corporation concerning either the stock or the dividend for seven years after the dividend became payable), the "holder" (corporation or other business entity) is obligated to file a report regarding the property with the appropriate state administrator (treasurer, controller, department of revenue, etc.).

In general, the report must contain:

- The name, if known, of the owner of the property (except for traveler's checks and money orders);
- The nature of the property and any identifying number;
- The date when the property became payable, demandable, or returnable or the date of the last transaction by the owner with respect to the property; and
- Any other information prescribed by rule or regulation to be included.

The report must be verified by an officer, partner, or chief fiscal officer of the entity (holder) filing the report.

.01 Filing Dates

The report must be filed before November 1st and indicate abandoned property held by the holder as of the preceding June 30th. Life insurance corporations must file the report before May 1st "as of December 31 next preceding." The purpose of this cut-off period is to allow the holder to close its books, determine what items of abandoned or escheated property it is holding, and prepare and file the report with the state. Some holders also use the time between the close of books and the report date to attempt to make contact with the owners before the state notification procedures are triggered by the filing of the report. Some states also require that the holder mail a special notice to the owner advising him/her that the property is about to escheat. Several states have modified the reporting dates. For current information on due dates for all states see www.unclaimed.org.

.02 Notification or Publication

After the state receives the report, it must publish notices in newspapers and/or mail a notice to the last known address of each owner of property specified in the report. If the property's value is less than a certain amount (such as $25.00), the state is usually not required to publish or mail the notice.

The aggregate amount (the floor amount for detailed reporting, e.g., name, address, social security number, etc.) in the 1995 Act has been raised from the UUPA 1981 requirement of $25.00 to $50.00.

See ¶ 705–¶ 710 for a complete discussion on filing reports.

¶ 315 Payment to State

Within the time specified by state law following the filing of the report or publication of notice, the holder must pay for or deliver the abandoned property listed in the report to the state. However, if, before the date specified for payment, the owner has appeared and established his ownership of the property to the holder's satisfaction, the holder need not pay for or deliver the property to the state if he/she files a verified written explanation or some other reason why the "presumption of abandonment is erroneous." Upon such payment or delivery, the state becomes charged with the custody and safekeeping of the property, and the holder is relieved from any further liability with respect to the property (to the extent of its value).

The 1995 Act contains a very significant change: the remittance of the funds representing the various categories of unclaimed property is due at the same time as the report. This change was welcomed both by holders and state unclaimed property administrators. A number of states that retained the 1981 Act did adopt the 1995 Act's "report and remit" provision. The 1981 Act had provided that remittance was due six months after the report date.

.01 Right of Owner to Income from Property

After property other than money, i.e., securities, has been paid or delivered to the state, the owner is entitled to receive any income or increments accruing to the property. Some states, however, pay interest to the owner when money is paid to the state that was interest bearing while in the holder's possession. Older versions of the Uniform Act, 1954 and 1966, did not entitle the owner to receive any amounts subsequently paid to the state such as a dividend on a stock, etc.

.02 Effect of Statute of Limitations

The running of a statute of limitations that would bar an owner from recovering the property from the holder does not relieve the holder from the obligation to report or pay or deliver the property to the state, unless the period of limitations has run prior to the effective date of the provision abrogating the defense.[1] However, the state may be subject to a statute of limitations defense in an action to collect escheated property if the holder has reported the property to the state (see ¶ 215).[2]

.03 State Sale of Property

Property other than cash delivered to the state must be sold by the state, usually at public sale or auction. The purchaser at the sale is given title to the property free from any claims of the prior owner, the holder, or their successors.

---

[1] *Douglas Aircraft Co. v. Cranston*, 58 Cal. 2d 374, P2d 819 (1962).

[2] *Blue Cross of Northern California v. Cory*, 120 Cal. App. 3d 723, 174 Cal. Rptr. 901 (1991).

.04 Recovery by Owner

UUPA 1981 and all of its prior versions are custodial in nature. The owner may recover escheated property paid or delivered to the state at any time by filing a claim with the state administrator. At the option of the holder, an owner may be repaid by the holder, in which case the holder may obtain reimbursement directly from the state.

.05 Examination of Records

The state official or agency charged with administering the unclaimed property act is empowered to conduct examinations of the records of any "person" (natural, corporate, etc.). Holders, primarily banking and financial institutions, had argued that the authority of state officials to examine records may be limited, however, where federal law confers such authority exclusively on a federal regulatory agency.[3] For example, some national banks contended that under federal law (12 U.S.C. 484), only the U.S. Comptroller of the Currency may exercise "visitorial" powers over a national bank.[4]

> ***CAUTION:*** However, national banks are no longer able to make this argument because 12 U.S.C. 484 was amended to specifically permit examination by state auditors for the purpose of ensuring compliance with unclaimed property or escheat laws. Similarly, in *United States v. Alabama,*[5] it was held that federal law did not preempt the state's authority to examine federal credit unions for unclaimed property.

.06 Penalties for Failure to Report or Deliver Property to the State

UUPA 1981 empowers the state administrator to bring civil actions to enforce delivery by any person who refuses to deliver property to the state, as required by the Act. Further, the Act provides for imposition of fines for willful failure to file reports or perform other duties required under the Act, and fines and/or imprisonment for willful failure to pay or deliver property to the state. However, there are no reported cases on this provision of the Act.

¶ 320 Specific Property Covered by UUPA 1981

UUPA 1981 contains separate sections pertaining to specified categories of property. In addition, the Act includes an "omnibus" or "catch-all" provision designed to apply to property not specifically mentioned in the other sections. Therefore, intangible personal prop-

---

[3] *Minnesota v. First Nat'l Bank of St. Paul,* 313 NW2d 390 (1981).

[4] *Clovis Natnl. Bank v. Callaway,* 69 N.M. 119, 364 P2d 748 (1961).

[5] 434 F. Supp. 64 (1977).

erty of virtually every category is covered regardless of type, unless exempted by a specific section in the unclaimed property law of a particular state.

The 1995 Act took a significant departure from NAUPA recommendations by combining all property categories into a single section, Act Sec. 2. The rationale for this unification of categories is stated in the comment following Act Sec. 2, "With limited exceptions, this reorganization does not alter the bases for presuming abandonment of the property from that established in the 1981 Act, but merely restates those standards in a unified section, more easily applied, with less repetition." Although the 1995 Act combined the property categories, holders will find little substantive change in types of property covered.

.01 Deposits Held by Depository Institutions

Act Sec. 6 of UUPA 1981 sets forth the criteria for escheat or presumption of abandonment of deposits held by banks and other financial organizations, such as savings and loan associations and credit unions.

"Deposits" include:

- Demand (checking) accounts,
- Savings accounts,
- Time deposits, such as certificates of deposit,
- Share accounts in credit unions and savings and loan or building and loan associations, and
- NOW (negotiable order of withdrawal) accounts.

However, it is unclear whether NOW accounts are classified as savings or demand deposits because they have characteristics of both. In most states, the distinction would be immaterial, but some states have different escheat periods for demand and savings accounts or allow service charges only on demand accounts.

With respect to deposits, the presumption of abandonment arises when the owner, for a period of five years, has neither:

- Increased or decreased the deposit, or presented the passbook for crediting of interest,
- Corresponded in writing with the holder concerning the deposit, or
- Otherwise indicated an interest in the deposit as evidenced by a written memorandum on file with the holder.

In those situations in which an owner has several accounts with the holder but has not initiated activity with respect to all of the accounts, the inactive accounts would escheat, notwithstanding the activity of the other accounts. However, some states have administratively interpreted the law so that activity or contact by the owner regarding any account with the same holder will be considered as contact or activity regarding all such accounts. This practice is commonly referred to as "cross referencing."

PLANNING NOTE: The holder of such accounts would be well advised to check the policies of each state.

Act Sec. 6 also permits the holder to deduct service charges conditioned upon certain prerequisites. However, some charges may not be lawful (see detailed discussion in Chapter 4).

The 1995 Act combined in a single section, renumbered as Act Sec. 5, all the provisions relating to dormancy charges that had previously been part of several different sections of UUPA 1981. Renumbered Act Sec. 5 applies to all categories of intangible abandoned property, regardless of the particular property category or holder industry, i.e., commercial money order issuer or financial institution.

IRAs and similar retirement accounts. The 1995 Act also addresses individual retirement accounts (IRAs) and similar plans. Currently, the Internal Revenue Code provides a "window" (age 59 1/2 to age 70 1/2 years) during which time the individual may withdraw his contributions without penalty. Some state administrators had questioned which age initiated the dormancy period. The Conference proposed:

> three years after the earliest date of the distribution or attempted distribution of the property, the date of the required distribution as stated in the plan or trust agreement, or the date, if determinable by the holder, specified in the income tax laws of the United States by which distribution of the property must begin in order to avoid a tax penalty . . .

.02 Written Instruments Issued by Banking Institutions

Act Sec. 5 of UUPA 1981 also applies to sums payable on certified checks and other written instruments such as cashier's checks and any instruments on which a banking or financial organization or business association is directly liable. Under Act Sec. 5, sums payable on written instruments escheat five years from the date they become payable or from the date of issuance if payable on demand.

CAUTION: Note that it is the "sum payable" on the instrument that escheats, not the instrument itself.

In *Blue Cross of Northern California v. Cory,*[6] the state sought to escheat amounts payable on outstanding checks issued by Blue Cross.

[6] 120 Cal. App. 3d 723, 174 Cal. Rptr. 901 (1981).

The court rejected the argument that the state was barred from recovering the sums because it could not meet the burden of proving delivery for the checks or produce the checks themselves, such as would be required of an "owner" bringing an action on such a check. The court pointed out that the state was not seeking to recover uncashed checks or maintain an action thereon but was seeking to recover money (not checks) that had escheated to the state pursuant to the state's unclaimed property law.

.03 Money Orders and Traveler's Checks

Money orders, traveler's checks, and similar written instruments are now escheatable by the state in which they were sold, or issued,[7] notwithstanding the 1972 U.S. Supreme Court decision in *Pennsylvania v. New York,*[8] which held that the *Texas v. New Jersey*[9] rule was applicable to such instruments, e.g., that they were escheatable by the state of the owner's last known address as shown on the holder's records or, if no address was shown, by the state of the holder's domicile.

Under the 1966 Act, the names and last known addresses of the owners of money orders and traveler's checks are not required to be reported to the state. Various efforts have been made to impose service charges on escheatable sums payable on both these items and other written instruments. The lawfulness of such charges is discussed in detail in Chapter 4.

UUPA 1981 unified the regulation of all categories of service charges.

.04 Life Insurance Benefits and Proceeds—"Unclaimed Funds"

Act. Sec. 7 of UUPA 1981 provides for the presumption of abandonment of "unclaimed funds" held and owing by life insurance companies. "Unclaimed funds" is defined to mean all moneys held and owing by life insurance corporations unclaimed and unpaid for more than five years after the moneys became due and payable "as established from the records of the corporation" under any life or endowment insurance policy or annuity contract "which has matured or terminated."

Act Sec. 7 contains a provision whereby a life insurance policy not matured by actual proof of death of the insured will be "deemed" to be matured and the proceeds due and payable if the insured would have attained the limiting age under the mortality table on which the reserve is based.[10]

---

[7] 12 U.S.C. 2501-2503.

[8] SCt, 407 US 206, 92 SCt 2075 (1972).

[9] SCt, 379 US 674, 85 SCt 626 (1965).

[10] *Schell v. Metropolitan Life Ins. Co.*, 3 SW2d 269 (1928).

COMMENT: Obviously, this provision is intended to prevent a life insurance company from never being required to pay off on a policy simply because no "proof of death" or claim is received by the company.

For purposes of UUPA 1981, Act Sec. 2 dispenses with any requirement that the life insurance policy or contract be surrendered to the company as a condition of liability on the policy.

Generally, the reports of life insurance corporations are due by May 1st and report property is presumed abandoned or escheatable as of the preceding December 31st.

CAUTION: Note that under Act Sec. 17(d) of UUPA 1981, life insurance corporations report and remit unclaimed funds at different dates than those specified for other classes of holders (see ¶ 310 and ¶ 315).

Unclaimed moneys owing under insurance policies other than life or endowment policies or annuity contracts ordinarily are presumed abandoned under the Act Sec. 2 "catch-all" provision. The 1995 Act proposes that the dormancy period be reduced from five years to three.

.05 Utility Deposits and Refunds

Act Sec. 8 of UUPA 1981 provides for the presumption of abandonment of deposits or refunds held or owing by public utilities.

Deposits made by subscribers to secure utility services or refunds ordered to be paid by a utility are presumed abandoned if unclaimed for more than one year after services were terminated, in the case of deposits, or after the refund became payable.[11]

Utilities are permitted to withhold "any lawful deductions," which allows a utility to offset against the amount of the deposit or refund any amount owing to it by a subscriber for utility services. Other property held or owing by utilities in the ordinary course of business, such as vendor payments, etc., would be reportable under the omnibus provision in Act Sec. 2.

.06 Stocks, Dividends, and Other Distribution—Corporate Issuers

Act. Sec. 10 of UUPA 1981 applies to stock or other certificates of ownership, dividends, profits, distributions, interest, payments on principal, or other amounts held or owing by a business association for or to a shareholder, certificate holder, member, bondholder, other security holder, or participating patron of a cooperative. UUPA 1981 applies

[11] *South Carolina Tax Comm'n v. York Electric Cooperative,* 275 S.C. 326, 270 SE2d 629 (1980); *Arkansas v. City of N. Little Rock,* 280 Ark. 512, 659 SW2d 937 (1983); *Cory v. Public Utilities Commission,* 33 Cal. 3d 522, 658 P2d 749, 189 Cal. Rptr. 386 (1983).

regardless of whether the certificate is in the possession of the issuer, a broker, or the apparent owner.

When a shareholder for seven years has neither claimed a dividend nor corresponded in writing or otherwise indicated an interest as evidenced by a written memorandum on file with the corporation, the shares escheat. The shares must then be reported to the state administrator, and subsequently, the corporation must issue a duplicate certificate in the name of the state administrator representing such escheated share.

Nondividend-paying stock. Nondividend-paying stock presents a special problem in determining when, if ever, the escheat period begins to run. California has dealt with the problem by administrative interpretation that allows the holder to assume that it knows the location of the shareholder if:

- The corporation conducts annual shareholders' meetings and provides notification of such meetings to all shareholders by first class mail;
- The corporation maintains reliable records of all such notifications to shareholders which are returned undelivered by the post office; and
- The notification mailed to a particular shareholder was not returned undelivered by the post office.

However, if the last such notification to a shareholder is returned by the post office as undelivered, the corporation may not assume that it knows the location of the shareholders and must report the shares to the state unless:

- The corporation had a positive contact with the shareholders, as specified in Cal. Code of Civ. Proc. § 1516, during the preceding seven-year period; or
- The corporation is successful in locating the shareholders prior to the statutory deadline for reporting the shares.

UUPA 1981 handles the problem of escheat of nondividend stock by not escheating "intangible interests" (shares) unless the corporation has paid at least seven dividends during the escheat period and none of those dividends have been claimed by the owner. Thus, if the corporation had not paid the requisite number of dividends during the seven-year period, the shares would not escheat or be "presumed abandoned."[12] Corporate bonds, debentures, notes, and other such securities are also covered by Act Sec. 10 of UUPA 1981.[13]

A "payment on principal" of a bond, for example, would be presumed abandoned seven years after the bond matured or the "payment" otherwise became due. Interest payments on such securities would be presumed abandoned seven years after each interest payment became payable. In the case of "bearer issues," some states have taken the position that moneys representing nonpresented coupons escheat at the same time that the payment on principal escheats. This is to prevent a bondholder from having to claim his or her unclipped coupons from the state when the bond itself is surrendered for redemption.

The 1995 Act, in Act Sec. 2, attempts to clarify the event that initiates the dormancy period. This provision specifies that in the case of automatic reinvestment or nondividend paying stock, the dormancy period commences at the earlier of the following two events:

> the date of the second mailing of a statement of account or other notification or communication that was returned as undeliverable, or after the date the holder discontinued mailings to the apparent owner, whichever is earlier.

.07 Liquidation Dividends and Distributions

Act Sec. 11 of UUPA 1981 provides for the presumption of abandonment of intangible personal property distributable in the course of a voluntary or involuntary dissolution of a business association that is unclaimed by the owner within one year after the date of final distribution. Under Act Sec. 11, the one-year period does not start to run until there has been a "final distribution," e.g., all of the property of the entity has been distributed (or at least has become distributable) to shareholders, creditors, employees, or others entitled to receive portions of the entity's assets.

When final distribution is delayed for a lengthy period and periodic liquidating dividends or distributions are made, each of those distributions is held in a fiduciary capacity, such as when the dissolution is accomplished through a liquidating trust. Thus, even though there has been no final dissolution of the entity, partial distributions may escheat or be presumed abandoned after seven years.

.08 Property Held by Fiduciaries

Intangible personal property and any income or increment thereon, held in a fiduciary capacity for the benefit of another, is

[12] Act. Sec.10(b) of UUPA 1981.

[13] *Oregon ex rel. Mallicoat v. Coe,* 254 Ore. 365, 460 P2d 357 (1969).

presumed abandoned under Act Sec. 12 of UUPA 1981 if the owner has not within five years after the property became payable or distributable:

- Increased or decreased the principal,
- Accepted payment of principal or income, or
- Corresponded in writing with the holder concerning the property or otherwise indicated an interest in the property as evidenced by a written memorandum on file with the holder (fiduciary).

Although the most obvious type of fiduciary property would be trust funds or other property held by trustees, a wide range of property may fall into this category, such as escrow deposits, earnest money, and funds held by brokers, agents, factors, guardians, conservators, receivers, attorneys, and labor unions. Dividends on corporate stock (covered under Act Sec. 10 of UUPA 1981) may also be held in a fiduciary capacity if the corporation segregates a fund for payment and places it in a special account.

Does a fiduciary relationship exist? In order for the property to be held in a fiduciary capacity, something more than a mere debtor-creditor relationship must exist. Generally, a relationship of trust or confidence must be found to exist. To determine whether a fiduciary relationship exists, the law of the particular state involved should be consulted. In most instances, the distinction between fiduciary property and ordinary debts will not be critical because debts would normally be covered under other provisions of UUPA 1981. However, this distinction may be critical when considering the application of the statute of limitations (see ¶ 215).

.09 Property Held by Public Officers and Agencies

Any intangible personal property held for the owner by any court, public corporation, public authority, public officer, or state or governmental subdivision of the state which is unclaimed by the owner for more than one year is presumed abandoned by Act Sec. 13 of UUPA 1981. Act Sec. 13 may apply to property such as condemnation deposits, court trust deposits, or exonerated bail funds. Some states have special statutes providing for the disposition of property held by governmental agencies or may completely omit such property from their unclaimed property laws.

The property categories recovered from state or local agencies are myriad: unclaimed school district bonds, utility deposits held by the municipality, wages/bonuses/sick leave, and vacation checks.

.10 Miscellaneous Property—The "Catch-All" or "Omnibus" Provision

Act Sec. 2 contains the so-called "omnibus" or "catch-all" provision of UUPA 1981. The similar provision in the 1995 Act is Act Sec. 2(a)(15). The language used in Act Sec. 2 is very broad because it applies to property "held or owing in this state in the ordinary course of the holder's business" which has remained unclaimed for five years after it becomes payable or distributable. The Commissioners intended this section to include all categories of property not otherwise mentioned.

A wide range of property is encompassed within the scope of Act Sec. 2. A partial list of such property includes:

- Sums owing on or arising out of credit balances,
- Credit memoranda,
- Unredeemed gift certificates of "scrip,"
- Obligations owing vendors,
- Wages and commissions,
- Layaways,
- Unused airline or bus tickets,
- Oil and mineral royalty payments,
- Product credits,
- Retirement, death or disability benefits,
- Vacation and holiday pay,
- Profit sharing,
- Severance pay,
- Employee savings,
- Health insurance payments, and
- Innumerable other obligations.

PLANNING NOTE: It must be emphasized that whether a holder has any obligation to report or pay any type of unclaimed property to a state depends upon the nature and extent of the holder's obligation to the owner of the property, because the state's rights are derivative of the owner. This concept is discussed in detail at ¶ 210.

In *Callahan v. Marshall Field & Co.,*[14] the defendant argued that the Illinois version of Act Sec. 2 (formerly Act Sec. 9 of the 1954 Act)

[14] 83 Ill. App. 3d 811, 404 NE2d 368, 38 Ill. Dec. 944 (1980).

did not apply to unclaimed intangible property held by business associations, unless the holder is one of those mentioned in the specific sections of the Act. The court rejected the argument, stating:

> We believe the language of section 109 [Act Sec. 2 of UUPA 1981] is clear, unambiguous, and susceptible to only one logical interpretation. In order to be covered by this section the property must be: (1) intangible personal property; (2) not otherwise covered by the Act; (3) held or owing in this state in the ordinary course of the holder's business; and (4) unclaimed by the owner for a specified period. The legislature did not indicate that only holders of subject property under other sections of the Act would be covered by section 109. The section refers to property held in the holder's ordinary course of business. We take this requirement to mean that any entity holding unclaimed intangible personal property in the ordinary course of its business must comply with the Act.
>
> In addition to being contrary to the over all policy of the Act, Field's interpretation would result in an illogical statutory scheme. For instance, business associations holding one isolated item of covered property as a fiduciary under section 107 would consequently be required to report all unclaimed intangible personal property held while a business association not holding any in a fiduciary capacity would be free to retain any unclaimed intangible personal property. We shall not attribute such an intention to our legislature.

Act Sec. 2 also applies to property covered by specific sections of the Act. Act Sec. 2 has also been held to apply to categories of property covered by specific sections of the Act. In *Travelers Express Co., Inc. v. Minnesota,*[15] Travelers sought a declaratory judgment on the grounds that the state lacked authority under its own law to take custody of money orders sold by it (a Minnesota corporation with its principal place of business in Minnesota) in other states. Pointing to the specific money order provision in Minn. Stat. § 45.32(c), which applied to "written instruments issued in this state," Travelers Express argued that the state's own law precluded it from demanding the sums payable on money orders sold in other states, even though federal law[16] permitted it to do so when the state in which the money orders were sold did not provide, by law, for the escheat or presumption of abandonment of such items or the holder did not maintain a record of the state of sale. Because the specific section covered money orders, Travelers argued that they were excluded from any further coverage under the omnibus section.

The court disagreed, stating that such an interpretation is not required by the language of the provision and conflicts with its role as an omnibus section. The court noted that other types of property covered under the specific sections are also covered under the omnibus section. Citing the Commissioner's Comment to Act Sec. 9 of the 1954

[15] CA-8, 664 F2d 691 (1981).

[16] 12 U.S.C. § 2503.

Act, the court concluded that the omnibus section clearly intended to include property of the type dealt with elsewhere in the Act.

PLANNING NOTE: It should be noted that Act Sec. 2 of UUPA 1981 permits the holder to deduct from property payable to the state under this provision "any lawful charges." Although UUPA 1981 does not define the phrase "lawful charges," California law defines the term to mean those charges that are specifically authorized by statute or by a valid, enforceable contract (see Chapter 4).[17]

¶ 325 Burden of Proof

In the typical situation, it is usually obvious that the property is in fact owed to someone. However, many property and casualty insurance carriers have taken a contrary position. The carriers argue that the failure by the payee (either their insured or a third party allegedly injured by their insured) to cash the check or draft meant the payee had rejected the carrier's offer of settlement.

Act Sec. 6 of the 1995 Act squarely addressed this issue:

> A record of the issuance of a check, draft or similar instrument is prima facie evidence of an obligation. In claiming the property from a holder who is also the issuer, the administrator's burden of proof as to the existence and amount of the property and its abandonment is satisfied by showing issuance of the instrument and passage of the requisite period of abandonment. Defenses of payment, satisfaction, discharge and want of consideration are affirmative defenses that must be established by the holder.

In a recent New Jersey case, the New Jersey Supreme Court stated that the burden of proving payment is on the party asserting it.[18] The lack of bank records is not evidence of payment, even though the bank had complied with its record keeping guidelines. In this case, the state claimed the balances in 20-year-old passbook accounts. The bank no longer had any record of such accounts.

CAUTION: UUPA 1981 represents a comprehensive, systematic approach to abandoned property. Although many states have adopted it, numerous refinements and modifications have been made by the enacting states to UUPA 1981's basic provisions. The foregoing general analysis is intended to familiarize the reader with the general scheme of UUPA 1981. However, particular state statutes and cases should be carefully reviewed when specific issues arise with respect to individual states.

[17] Cal. Code of Civ. Proc. § 1520.

[18] *Pagano v. United Jersey Bank*, 143 N.J. 220, 670 A2d 509 (1996).

Chapter 4

LAWFULNESS OF CHARGES ON UNCLAIMED PROPERTY

¶ 401 Overview

The 1981 Uniform Unclaimed Property Act (UUPA 1981) permits the holder of certain categories of property to deduct lawful charges. Such charges are discussed at ¶ 405. The Act also imposes some restrictions, which are discussed at ¶ 410. In determing whether charges are lawful, a four-prong test is applied; this test is described at ¶ 415.

¶ 405 Lawful Charges

In various places, UUPA 1981 permits the holder of certain categories of property to deduct "lawful charges," "lawful deductions," or "any charges due to dormancy or inactivity." While UUPA 1981 does not define these terms, a few cases and statutes have sought to clarify their meaning. For example, under Cal. Code of Civ. Proc. § 1520, the omnibus or "catch-all" provision, in order to deduct "lawful charges" from unclaimed property, the charges must be:

- Permitted by the applicable provision of the unclaimed property statute, and
- Legally authorized by either a valid, enforceable contract or a statute other than UUPA 1981.

The necessity of these criteria was impliedly recognized by the court in *Cory v. Golden State Bank*.[1] In that case, the bank sought to withhold service charges from sums payable on uncashed money orders issued by the bank. The statute relating to the escheat of such sums allowed the exclusion from escheat of "any charges that may lawfully be withheld."

The bank argued that the service charges were authorized by statutes providing for warehouseman's and banker's liens and by contract created by language set forth on the customer's receipt attached

[1] 95 Cal. App. 3d 360, 157 Cal. Rptr. 538 (1979).

to the money order form, referring to the right to assess a service charge. The court stated that the evidence "adequately demonstrated that the Bank was not, as a matter of law, legally entitled to withhold service charges under any of its theories, contractual or statutory."

Prior to the decision in *Golden State Bank,* in a memorandum opinion in *Bank of America v. Cory,*[2] the California superior court judge had also upheld the requirement that there must be some contractual or statutory (other than UUPA 1981) basis in order for service charges to be "lawfully withheld." Basically, the case involved the state's claim that service charges withheld by the Bank of America from savings and demand deposits and from sums payable on written instruments that were escheatable to the state were unlawful. The state also challenged the bank's practice of terminating interest on escheatable savings deposits. In answer to the bank's contention that the provisions of California's Unclaimed Property Law relating to service charges on unclaimed deposits were void for vagueness, the court said:

> The phrases "reasonable service charge" and "may be lawfully withheld" as set forth in the Law do not seem vague to the Court. "Reasonable service charge" would seem to mean a charge that is appropriate in relation to the service performed, while "may be lawfully withheld" requires that the service charge be based on contract or statute since this clearly is the only charge a depositor could be required to pay. The "Derivative Principle" again is in point.

An additional ground cited by the courts for finding that service charges may not be withheld from unclaimed property is that the charges were not imposed against customers or owners by the holder but were only deducted if the property escheated to the state. In such cases, the holders were held to have "waived" whatever rights they may have had to withhold the charges. As the court stated in *Golden State Bank:*

> We note finally that even if it is assumed, for sake of argument, that the service charges provision appearing on the Bank's money orders does create some sort of contractual obligation on indebtedness owing to the Bank, the Bank would nonetheless be estopped from claiming the right to withhold the funds in question from Cory by virtue of an admission it made during discovery to the effect that it does not, in general, seek to enforce the service charge provision against members of the public. "The Bank may not waive its contractual rights as to a purchaser . . .; and then enforce those same rights as against the State and the Controller."[3]

Thus, having a statutory or contractual basis for imposing service charges may be of no aid to the holder if its general policy or practice is

[2] Sacramento Sup. Ct. No 357509, (1976).

[3] *Bank of America v. Cranston,* 252 Cal. App. 2d 208, 60 Cal. Rptr. 336 (1967).

not to assess the charges when owners claim the property from the holder.[4]

¶ 410 The 1981 Uniform Unclaimed Property Act Restrictions

UUPA 1981 imposes similar restrictions on service charges. For example, charges imposed on amounts payable on money orders and traveler's checks by reason of the failure to present such instruments for payment may be deducted from funds turned over to the state only if there is a valid, enforceable contract providing for such charges and the holder regularly imposes the charges. UUPA 1981 includes similar restrictions on service charges imposed on sums payable on other written instruments and on deposits made with banks and other financial institutions.

Act Sec. 4(c) of UUPA 1981 states:

> No holder may deduct from the amount of any traveler's check or money order any charges imposed by reason of the failure to present those instruments for payment unless there is a valid and enforceable written contract between the issuer and the owner of the property pursuant to which the issuer may impose those charges and the issuer regularly imposes those charges and does not regularly reverse or otherwise cancel those charges with respect to the property.

In essence, Act Sec. 4(c) creates a prohibition against the taking of service charges on written instruments if the instrument is paid at face value by the issuer.

COMMENT: The final word on the service charge issue may not have been heard yet. However, the trend of the courts and legislatures appears to be toward restricting or eliminating charges against unclaimed property. This seems particularly true where the charges are simply a device to decrease or totally defeat the state's entitlement to the property.

A recent case decided in the Pennsylvania Commonwealth Court again restricted a financial institution's attempt to impose service charges and withhold interest on dormant savings accounts. In *First Federal S & L Ass'n of Hazleton v. Office of State Treasurer,*[5] the State Treasurer demanded that the monies representing the service charges and unapplied interest be reported and remitted as abandoned property. First Federal had argued that, under federal law, the Federal Home Loan Bank Board had the exclusive authority to regulate savings

[4] See also *Travelers Express Co., Inc. v. Regan,* 498 N.Y.S.2d 569, 114 A.D.2d 194 (1986).

[5] 650 A2d 1166 (PA Commonwealth 1994).

and loan associations. When the treasurer rejected this argument, the lender filed suit.

The court found that there was no conflict between federal oversight of lending practices and state regulation of dormant property. Accordingly, the Commonwealth Court ruled against the lender.

¶ 415 Applying the Lawfulness Test—The Four Elements

In applying the acid test to any type of charge or deduction from property, the appropriate analysis is comprised of four elements:

1. Is there a valid, enforceable contract that permits the taking of the charge or is there a specific statute other than the unclaimed property law that specifically permits such charge?

CAUTION: It is important to note that pre-printed contracts that contain fine print are many times viewed as adhesion contracts and charges taken pursuant to such contracts may well not be enforceable.

CAUTION: The adoption of a resolution of the board of directors authorizing the taking of a charge may not be sufficient to claim that the charges were taken pursuant to a valid or enforceable contract unless notice is given to the owner of such charges.

Likewise, the adoption of a bylaw or charter provision by a corporation that authorizes charges may not be sufficient to meet notice requirements to owners unless it is provided to an owner.

CAUTION: Contracts that contain provisions that bind owners to future changes to the amount of a charge are generally invalid as illusory contracts because they appear to bind the owner but in fact do not bind the owner due to a lack of specific notice. A material adverse change to an owner's property right(s) requires notice.

2. Does the holder regularly impose the charge against all property, both active and inactive? The holder may not treat an inactive item of property differently than an active one solely on the basis of its inactivity.

3. Is it the policy of the holder to refund or reinstate the charge if the owner reactivates or claims the property?

PLANNING NOTE: A policy or practice of refunding the charge to the owner will normally evidence a waiver on the part of the holder and will invalidate the charge as being lawful. The policy to refund or waive can be established from transaction evidence in the holder's records such as refunded charges and the burden of proving that these refunds do not constitute a waiver will fall upon the holder.

CAUTION: The reason a charge is refunded is not relevant in the analysis of whether a waiver has occurred. The fact that a charge is refunded for customer goodwill or good business practice does not legitimize the waiver. This subjective reason for the waiver does not overcome its poisonous effect.

PLANNING NOTE: No specific number of refunds or percentage of refunds out of a total population is absolutely determinative that the holder has a "policy or practice" of waiving a charge. The actual fact pattern of each individual case must be carefully reviewed.

A simple test that is routinely applied by unclaimed property examiners is asking the question, "How would you treat the owner of an account that had been service charged if they appeared in person and requested the balance of the account?" If the owner who appears and claims the property is refunded the charge or fee, the state will claim that the fees are not lawful under the waiver theory.

4. Is the charge reasonable? This is a subjective test based on the facts and circumstances of the nature of the property, the "service" provided, and the earnings credit that may be attributable to the value of the property, if any.

Example: It would be impossible to show that a service charge of $10 per month was reasonable on a $50,000 passbook savings account on the basis of even the smallest earnings credit for the account. The direct costs of maintaining such an account, including paying the passbook rate of interest would certainly show a profit when the earnings credit on the account was applied.

CAUTION: Without careful planning when implementing or changing service charge policies, the potential of a state disallowing such a charge when applied to unclaimed accounts is a certain risk.

Chapter 5

RULES OF JURISDICTION—WHERE TO REPORT UNCLAIMED PROPERTY

¶ 501 Overview

In the context of escheat law, "jurisdiction" refers to the power of a state to take custody of unclaimed property (¶ 505). The rules of jurisdiction are based on U.S. Supreme Court cases that are discussed in ¶ 510 and ¶ 515. The federal "place of sale" test of P.L. 93-495 is also discussed at ¶ 515.

¶ 505 Definition of "Jurisdiction"

"Jurisdiction," in a legal sense, may refer to various concepts:

- The power of courts to hear and decide cases,
- The power of a sovereign to govern or legislate, or
- In the context of escheat law, the power of one state to take custody of unclaimed property to the exclusion of other states.

According to the U.S. Supreme Court, it has always been the settled rule that real property and tangible personal property are escheatable only by the state in which the property is located.[1]

¶ 510 Jurisdiction to Escheat—The Rules of Jurisdiction

The rules of jurisdiction in unclaimed property law are unique. They are based on three U. S. Supreme Court cases: *Texas v. New Jersey, Pennsylvania v. New York* (discussed later in this paragraph), and *Delaware v. New York* (discussed at ¶ 515). Concepts of nexus and "doing business," which are familiar in the tax arena, do not apply in unclaimed property law. The state to which property must be reported

[1] *Texas v. New Jersey*, SCt, 379 US 674, 85 SCt 626 (1965).

is based on an "address test," e.g., the last known address of the owner of an unclaimed property item. The rules were originally established in 1965 in *Texas v. New Jersey,* which is still the controlling law.

The right of states to take custody of abandoned property, by proper procedures, is well settled. However, the U.S. Supreme Court has considered, in both a constitutional context and a practical one, the power of a state to escheat when the potential exists that other states may claim the same property.

.01 *Connecticut Mutual Life Insurance Co. v. Moore*

As discussed at ¶ 205.06, the case of *Connecticut Mutual Life Insurance Co. v. Moore*[2] involved New York's attempt to collect proceeds of life insurance policies issued for delivery in New York on the lives of New York residents by companies incorporated in other states. Nine such insurance companies sued to obtain a declaration that New York had no power to "sequester" the funds and that the New York statute would deprive the insurance companies of their property without due process of law in violation of the Fourteenth Amendment.

The U.S. Supreme Court approached the problem by examining whether New York had "sufficient contacts" with the transactions in question "to justify exertion of the powers to seize abandoned money due its residents."

Concluding that New York did indeed have sufficient contacts, the Court stated that "it is the beneficiary of the policy, not the insurer, who has abandoned the moneys." The Court, however, declined to deal with the question of what it would do if another state claimed the same property.

In separate dissenting opinions, Justices Frankfurter and Jackson argued that the Court should not decide the case because other states possessing possible interests were not parties to the suit. Justice Jackson contended that if the Court was going to decide the suit, a more definite standard than "sufficient contacts" should be developed. Prophetically, he stated: "[w]hile we may evade it for a time, the competition and conflict between States for 'escheats' will force us to some lawyerlike definitions of State power over this subject." But it would be more than 15 years before the Court would once again face a situation in which several states would each claim the right to escheat the same property on the basis of some contact with the transaction or parties.

---

[2] SCt, 333 US 541, 68 SCt 682 (1948).

.02 *Standard Oil Co. v. New Jersey*

Meanwhile, in 1951, the Court decided *Standard Oil Co. v. New Jersey.*[3] Under its statute, the state of New Jersey obtained an escheat judgment regarding shares of stock and unpaid dividends owing or unclaimed for more than 14 years to persons whose last known addresses were outside New Jersey. The corporation, however, was domiciled in New Jersey—the reverse of the situation in *Connecticut Mutual.*

In *Standard Oil,* the New Jersey Supreme Court affirmed the escheat judgment and the U.S. Supreme Court, in a five-to-four decision, upheld that ruling. In *Standard Oil,* the Court once again relied on the fact that Standard Oil Co. was "amenable to process" in New Jersey and, thus, had sufficient contacts with the state so that service of process effected seizure of the obligation owing by the corporation. The Court reasoned that the rights of the owners of the stock and dividends came within the reach of the court by the notice, i.e., service by publication. That power enables the escheating state to compel the issue of certificates or payment of the dividends. The majority concluded that Standard Oil Co. would not be subjected to double liability because the full faith and credit clause of the Constitution[4] would require that other states respect the judgement of the New Jersey courts.

However, Justice Frankfurter, dissenting again, argued that:

> [t]he Constitution ought not to be placed in an unseemly light by suggesting that the constitutional rights of the several States depend upon, and are terminated by, a race of diligence.

.03 *Western Union Telegraph Company v. Pennsylvania*

Probably the most confusing and seemingly inconsistent unclaimed property case to be decided by the U. S. Supreme Court was *Western Union Telegraph Co. v. Pennsylvania.*[5] In *Western Union,* the Court departed from its prior pattern of upholding the rights of states to exercise jurisdiction to escheat by deciding that Western Union would be denied property without due process because the courts of Pennsylvania lacked the power to protect the company against the claims of other states for the same property. Pennsylvania sought to escheat amounts payable on unclaimed telegraphic money orders purchased in that state for transmittal to payees in other states. Unlike the situations in *Connecticut Mutual* and *Standard Oil,* Western Union was not a domestic corporation, and the subject property's last known owners were not residents of the state in which the property was located.

---

[3] SCt, 341 US 428, 71 SCt 822 (1951).

[4] U.S. Constitution, Art. IV, Sec. 1.

[5] SCt, 368 US 71, 82 SCt 199 (1961).

Justice Black, writing for the Court, noted that although New York claimed a part of the same property, neither New York nor any other possible claimant state was a party to the suit. Therefore, the Pennsylvania courts did not possess the power to protect Western Union from these rival claims. The Court explained that "a state court judgement need not be given full faith and jurisdiction of the court that rendered it."

Seeming to invite an opportunity to straighten out this jurisdictional tangle, the Court asserted that "the rival State claimants here can invoke our original jurisdiction." In an effort to harmonize its decision with prior decisions, the Court pointed out that in *Connecticut Mutual,* New York had been permitted to take the property only as a custodian, and other claimants could have brought actions to recover it at any time. Thus, the Court appeared to be resurrecting the true escheat-custodial distinction despite its statement in *Standard Oil* that such distinction was not significant.

.04 *Texas v. New Jersey*—The Rules of Jurisdiction "Invented"

Fortunately, the confusion created by the *Western Union* decision was relatively short-lived. In its decision in *Texas v. New Jersey,*[6] the U.S. Supreme Court finally had before it the type of factual situation and the variety of parties for which it had long been waiting. Invoking the Court's original jurisdiction, Texas brought an action for injunction and declaration of rights against New Jersey, Pennsylvania, and Sun Oil Company "to settle a controversy as to which State has jurisdiction to take title to certain abandoned intangible personal property through escheat."

The property consisted of various small debts owing by Sun Oil Company over a period of from seven to 40 years prior to the filing of the action. Sun Oil Company claimed no interest in the property but contended that it should be protected from possible multiple liability to more than one state for the same debt.

Texas argued that it should have the right to escheat since the debts were shown on the books of Sun Oil Company's two Texas offices and since the last known addresses of many of the creditors were in Texas. New Jersey claimed the right to escheat based on the fact that Sun Oil Company was incorporated in that state. Pennsylvania claimed the power to escheat on the ground that Sun Oil Company's principal business offices were in that state. Florida was permitted to intervene and argue that it should be entitled to escheat obligations owing to persons whose last known addresses were in Florida. Illinois, however,

[6] SCt, 379 US 674, 85 SCt 626 (1965).

was denied leave to intervene and argue its position that jurisdiction to escheat should depend on the laws of the state in which the indebtedness was created.

The Court, having referred the case to a Special Master, adopted the Master's recommendation. The Court prefaced its ruling by noting:

> Since the States separately are without constitutional power to provide a rule to settle this interstate controversy and since there is no applicable federal statue, it becomes our responsibility in the exercise of our original jurisdiction to adopt a rule which will settle the question of which State will be allowed to escheat this intangible property.

The Court rejected the "most significant contacts" test advanced by Texas (and, incidentally, enunciated by the Court in earlier cases), stating that the question "should be settled once and for all by a clear rule which will govern all types of intangible obligations like these and to which all States may refer with confidence."

The "clear rule" handed down by the Court to finally settle the question as to which state has the exclusive power, or "superior" right, to escheat intangible property is as follows:

1. Unclaimed or abandoned intangible property "is subject to escheat only by the state of the last known address of the creditor, as shown by the debtor's books and records."
2. If the records of the debtor do not show the state of the last known address of the creditor, the property is subject to escheat by the State of corporate domicile of the debtor.
3. If the records of the debtor show that the last known address of the creditor is in a state that does not, "at the time in question," provide for the escheat of such property, the property is subject to escheat by the state of corporate domicile of the debtor.

The Court indicated, however, that in situation 2, above, another state could later escheat the property (presumably from the domicile state) "upon proof that the last known address of the creditor was within its borders." In situation 3, above, the Court indicated that the debtor's domicile state could escheat the property

> subject to the right of the state of last known address to recover it if and when its law made provision for escheat of such property. In other words, in both situations, the state of corporate domicile should be allowed to cut off the claims solely of private persons, retaining the property for itself only until some other state comes forward with proof that it has a superior right to escheat.

The Court conceded that its decision was not controlled by constitutional or statutory law, nor was it necessarily logical. The Court, however, was impressed with the apparent ease of administration and equity of its rule.

Notwithstanding the Court's delight with the assumed beauty and simplicity of its decision, various questions remained unanswered, such as which state has the right to escheat if the debtor (holder) has no last known address of the creditor (owner) on its records and the creditor's corporate domicile is in a state that does not provide for the escheat of the property? What rule should apply if the debtor has deliberately destroyed its records of last known addresses? Must an address be a description of location sufficient for the delivery and receipt of mail or does a computer code purportedly representing the state of residence of an owner or payee constitute a last known address? What if the creditor's last known address is in a foreign country?

In *Nellius v. Tampax, Inc.,*[7] a Delaware Chancery Court strictly applied the *Texas* rule and rejected Delaware's escheat claim based on the domicile of the holder since the corporation's records showed the owner's last known address in Massachusetts, but other evidence indicated that the property had been transferred by such person.

At its next opportunity, the Supreme Court would demonstrate that the case of administration, rather than equity or logic, was its prime concern in this area.

.05 *Pennsylvania v. New York*

In a 1972 case, the Supreme Court was once again asked to resolve a dispute concerning state power to escheat proceeds of unclaimed money orders. In *Pennsylvania v. New York,*[8] the Court was also given the chance to modify or refine the *Texas v. New Jersey* rule. This time Pennsylvania filed an original action in the Supreme Court against New York and other states, asking that the Court resolve the conflicting claims as to which state had jurisdiction to escheat sums owing on money orders purchased in Pennsylvania.

Pennsylvania argued that because Western Union's records did not generally show addresses of the purchaser or payee, strict application of the *Texas v. New Jersey* rule would result in a bonanza for New York, Western Union's State of incorporation. Thus, Pennsylvania argued for an exception to *Texas v. New Jersey,* covering transactions in which the debtor does not ordinarily keep a record of the address of the creditor.

The Court conceded that Pennsylvania's proposal had some surface appeal but observed that the only arguable basis for such an exception was that money orders involve a higher percentage of unknown ad-

[7] 394 A2d 233 (1978).

[8] SCt, 407 US 206, 92 SCt 2075 (1972).

dresses. In refusing to depart from *Texas v. New Jersey,* the Court states:

> to vary the application of the *Texas* rule according to the adequacy of the debtor's records would require this Court to do precisely what we said should be avoided—that is, "to decide each escheat case on the basis of its particular facts or to devise new rules of law to apply to ever-developing new categories of facts."

The Court seemed to believe, however, that states such as Pennsylvania had an adequate remedy for the future: "[a]s for future money order transactions, nothing we say here prohibits the States from requiring Western Union to keep adequate address records."

¶ 515 Congress Reacts—P.L. 93-495 Enacted to Create a "Place of Sale" Rule

In 1974, Congress finally decided to get involved, to a limited extent, in the tug-of-war between the states. Effective October 28, 1974, P.L. 93-495 established the "place of sale test," specifying which state has jurisdiction to escheat sums payable on money orders, traveler's checks, and "similar written instruments." Demonstrating its intention to supplant the Supreme Court's decisions in *Texas v. New Jersey* and *Pennsylvania v. New York* (see ¶ 510), insofar as they affected jurisdiction to escheat this type of property, Congress made the new test applicable to all sums payable on money orders, traveler's checks, and similar written instruments "deemed abandoned on or after February 1, 1965, except to the extent that such sums have been paid over to a State prior to January 1, 1974."

Whether states must, by legislation, expressly extend their escheat laws to reach those sums now made escheatable to them by P.L. 93-495 is uncertain. California has adopted such legislation. However, a federal district court in Minnesota interpreted Minnesota's pre-1974 statute as applying to money order proceeds brought within the state's jurisdiction simply by virtue of P.L. 93-495. This part of the district court's decision was disapproved by the Eighth Circuit Court of Appeals.[9] However, the Court of Appeals held that under Minnesota's "omnibus" or "catch-all" provision, Minnesota could take custody of sums payable on uncashed money orders sold in states that did not have applicable escheat or custodial laws.

---

[9] *Travelers Express Co., Inc. v. Minnesota,* 664 F2d 691 (1981). Cert. dismissed, 456 US 920, 102 SCt 1780 (1982).

.01 *Delaware v. New York*

In 1988, Delaware sought the Supreme Court's guidance in its claim that New York's escheat of certain monies violated the priority rules of *Texas v. New Jersey* (see ¶ 510.04).[10] The monies at issue were unallocated distributions from securities. The owners of the securities were in fact unknown as the securities were held in the brokerage's nominee or "street" name. Because this property had no owner information, it would be escheatable to the state of the holder's domicile (here, Delaware) under the existing priority rules. New York claimed that the brokers, and not the securities purchasers, were entitled to the monies at issue. Because the brokers had trading addresses in New York, New York argued that the monies should be escheatable there.

Texas intervened, asserting that the holder was not the brokerage house but was, in reality, the issuer of the securities. Under this theory, the monies due the unknown owners would go to the state of the issuer's domicile. More than 35 states intervened to support Texas' argument. Subsequently, California and five other jurisdictions intervened, advancing a commercial proportionality rule wherein these unknown monies would be distributed on an apportionment basis, such as the percentage of stockholders in each state.

All the states (except the California group) insisted that *Texas v. New Jersey* should be upheld: their quarrel rested with the definition of "owner"—securities purchaser or brokerage house—and "holder"—issuer or broker. As is its practice in cases of original, versus appellate, jurisdiction, the Supreme Court appointed a Special Master to review the extensive pleadings and briefs, to consider evidence and propose findings of fact and conclusions of law. This practice had been followed in both *Texas v. New Jersey* and *Pennsylvania v. New York;* in both cases, the Supreme Court adopted the Special Master's recommendation (see ¶ 510).

The Special Master's report adopted Texas' argument, but with a twist. The report agreed that the issuers (and not the brokerages which the Special Master labeled as "intermediaries") were the holders but recommended that the test for corporate domicile be changed to "principal executive office" rather than state of incorporation.

Both Delaware and New York, disappointed by the Special Master's recommendation, filed exceptions to the report. The Supreme Court nonetheless abided by its prior decisions. Thus, the precedent established by the 1965 *Texas v. New Jersey* decision and affirmed by

[10] *Delaware v. New York,* SCt, 507 US 490, 113 SCt 1550 (1993).

the 1972 *Pennsylvania v. New York* decision was reaffirmed on March 30, 1993 with this case. Specifically, the Court stated as follows:

> Only by adhering to our precedent can we resolve escheat disputes between states in a fair and efficient manner. We have repeatedly declared our unwillingness "either to decide each escheat case on the basis of its particular facts or to devise new rules of law to apply to ever-developing new categories of fact." To craft different rules for the novel facts of each case would generate "so much uncertainty and threaten so much expensive litigation that the states might find that they would lose more in litigation expenses than they might gain in escheats."

In rejecting the Special Master's contention that the issuer was the holder, the Court looked to the Uniform Commercial Code "which is the law of all 50 states and the District of Columbia." Because the facts of this case revealed that all of these distributions were registered in the nominee or "street" name of the intermediary brokerages, banks, or depositories, the Court relied upon U.C.C. Sec. 8-20738 to conclude that these intermediaries were the only holder to whom the apparent owners could look for payment:

> [U]nlike an issuer, which discharges all liabilities upon payment to a record owner, an intermediary remains liable should a "lost" beneficial owner reappear to collect distributions due under a contract with the intermediary.

In rejecting the Special Master's own suggestion (no state had raised this issue) that the test of corporate domicile be changed, the Court noted that a "principal place of business" test had been suggested in *Texas v. New Jersey*. However, the Court resoundingly rejected that argument in 1965 and succinctly restated its opposition in this case as follows:

> The mere introduction of any factual controversy over the location of a debtor's principal executive offices needlessly complicates an inquiry made irreducibly simple by Texas' adoption of a test based on the state of incorporation.

Clearly the Supreme Court will not change the jurisdictional rules in the foreseeable future. The Court, however, recognizing that all states (except Delaware) would be disappointed with its decision, suggested a different venue:

> If the states are dissatisfied with the outcome of a particular case, they may air their grievances before Congress. That body may reallocate abandoned property among the states without regard to this court's interstate escheat rules. Congress overrode Pennsylvania by passing a specific statute concerning abandoned money orders and traveler's checks [citation omitted] and it may ultimately settle this dispute through similar legislation.

The result of *Delaware v. New York* was a settlement by all the states that resulted in a lump sum payment (amounts varied based on population). In exchange, no federal legislation would be introduced to change the backup rule reiterated by the Supreme Court in that case.

COMMENT: It is anticipated that in 2005, when the settlement agreement with all the states expires, federal legislation will be proposed that creates some type of apportionment rule for no-address property that will reverse the current "winner-take-all" backup rule.

PLANNING NOTE: In practice what constitutes an address for purposes of reporting property to many states can become quite problematic. Careful analysis of what records of owner's addresses are actually extant is critical in reporting correctly under the primary and backup rules.

Chapter 6

TANGIBLE PERSONAL PROPERTY: ABANDONED, LOST, AND MISLAID PROPERTY—FINDER'S LAWS

¶ 601 Overview

Most of the law of unclaimed property that is the subject of the 1981 Uniform Unclaimed Property Act (UUPA 1981) relates to intangible personal property, money rights, and obligations that are not physical in nature. However, many holders find that they come into possession of tangible personal property and frequently need guidance on how to treat such property from a legal perspective.

UUPA 1981 addresses tangible property in two places:

1. The contents of safe deposit boxes, and
2. The omnibus or catch-all provision that in some states covers both "tangible and intangible property not otherwise covered" (by another section of the Act).

The discussion in this chapter is meant to give general guidance to those who "find" or come into possession of unclaimed tangible property as holders.

Most states have statutes separate and distinct from the unclaimed property law that cover lost, mislaid, or abandoned tangible property. These statutes vary widely and are beyond the scope of this discussion. However, the basic common law regarding this type of property is covered in the following paragraphs as a starting point for further research.

"Tangible property" is defined at ¶ 605. A discussion of where tangible property escheats is at ¶ 610. The state's option to reject reported property under the 1981 Act is explained at ¶ 615. The sale of unclaimed property is discussed at ¶ 620. A discussion of property and property rights by classification may be found at ¶ 625. A detailed discussion of abandoned, lost, and mislaid tangible property is located at ¶ 630.

¶ 605 Definition of "Tangible Property"

Tangible property is property that has a physical existence, i.e., it may be seen, touched, or otherwise detected with the senses. On the other hand, intangible property has no spatial existence. While intangible property may be represented by a tangible item, such as a stock certificate, note, or paper money, the property is not the nominal value of the piece of paper itself but the value, or "property," represented by the piece of paper. Tangible property may be real or personal. Real property is land or things affixed to land; personal property is all property other than real property.

¶ 610 Where Tangible Property Escheats—Situs

In *Texas v. New Jersey* (see ¶ 510.04), the U.S. Supreme Court noted that with respect to tangible property, "it has always been the unquestioned rule in all jurisdictions that only the State in which the property is located may escheat." However, UUPA 1981, which most states have adopted, sought to take advantage of this power only in a piecemeal manner. Specifically, UUPA 1981 applies to all sorts of intangible unclaimed property, but it covers tangible property only where it is removed from a safe deposit box or other safekeeping repository. It may have been concluded that most items of unclaimed tangible property were worthless or of such nominal value as not to justify the expense and inconvenience associated with the handling, safekeeping, and sale of the property. Nevertheless, a number of states have enacted comprehensive provisions relating to unclaimed tangible property. Most states have also enacted special statutes providing for the disposition of tangible property held by consignees, bailees, warehousemen, police agencies, etc. Such special statutes are not covered in this discussion.

Documents removed from safekeeping repositories, such as deeds, vehicle titles, stocks, bills of sale, checks, etc., are ordinarily mere evidences of ownership of property and have no intrinsic value.

The state' s right to the underlying property represented by such documents is dependent upon other provisions of the law. In some instances, documents may have special value, such as "Lincoln letters," ornate or unusual stock certificates that no longer have any commercial value, or other collector's items.

It should also be borne in mind that possession of literary manuscripts, film, recordings, or other copyrighted material does not result in escheat of the copyright. Possession or ownership of the tangible object by lawful means pursuant to statute does not terminate the copyright owner's control over publication of the copyrighted material.

¶ 615 Option to Reject Property Reported

Under Act Sec. 27 of UUPA 1981, the state unclaimed property administrator may decline to receive any property reported if he/she deems the property to have a value less than the cost of publishing notice and holding a sale. The administrator must exercise this option by notifying the holder within a specified time after the filing of the report. Without the right to make this election, states would find themselves burdened with many valueless, unwanted items. Some statutes, such as California's, allow the state administrator to destroy or otherwise dispose of property delivered to the state that has "no apparent commercial value."[1]

¶ 620 Sale of Unclaimed Property

Act Sec. 22 of UUPA 1981 requires the state administrators to sell, within one year following delivery to the state, all abandoned property other than cash or securities. The property must be sold to the highest bidder at public sale, but the administrator may decline to accept the highest bid if it is considered insufficient. The time within which the sale must be held varies from state to state. Some states, such as California, have no time limit to sell the property. The purchaser at the public sale receives title to the property free and clear of any claims of the owner or prior holder.

¶ 625 Property and Property Rights

A basic working knowledge of the law of property is essential to properly report it as "abandoned" or "unclaimed."

.01 Classifications of Property

Property, as used in this discussion, means anything that may be owned, such as land, buildings, automobiles, money, shares of stock, bonds, or patent rights. It is classified as movables and immovables; lands and chattels; real property and personal property; and tangible personal property and intangible personal property.

Under the civil law (which is still the basic law of the state of Louisiana), property was divided into movables and immovables. Movables are objects of property that a person may take with him or her wherever he or she goes—such as money, securities, and furniture. Immovables are tangible (touchable) things that cannot be moved from place to place—such as land and buildings.

[1] Cal. Code of Civ. Proc. § 1533.

Land and chattels. Under the common law of England (which forms the basis of most American property laws), property was formerly divided into lands and chattels. "Lands" means the soil and everything of a permanent character attached to it by the course of nature or by the hand of man—the soil itself, the trees growing in it, and the house built on it. Chattels include all movable and immovable property except freehold estates in land, which are estates of inheritance and estates for life. Chattels are divided into two classes: real and personal.

Real and personal property. According to modern classifications, all property is divided into two main groups: real property and personal property. The usual distinction between the two, which is adequate for practical purposes, is that real property is land and anything attached to the land with the intention that the attachment shall become a fixture, whereas personal property is all property except real property.

Tangible and intangible personal property. "Tangible personal property," as the term implies, is property that can be touched, has physical substance, and is not a mere evidence of value but has value in and of itself. "Intangible personal property" is property that cannot be touched or realized with the senses. A certificate of stock is classified as intangible because although the certificate as a piece of paper is a tangible thing in that it can be touched, it is only evidence of a right. The right is the stockholder's claim on the profits and assets of the company. If the certificate was lost, destroyed, or stolen, the stockholder would not lose his right, but he would have to take certain prescribed steps to prove that right. The same holds true for notes, bonds, and other evidences of debt: they are valuable not in and of themselves but only as evidence of rights.

> ***CAUTION:*** It should be stated, however, that laws have been enacted that treat bonds, notes, certificates of stock, and the like as if they were tangible personal property. This is particularly true of tax laws.

.02 Property Rights

"Property rights," as the term is employed here, are the rights that a person has with respect to property that he or she owns or in which he or she has an interest. Naturally, his or her rights are dependent on the kind or degree of his or her ownership. An absolute owner is one who has the exclusive right of possessing, using, enjoying, and disposing of property. The rights of possession, use, enjoyment, and disposition are called the "incidents of absolute ownership." In a limited ownership one or more of these rights are either absent or reduced.

.03 Method of Acquisition and Disposition of Property

The acquisition and the disposition of property may be treated together, for these actions, in a sense, are reciprocal.

Acquisition of disposition by descent and by purchase. All the ways of acquiring or disposing of property may be grouped into two main categories: by descent and by purchase. In general, the phrase "by purchase" means the acquisition or the disposition of property by every method other than descent.

The word "purchase" is not used here in the sense of bargain and sale. It refers, rather, to such ways of acquiring or disposing of property as the following:

- Escheat—the falling back of property to the state because of lack of heirs.
- Occupancy—the taking possession of property that is without an owner (such as public lands acquired by homesteading and the capture of wild beasts) with the intention of appropriating it to one's own use.
- Prescription—the possession or use of property for a period of time long enough, under the law, to obtain for oneself a title or right of possession as against others.
- Adverse possession—the occupancy of real property as if by right and without molestation (occupation that may at length ripen into ownership).
- Forfeiture—the divesting of a person of property by or in consequence of a wrong, default, or breach of condition.
- Alienation—any method by which property is voluntarily transferred from one person to another, such as by sale or gift or by a bequest or devise.

Acquisition or disposition by other methods. There are many methods of acquiring or disposing of property other than by buying or selling it. The principal ones are by:

1. Gift between living persons.
2. Gift because of approaching death.
3. Declaration of trust.
4. Survivorship under joint tenancy.
5. Intestacy.
6. Will.
7. Abandonment.

When a person dies without leaving a will, he is said to die intestate. His real property descends according to the laws of descent in the state in which it is located, and his personal property is distributed by the administrator according to the laws of distribution in the state in which the decedent had his or her residence. In some states the distinctions between real and personal property with respect to descent and distribution have been largely abolished, and all property passes according to certain rules that apply to real and personal property alike. The estate of the heirs in the real property and the interest of the distributees in the personal property are subject to the rights of the surviving spouse.

¶ 630 Abandoned, Lost, and Mislaid Tangible Property

.01 Abandoned Property

The term "abandonment" as applied to property and property rights has acquired a well-defined and technical meaning. In its general sense, "abandonment" means the act of intentionally relinquishing a known right absolutely and without reference to any particular person or for any particular purpose. Abandoned property is that to which the owner has voluntarily relinquished all right, title, claim, and possession with the intention of terminating his ownership, but without vesting it in any other person and with the intention of not reclaiming future possession or resuming its ownership, possession, or enjoyment.

.02 Lost and Mislaid Property

"Lost property" is defined in law as property with which the owner has involuntarily parted through neglect, carelessness, or inadvertence, that is, property that the owner has unwittingly suffered to pass out of his possession and of whose whereabouts he has no knowledge. While in a popular sense property is lost when the owner does not know, and cannot ascertain, where it is, the essential test of lost property in contemplation of law is whether the owner parted with the possession of the property intentionally, casually, or involuntarily; only in the latter contingency may it be lost property. The distinction between loss and abandonment of property is that the first is involuntary and the second is by intent or design.

"Mislaid property" is property that the owner voluntarily and intentionally laid down in a place where he or she can again resort to it and then forgets where he or she put it. Property is not "lost" unless the owner parts with it involuntarily and unintentionally and does not at any time thereafter know where to find it.

Place of finding as a factor in determining character of property as lost or mislaid. The place where money or property claimed as lost is found is a potent factor in the determination of whether it was lost or only mislaid. If the owner laid the property down in a public place, in a place of business (as in a private compartment of a safe-deposit company), or other place and then forgets that he or she has done so and cannot find it, or if he or she hides the property and does not remember and cannot discover the hiding place, it is not lost but mislaid property that is still in the constructive possession of the owner. However, when articles are accidentally dropped in any public place, public thoroughfare, or street, they are lost in the legal sense. In short, property will not be considered to have been lost unless the circumstances are such that considering the place where and the conditions under which it is found, there is an inference that it was left there unintentionally.

Property in the possession of another cannot be found in the sense of the law of lost property. Thus, when property is discovered in a place where only customers of the owner of the premises have a right to be, for example, when property is discovered in the safe-deposit vault area of a bank, the bank, as agent or trustee for the true owner, has the right to the custody of any property found. If the finder of such property is the servant of the fiduciary and he or she finds it in his or her character as such servant, the right of custody of the property is in the fiduciary and not in the individual servant or agent who recovers its physical possession.

.03 Treasure-Trove and Property Embedded in the Earth

According to the common law, treasure-trove is any gold or silver in coin, plate, or bullion whose owner is unknown that is found concealed in the earth or in a house or other private place, but not lying on the ground.

It is not essential to its character as treasure-trove that the thing is hidden in the ground; it is sufficient if it is found concealed in other articles, such as bureaus, safes, machinery, etc. While strictly speaking treasure-trove is gold or silver, it might include the paper representatives thereof, especially when found hidden with those precious metals. Treasure-trove carries with it the thought of antiquity; to be classed as treasure-trove, the treasure must have been hidden or concealed so long as to indicate that the owner is probably dead or unknown.

Treasure-trove differs from lost property in that property is not lost unless the owner parted with it involuntarily, while it is essential to the character of treasure-trove that it was concealed by the owner for safekeeping. Treasure-trove is also to be distinguished from a class of discovered property known as "property embedded in the soil," which includes anything other than gold or silver that is so buried.

Thus, an aerolite, a prehistoric boat, valuable earthenware, and gold-bearing quartz found embedded in the soil under circumstances indicating that some person had placed it where it was found have all been placed in this class.

.04 Rights of Finder in and to Property

Abandoned property. Property that is abandoned by the owner who relinquished it with the intention of terminating his ownership interest in it and without intending to vest ownership in another goes back into a state of nature, or, as more commonly expressed, it returns to the common mass of things in a state of nature and becomes subject to appropriation by the first taker, occupier, or finder who reduces it to possession. Such person thereupon acquires an absolute property interest therein as against both the former owner and the person upon whose land it happens to have been left.

Lost property. The finder of a lost article does not acquire an absolute property right or ownership, but he or she does acquire such property interest or right as will enable him or her to keep it against all the world but the rightful owner. The place of finding, or the relation of the finder to a third person, does not affect this rule. The finder of lost property has a right to possession of the article superior to that of the owner or occupant of the premises where it is found. Under this rule a servant is, as against his or her master, entitled to property that he or she finds on the employer's premises. The finder of a valuable secreted in an article sold also has the right to possession as against the purchaser of the particular article.

The right of the finder to possession against all persons other than the owner is not lost by the fact that the property has gotten out of the finder's possession, either by its loss and finding by another or by the fact that he or she surrendered it to another. In other words, a finder's right to the property is not dependent upon his or her possession, and he or she may bring an appropriate action to recover it notwithstanding his or her loss of possession.

Joint finders. If lost property is found by several persons under such circumstances that the finding is the joint act of all, they have equal rights in the thing found, and if it is divisible, they become tenants in common thereof and each is entitled to the possession of a part and charged with the duty of holding it for the owner until he can be ascertained. Whether several persons present at a finding are to be deemed joint finders is sometimes a difficult question when the evidence shows that some of them saw the property before the others or had a greater share of the work of which the finding was an incident. Generally, the courts have inclined, in doubtful cases, to regard the finding as joint and all persons present and to any degree participating as joint finders.

Treasure-trove. Originally, under the English law, treasure-trove belonged to the finder if the owner was not discovered. Later it was judged expedient for the purposes of the state and particularly for the coinage that it should go to the sovereign. It was this supervision by the state and the right of the Crown that created a distinction between treasure-trove and lost property at common law.

In this country, in the absence of legislation, the rule is that the title to treasure-trove belongs to the finder against all the world except the true owner, and the doctrine of the English common law in regard to treasure-trove has become merged into the law respecting the finding of lost property, in so far as the rights of the finder are concerned. The result is that the finder of treasure-trove has a right thereto as against the owner or occupant of the premises where it is found, and the fact that the finder is an employee of the owner of the premises where it is found does not affect his or her right.

Property embedded in the earth. A person who finds property that is embedded in the soil but that is not treasure-trove acquires no title thereto, because the presumption is that the possession of the article found is in the owner of the place in which it is found. When property is embedded in the earth and the owner of the realty dies, such rights as he or she has in the embedded property pass with the realty to the person to whom it is devised and the deceased owner's executor has no cause of action for its recovery as against the finder.

Mislaid property. A person who finds mislaid property acquires no special rights in it, and when such property is found upon another's premises, the finder has no right to its possession; this is true whether the finder is an employee of the owner or occupier of the premises on which the mislaid article is found or a customer of the owner or occupant. The finder has no right to the property that he or she found on the premises of another and cannot recover it from the latter if the owner does not turn up or cannot be located.

The right of possession as against all except the true owner is in the owner or occupant of the premises where the property is discovered, because mislaid property is presumed to have been left in the custody of the owner or occupier of the premises upon which it is found. The result is that the proprietor of the premises is entitled to retain possession of the thing pending a search by him or her to discover the owner or during such time as the owner may be considered to be engaged in trying to recover his or her property.

.05 Rights of Owner or Former Owner

Abandoned property. Abandonment divests the former owner of title to the property, so that he or she never had any right or interest in it. The owner cannot thereafter reassert his or her rights of ownership to the prejudice of those who may have in the meantime appropriated the property. However, the owner of abandoned property of which the state has assumed protective custody may reclaim it from the state at any time, and even when such property has escheated to the state, the former owner may have a statutory right to reclaim it within a stated period of time.

A person does not lose his or her right to property by the fact that it has been carried by a flood and has become stranded upon another's land. It continues to be his or her property; he or she may enter and take it away, and he or she has a right of action if the landowner appropriates it to his or her own use. However, the landowner is under no legal obligation to preserve it for the true owner and the landowner may free the land from the encumbrance, provided in so doing he or she does no unnecessary harm to the property.

Lost property, treasure-trove. The finder of lost property or of treasure-trove only acquires the right to possession and custody, and the owner of such property or his or her personal representative has, unless otherwise limited by statute, the right to reclaim it from the finder. However, the owner's right to such property may be cut off if the finder has complied with the statutory provisions relating to the posting and advertising of his or her find and the owner does not claim it within the statutory period. If the owner of lost property has offered a specific reward for its restoration, the finder is entitled to retain possession until the reward has been paid.

The finder of lost property is rightfully in possession and such possession of itself creates no right of action in favor of the loser. Something must first occur to make the possession wrongful as when, upon demand and appropriate evidence to title, the finder refuses to deliver the property or when, in the absence of such demand and refusal, the finder is guilty of some misconduct toward the property, as when he or she abuses or wrongfully uses it.

As between the owner and third persons, the title of the former must be deemed perfect, except as to money or negotiable instruments the title to which may be acquired by a bona fide purchaser without notice of the rights of the true owner.

Mislaid property. The owner of mislaid property is constructively in possession of such property although its custody may be in another on whose premises it has been left, and he has a right to reclaim it from any person who has assumed custody.

Statutes providing a method by which title to lost property may be acquired by the finder have no application to mislaid property.

.06 Duties and Liabilities of Finders and Bailees

The right of a person who finds property, and of any person other than the true owner who claims it, are fixed at the time of the findings and the fact that the owner subsequently appears or that the owner cannot be found does not affect the status of either party as to the right of possession at that time.

The owner of property that has been carried away by flood and has become stranded upon another's land does not lose his or her title, and the person upon whose land it is stranded becomes an involuntary bailee with the right to possession as against everyone but the owner.

Lost property. A person who finds lost property is not bound to take charge of it, but if he or she chooses to undertake its custody he or she binds himself or herself to the owner for its safekeeping and its return if demanded. In the absence of a statute imposing a greater duty, a finder's liability for any loss occurring to the property is that of a gratuitous bailee. At common-law, the finder of lost property had a duty to look for the owner and was absolutely liable if he or she delivered the property to anyone other than the true owner. This duty has been changed by statute in some states so that if the finder follows the procedure prescribed, and the owner does not claim it within the statutory period, there is no liability for delivering it to a person other than the owner.

> ***CAUTION:*** Aside from the common-law duty of the finder of lost property to deliver it to the real owner, the criminal statutes may require the finder to make reasonable and just efforts to find the owner and restore his or her property to him or her, and a finder who appropriates property to his or her own use with knowledge of, or the immediate means of ascertaining, the owner thereof may be guilty of larceny.

Some statutes impose upon the owner of lost property a duty to reward the finder. Such statutes have been held constitutional against the contention that they operate to deprive the owner of his property without due process of law. Registered and nonnegotiable savings bonds and corporate stock certificates stolen from the owner, which were of no value to the finder, have been held not to be within the meaning of the statute; although money taken from its owner by force and concealed by robbers was considered to be lost so as to entitle the finder to a reward.

Reimbursement of finder for expenses; right to reward. Some authorities hold that the finder of lost property is entitled to recover from the owner his or her necessary expenses in its preservation, while others hold that he or she is not. Even admitting the finder's right to compensation, he or she has no lien on the property but must surrender possession and resort to a civil action against the owner to recover expenses.

In the absence of a statute imposing upon the owner of lost property a duty to reward the finder, or in the absence of an offer of a reward by the owner, the finder has no right to a reward and, therefore, no lien on the property.

> ***PLANNING NOTE:*** Although we have attempted to cover most of the common law concepts regarding tangible personal property that has parted ways with its owner, a careful review of state and local law in the particular state where such property is located is essential to resolve ownership claims.
>
> Many states and local jurisdictions have enacted specific legislation to handle lost and mislaid property; in a few jurisdictions, treasure trove and other categories of tangible property are covered.

Chapter 7

FILING REPORTS, AMNESTY PROGRAMS, IMMUNITY AND INDEMNITY

¶ 701 Overview

The requirements for reporting unclaimed property are discussed at ¶ 705. A discussion of the necessary forms, how to obtain them, various methods of reporting, amnesty programs, and reimbursement of a holder's costs are may be found at ¶ 710. Immunity and indemnity for holders for reported property is discussed at ¶ 715.

¶ 705 Reporting in General

Reports of unclaimed property are not complicated by their nature, but the underlying rules for reporting property correctly can become complex. The rules of jurisdiction discussed in Chapter 5 are the foundation for filing all unclaimed property reports with the states. The report form for each state is basically a listing of all owners that have not claimed their property for the requisite time period, one year, three years, or five years, in most cases.

Property items that are less than a certain dollar value (the "aggregation limit") may be reported as one line item on the report such as "299 payroll checks, each less than $50" for a total of $822.95. Also, owners of property items where no names or addresses exist may be reported in the aggregate such as "32 expense checks, no names or addresses" for a total of $3,657.00.

> ***CAUTION:*** One common misconception of holders is that if no name or address can be located for an owner, the property is not reportable to any state. Property that can be identified in the books and records of a holder must be reported just like any other item of property; however, there will be no name or address to report.

¶ 710 Reporting Forms

The National Association of Unclaimed Property Administrators (NAUPA) has grappled with the problem of uniformity not only in the statute but also in the administrative processes relating to unclaimed property compliance administration. As a result, a uniform reporting form has been adopted by the NAUPA that is currently in use by many states (see ¶ 11,020). This is one of the many steps the states are taking in an attempt to secure better holder compliance with their unclaimed property statutes.

The reporting forms in each state are basically comprised of two elements. First, a verification or checklist is required. The checklist enumerates various categories of unclaimed property and also contains a verification under oath that the holder has reported all of the property covered by the 1981 Uniform Unclaimed Property Act (UUPA 1981).

Second, the reporting forms contain a schedule for listing each individual owner of unclaimed property and require the reporting of such information as:

- The owner's name and last known address,
- The owner's social security number,
- A description of the type of property being reported,
- The date of the last activity on the account or the item,
- The date of last contact with the owner that is documented in the holder's records,
- The amount that is due the owner,
- The amount of any service charges or offsets taken against the property while in the custody of the holder, and finally,
- The amount that is being reported to the state as unclaimed property under the law.

The report forms for the states that administer unclaimed property laws still contain substantial variances due to unique differences in specific statutes and variances with the various versions of UUPA 1981. In many cases, however, a holder may substitute certain detailed owner lists that are produced as a result of a computer run or listing instead of re-transcribing such information onto the forms provided by the state. In many instances, the instructions sent by the state will advise the holder that such a substitution is permissible. However, a holder should check to determine if a substitution is permissible. Many states permit the filing of the report on computer media such as diskette or magnetic tape, and many states require electronic reporting.

.01 Obtaining Reporting Forms

Most state reporting forms are available on NAUPA's web site which lists a link to most of the state unclaimed property divisions at www.unclaimed.org. In addition, state forms are available by calling or writing to each state at the phone number or address listed at the NAUPA site. Once a holder receives forms from a state and files a report, most states automatically send forms in the following year.

> ***CAUTION:*** Not receiving the reporting forms does not in any way relieve a holder from the duty to file a report if property is due. Some states require the filing of a negative report—one that declares that there is no property to report in that year. Many states will accept a letter from a holder indicating that there is no reportable property.

A sample reporting form may be found at ¶ 11,020.

.02 Software

Several companies have developed computer software to automate the report preparation process. Some of these programs can manage the data related to unclaimed items as a separate liability that can be listed in the current or long-term liability section of the balance sheet. Most of these vendors advertise on the NAUPA web site.

> ***CAUTION:*** Although all of these vendors advise that their software is updated for the most current changes in the states' laws, caution should be exercised in using any software package. The holder is ultimately responsible for the correct filing of the report.

.03 Reporting Services

In addition to software that has been developed for managing and reporting unclaimed property, several vendors provide reporting services for holders. These services generally involve the capture of data for stale-dated items of property that have not yet become three or five years old and preparing reports for each state in which property is owed. The reports are then submitted to the holder for signature and filing with the state along with the appropriate remittance. Many of these vendors advertise on the NAUPA web site at www.unclaimed.org.

> ***CAUTION:*** It is important to note that the holder is ultimately responsible for the completeness and accuracy of the reports filed with each state even though preparation has been out-sourced.

.04 Reciprocal Reporting

In an attempt to reduce the burden of reporting to many states, the states have developed reciprocal agreements that permit holders to report property for other states to a "home state." Each state provides a list of any states for which they accept reciprocal property.

Example: A state may have reciprocal agreements with 20 other states. This allows a holder to report all property for owners in those 20 other states on its home state's report.

Some of these reciprocal agreements also permit other states to audit for the home state.

CAUTION: Even though states have these reciprocal agreements, they prefer that holders report directly. In addition, property must be reported under the correct state's holding period and report and remit due dates. Therefore, it is probably easier to report directly to each state unless there is an occasional item that can be included in the home state report. The number of states that enter into reciprocal agreements changes frequently and the states' interpretations often differ.

PLANNING NOTE: It is recommended that holders report directly to each state under the rules of jurisdiction contained in *Texas v. New Jersey*. (See Chapter 5 for a discussion of the rules of jurisdiction in unclaimed property law.)

.05 Filing the First Report with a State

Compliance with unclaimed property laws is problematic for most holders because of the multi-state aspect of filing reports in all states where an unclaimed asset owner may reside. Many holders are not subject to the jurisdiction of more states than the one in which they are located. Reporting to foreign states is not a routine practice for any other matter than unclaimed property compliance. Therefore, many holders have only recently become aware that they have reporting responsibilities in several or all states and now must confront how to come forward and file an initial report. Will an initial report trigger an audit by a state? Will interest and penalties be assessed for tardy reports? In most cases, states receive initial reports from many holders each year and process them routinely. It is doubtful that an initial report will trigger an audit unless extraordinary circumstances are present.

The main concern for an initial report is how far back into its records does a holder need to research for unclaimed items. The answer is not an easy one. States have different reach-back periods. Some states are limited to a 10-year reach-back. Some states go back to the date their law was enacted. For example, California goes back to 1959, the year that the California statute was originally enacted. Each state will provide guidance in how far back a holder needs to research records or reconstruct records.

CAUTION: The guidance provided by the state may or may not be in concert with what its law requires. Generally, incorrect advice provided by a state official is not a defense against incorrect reporting. The issue of the reach-back for an initial report must be carefully analyzed to avoid leaving an open liability to a state or states.

.06 Amnesty Programs

Due to the concerns raised regarding filing an initial report, many holders have failed to file reports in one or many states. Recognizing that a holder coming into compliance and reporting into the future on an ongoing basis is good public policy, many states have adopted amnesty programs of one sort or another. These amnesty programs generally provide that holders who voluntarily come forward and report and remit past due sums will not be assessed any interest or penalties. The great majority of states operate in this fashion.

However, there are some exceptions that must be noted. For instance, California and New York historically have had policies to assess their statutory interest in all cases of late remittance of property. Some other states have taken the same position, but these positions change from time to time as new administrators take over these programs.

California passed legislation in 2000 to formally adopt an amnesty program for non-filers for all property that was reportable in 1999 and all prior years. The California interest section provides for interest at 12 percent per annum.[1] For property that is eight years old, that would translate into a 96-percent interest assessment on the initial amount due, and California may go back to 1959. Conditions that must be met are prescribed in a checklist (see ¶ 11,015).

New York now has an amnesty program that forgives interest and penalties. Holders should contact the state for details of this program.

The policy of not assessing interest and penalties does not apply when a state audits a holder and discovers unreported unclaimed property. The theory here is that the state has deployed scarce resources to identify and audit a scofflaw and that cost should be borne by the scofflaw and not the taxpayers. Many states have informal processes for waiving interest and penalties if a holder can show good cause for not reporting. This is a matter of administrative practice in each state and varies widely.

---

[1] Cal. Code of Civ. Proc. § 1577.

.07 Reimbursement of Holders' Costs

There is a gradually accumulating body of law a holder can cite as authority for the argument that the costs of record keeping and reporting to the state may be deducted from the unclaimed property or claimed from the state. For example, in *Pennsylvania v. New York,*[2] a case involving uncashed money orders, the U.S. Supreme Court stated:

> as a matter of fairness the claimant States, and not Western Union, bear the cost of finding and recording available addresses, and we shall remand to the Special Master for a hearing and recommendation as to the appropriate formula for distributing those costs.

However, this holding did not suggest that the auditing states reimburse Western Union.

In the case of *Arkansas Department of Finance and Administration v. City of North Little Rock,*[3] the Arkansas Supreme Court held that the City of North Little Rock should be allowed a credit for its record keeping and reporting cost against unclaimed customer deposits payable to the state. The court reasoned that it was fair and reasonable to impose such a charge on the state rather than the city since the unclaimed property statute imposed a financial burden on the city that the city would not have incurred had the law not been passed.

Also, Cal. Code of Civ. Proc. § 1564 (b)(4) suggests that the legislature may have intended that holders receive reimbursement "for any unpaid lawful charges or costs which arose from holding any specific property or any specific funds which were delivered or paid to the Controller, or which arose from complying with this chapter with respect to such property of funds."

¶ 715 Immunity and Indemnity for Holders for Property Reported

.01 The UUPA 1981 Provision

Act Sec. 20 of UUPA 1981, and the laws of those states that have adopted it, provides the holder relief from liability to the extent of the value of property paid or delivered to the state pursuant to its unclaimed property act. Act Sec. 20 also allows a holder who has paid escheated property to the state to pay the rightful owner the amount of the escheated property and then obtain reimbursement from the state upon presentation of proof of such payment.

Some states, such as California, have gone even further by requiring the state to "defend" and "indemnify" the holder against any claim

[2] SCt, 407 US 206, 92 SCt 2075 (1972).

[3] 280 Ark. 512, 659 SW2d 937 (1983).

brought by any person or another state to recover property turned over to the state under its unclaimed property law.

It should be noted that the immunity provision contains certain important limitations. First, the immunity provision applies only to property paid or delivered to the state under the provisions of its abandoned or unclaimed property law. Thus, if the property was erroneously turned over to the state (for example, because the holder failed to notice that its records showed a recent contact with the owner), presumably the holder could not avail itself of the statutory immunity if the owner or another person or state should sue the holder for the property. In most cases, the fact that the holder may not technically be entitled to immunity is somewhat academic since the holder would ordinarily have the right to recover property paid to the state under a mistake of fact or law.

If the property is other than cash, such as stocks or tangible property that may fluctuate in value, the immunity problem may become more complex.

The second limitation restricts immunity to the extent of the value of the property paid or delivered to the state. Again, this limitation may be of little practical concern if the property is cash because the money could be recovered from the state and any claim by an owner or another state against the holder would usually be only in the amount of such cash.

Property subject to fluctuations in value, however, presents additional complications. The limitation of immunity to the extent of the "value" of the property has been viewed by at least one court as adequate protection for holders.

In *Clovis National Bank v. Callaway,*[4] the New Mexico Supreme Court stated:

> [p]laintiffs also make reference to the fact that Sections 22-22-15, N.M.S.A. 1953, pocket supp., only protects them to the extent of the "value" of the property so paid or delivered. It seems to us that this protection afforded is as broad as it need be. If the banks have acted improperly or have become liable over and beyond the value of the property, it should be their responsibility, and as far as any property which might be lost through surrender of the same to the state is concerned, it would be our view that protection for the "value" of the property is all that they can demand or expect.

Most state laws not modeled after UUPA 1981 also contain similar immunity provisions.

---

[4] 69 N.M. 119, 364 P2d 748 (1961).

.02 Shares of Stock and Tangible Property

While statutory immunity and the right to recover the escheated property from the state are usually adequate protection for holders to guard against claims by owners or other states, such protection may not entirely alleviate the concerns of holders delivering stock certificates, tangible property, or similar items to a state. These items, by their nature, may fluctuate in value depending on the whims of the marketplace.

> **Example:** A corporation may deliver certificates to the state representing the shares of stock of certain owners; the shares are subsequently sold by the state at the prevailing market price. However, the owner may appear at a later date, contending that the corporation should pay him the current market value of the shares or "make him whole" by purchasing like shares off the open market, which cost may be higher than the state realized when it sold the stock.

If the shares met all the criteria for escheat under the law and were properly delivered to the state, the holder would appear to be protected from such an owner's claim, even though the value of the property had increased from the time the certificates were delivered to the state or sold by the state. (The relief from liability "to the extent of the value of the property" appears to refer to the property's value at any point in time; otherwise, the statutory immunity would be hollow indeed.)

If, however, the shares were not, in fact, escheatable because, for example, the corporation had overlooked a recent contact with the shareholder or the escheat period had not run, the corporation may be unable to invoke the immunity provision because it only applies when the property was paid or delivered to the state "under this act." The corporation may, therefore, be liable to the shareholder or his successor for the full amount of the resultant damages. Of course, even when delivery to the state was erroneous, the corporation's liability could be mitigated by recovering from the state the proceeds the state received from the sale of the stock, or the stock itself, if it has not been sold.

In addition to the express relief from liability and indemnity provisions found, respectively, in Act Secs. 20(a) and (e) of UUPA 1981, that Act provides further holder protection in two additional sections. Act Sec. 19 (Payment or Delivery of Abandoned Property) provides in subsection (d) that the issuer is relieved of all liability upon delivery of the duplicate certificate (the original presumably being in the hands of the missing owner) to any person (which would cover any official acting under a state escheat or abandoned property law).

Furthermore, Act Sec. 22 (Public Sale of Abandoned Property) provides in subsection (d) that the state administrator should hold the stock for three years before sale.

The administrator may, if the "best interest of the state" so requires, sell prior to the lapse of this three-year "state holding period," in which case the reappearing owner would be entitled to the greater of the sales proceeds or the prevailing market price. If the state sells after three years, the reappearing owner is entitled only to the sales proceeds and "no person" has a claim against the state or "the holder, any transfer agent, registrar or other person acting for or on behalf of a holder" for "any appreciation."

Clearly, states and holders should not be concerned about liability for appreciating property after the expiration of the three-year "state holding period." The holder (including any agent acting on its behalf) should be protected against liability for any appreciation by virtue of Act Sec. 19(d), even if the state administrator should exercise his discretion to sell the stock prior to the three-year period.

.03 California's Indemnity Provision

In addition to providing immunity from further liability for holders that pay or deliver escheated property to the state, California's Unclaimed Property Law also specifies that the state controller shall, upon receiving written notice of a claim against the holder for the escheated property, "defend the holder against the claim and indemnify him against any liability on the claim."[5] Again, this protection is available only when the property has "escheated" to the state. Note, however, that even property paid or delivered to the state under a mistake of fact or law may be recovered if the State Controller has not disposed of the property; otherwise, a refund of cash may be obtained.

The effect of Code of Civ. Proc. § 1561 is to require the state controller to defend the holder against a claim and indemnify him against "any liability," even one which conceivably might exceed the amount or value of the property paid or delivered to the state. Furthermore, the obligation to defend the holder is not limited to actions or claims brought against the holder in California but would extend to those brought in other states. However, any legal expenses or other costs incurred by the holder prior to giving written notice of the claim to the state controller would presumably be the responsibility of the holder. If the state controller failed or refused to defend the holder after receiving notice of the claim, the holder could seek reimbursement for any expenses incurred as a result of the breach of the controller's duty.

[5] Cal. Code of Civ. Proc. § 1561.

Other states may or may not have provisions similar to California's indemnity provision. Many states provide a written indemnity agreement as part of a settlement of disputed amounts in the audit arena. Whether a state may extend this level of protection to a holder without the underlying statutory authority has not been tested.

> ***COMMENT:*** The lack of reported cases dealing with immunity or indemnity under the unclaimed property laws suggests that the subject rarely, if ever, arises other than academically, or that states have been able to resolve such cases amicably. Based on the authors' experience, it appears that a combination of these two factors explains the absence of case law in this area.

Chapter 8

SPECIAL CATEGORIES OF PROPERTY: EXEMPTIONS AND LIMITATIONS

¶ 801 Overview

There are several categories of property that have been problematic in the field of unclaimed property law. This chapter attempts to identify and discuss the major problem areas that have been identified over the past several years.

This chapter covers the following types of property that have been the subject of litigation, exemption, and special treatment due to their unique nature: insurance drafts and checks (¶ 805), unclaimed court ordered refunds (¶ 810), mineral interests and oil and gas royalties (¶ 815), gift certificates (¶ 820), vendor-to-vendor checks and credits (¶ 825), ERISA property (¶ 830), and IRA accounts (¶ 835).

¶ 805 Insurance Drafts and Checks

Litigation involving amounts represented by unpresented drafts issued by insurance companies has created a split in the way that courts have viewed this category of property. The dispute generally focuses on whether the drafts or checks are mere offers to settle unliquidated claims and, therefore, represent only contingent liabilities of the company, or denote a fixed obligation that may be subject to escheat.

The first reported case to deal with the issue in any sort of direct way was *Insurance Co. of North America v. Knight.*[1] In that case, the insurance carrier, appealing from the trial court's denial of a motion for summary judgement, argued, among other things, that the Illinois unclaimed property statute could not constitutionally apply to outstanding drafts "which were offers of settlement of alleged claims under

[1] 8 Ill. App. 3d 871, 291 NE2d 40 (1972).

policies of liability insurance." Although the appellate court sustained the ruling of the trial court, it centered its attention on the allegations of the complaint and the state's answer thereto relating to whether there was "delivery" of the drafts in question:

> An allegation of "outstanding" checks connotes delivery of the instrument to the payee. If, in fact, there was no delivery, it would appear that the question cannot arise for no certain and fixed obligation would be owing. Allegations of the "issue" of drafts or checks, without more, denotes delivery.

The next case to confront the escheatability of sums represented by insurance claim drafts or checks was *Kane v. Insurance Co. of North America.*[2] In denying the state's claim to sums represented by checks, drafts, and credit memoranda, the court said:

> The fatal flaw in the Commonwealth's case is its failure to prove that those persons to whom the checks, drafts and credit memoranda were payable, or to whose accounts they were credited, were unqualifiedly entitled to same. The findings of the courts below that at least some of the items in question were drawn in anticipation of unliquidated claims never made, or liabilities never incurred, leaves the Commonwealth, whose rights in an escheat proceeding are derivative, in the position of attempting to create unliquidated claims where none exist.

The court went on to hold that the state had failed to meet its burden of proof in that it did not establish a prima facie case for escheat.

In *Blue Cross of Northern California v. Cory,*[3] Blue Cross argued that checks it issued to subscribers and health care providers pursuant to its medical insurance policies did not represent funds that were unconditionally owing because the checks allegedly were sent as offers of settlement of unliquidated claims. The court, noting that the checks were written and mailed pursuant to language in the policies providing that Blue Cross "shall pay" specified amounts for specified services, held that there was substantial evidence to support the trial court's finding that, when Blue Cross mailed the checks, the checks were not offers of settlement of unliquidated claims but were payment of unconditional obligations.

In *Allstate Insurance Co. v. Eagerton,*[4] the trial court held that unpresented drafts issued by Allstate represented funds subject to escheat. The Alabama Supreme Court reversed the trial court, stating that the parties had stipulated that the drafts were issued for the purpose of settling unliquidated claims and, therefore, did not constitute an acknowledgment by the company that it was liable to pay that amount. The court noted that if "the drafts were issued in payment of

---

[2] 38 Pa. Commw. 42, 392 A2d 325 (1978).

[3] 120 Cal. App. 3d 723, 174 Cal. Rptr. 901 (1981).

[4] 403 So. 2d 172 (1981).

fixed amounts due under the insurance contract, such as the face amount of a life insurance policy," the amounts of the unpresented drafts might well be subject to the Act. Here, however, Allstate retained the right to reject and litigate all claims not "settled" by accepting and presenting the drafts.

Citing *Kane v. Insurance Company of North America,* the court concluded that the drafts were offered in settlement of unliquidated and unconceded claims. Because they did not represent monies due and owing to the payee, the amounts represented by the drafts were not abandoned funds subject to the Act. Following the Allstate decision, the Alabama Supreme Court reached a similar result in *Aetna Casualty and Surety Insurance Co. v. State of Alabama.*[5]

The few cases in this area, while differing in result, have primarily turned on factual issues relating to whether the checks were issued as offers to settle disputed claims or whether the underlying claims for payment of which the checks or drafts were issued were fixed or liquidated.

Act Sec. 2 of the 1981 Uniform Unclaimed Property Act (UUPA 1981) will affect the outcome of future litigation involving insurance drafts and checks. Act Sec. 2(b) provides as follows:

> Property is payable or distributable for the purpose of this Act notwithstanding the owner's failure to make demand or to present any instrument or document required to receive payment.

Thus, although Act Sec. 2 does not address the problem of determining whether a draft merely represents an offer to settle an unliquidated claim, it does seem to remove the necessity for presentment mentioned in *Allstate* and *Kane.*

A decision by the Supreme Court of Wisconsin suggests that the tide may be turning in favor of the states. In *Employers Insurance of Wausau v. Smith,*[6] the court held that uncashed benefit checks issued by the Wisconsin Worker's Compensation Division were escheatable. Although the checks at issue represented payment for on-the-job injuries, the insurer still maintained that issuance of these checks was not an admission of liability. The insurer's unusual argument was premised on the worker's compensation provision that allowed an insurer to dispute liability even after it had issued a check. The court found this possibility unconvincing and agreed with the treasurer's rhetorical question: "Why is it that the person who cashed the check is entitled to get the money but the person who loses the check can no longer have the money?"

[5] 414 So. 2d 455 (1982).

[6] 154 Wis. 2d 199, 453 NW2d 856 (1990).

Act Sec. 6 of the 1995 Uniform Unclaimed Property Act includes language that would resolve this issue. Concerned that some insurers had misconstrued the Commissioners' Comment to Act Sec. 2 of UUPA 1981, the Commissioners added Act Sec. 6. This new Act Sec. 6 states:

> A record of issuance of a check, draft, or similar instrument is prima facie evidence of an obligation. In claiming property from a holder who is also the issuer, the administrator's burden of proof as to the existence and amount of the property and its abandonment is satisfied by showing issuance of the instrument and passage of the requisite period of abandonment. Defenses of payment, satisfaction, discharge, and want of consideration are affirmative defenses that must be established by the holder.

Act Sec. 6 shifts the burden of proof from the state to the holder. Legal challenges to this change have not yet occurred.

¶ 810 Unclaimed Court Ordered Refunds

A relatively new category of unclaimed intangible property consists of monies ordered to be refunded by a court or governmental agency. Court proceedings such as class actions, taxpayers' suits, and shareholders' derivative suits against corporate directors can present situations in which large amounts may remain undistributable because of the inability to locate all members of the class or group entitled to share in the recovery. Unclaimed refunds ordered by governmental agencies may arise when a regulatory board or commission, such as a public utilities commission, orders a regulated business to refund erroneous or improper fees or charges.

Unclaimed refunds may be subject to escheat under various provisions of UUPA 1981. Act Sec. 9 of UUPA 1981 specifically covers refunds ordered to be made by business associations. Other provisions of UUPA 1981 under which refunds may escheat are Act Sec. 12 (money or property held in a fiduciary capacity), Act Sec. 13 (money paid into court or the custody of a public officer or agency), Act Sec. 11 (property distributable in the course of a business's dissolution), and Act Sec. 2 (miscellaneous property held or owing in the ordinary course of business).

Two cases involving public utilities have reinforced the proposition that decisions of administrative bodies providing for particular dispositions of unclaimed refunds owed by regulated business may not override the state unclaimed property statutes in the absence of specific statutory authority to do so.

.01 Alabama

The first case to establish this principle was *Boswell v. Whatley*.[7] In 1976, the Alabama Public Service Commission ordered Mobil Gas Service Corporation to make certain refunds to its customers. The commission subsequently amended its order to provide that none of the refunds should escheat to the state, but that they should be distributed as a credit against the bills of its then existing customers. The Commissioner of Revenue sought to enjoin implementation of the order on the grounds that the Public Service Commission exceeded its authority in providing that none of the funds would be subject to escheat. The trial court refused to grant such relief.

The Alabama Supreme Court held that the statutory authority of the Public Service Commission does not include the power to extinguish the property of those who are served by the utilities. The court found that the legislature provided for unclaimed or abandoned property to be disposed of in accordance with Alabama's version of the 1954 Uniform Disposition of Unclaimed Property Act:

> But once the Commission made a final determination or order providing for a refund, those customers were entitled to their share, which constituted a chose in action. Should those remain unclaimed for more than two years, the provisions of the Uniform Disposition of Unclaimed Property Act would control them.

Therefore, the Commissioner of Revenue was entitled to injunctive relief.

.02 California

The California Supreme Court reached a similar result in *Cory v. Public Utilities Commission*.[8] After a series of decisions, the Public Utilities Commission (PUC) ordered Pacific Telephone and Telegraph Company (Pacific) to refund ratepayers over-collections of approximately $381 million. Approximately $6 million of the refunds owing to former customers were unclaimed, either because the refund checks were returned as undeliverable or because the checks were not cashed. The PUC ordered that the funds represented by the checks were to be credited to the accounts of current customers on a pro rata basis. The state controller contended that such amounts would be subject to the California Unclaimed Property Law if not claimed by the owners for seven years and, consequently, the PUC had no authority to redistribute the funds to current customers.

---

[7] 345 So. 2d 1324 (1977).

[8] 33 Cal. 3d 522, 658 P2d 749, 189 Cal. Rptr. 385 (1983).

The California Supreme Court reversed the decision of the PUC and held that the unclaimed refunds could not be redistributed to current customers of Pacific but had to be preserved and eventually reported to the state under the California Unclaimed Property Law. The court stated that there is nothing in the law indicating that the PUC,

> having ordered the refunds, is authorized to subsequently repudiate the property rights of unlocated former customers, declare a forfeiture, and provide a windfall for current customers who have already received the full refund to which they are entitled.

The court went on to say:

> [t]he Commission is not authorized to forfeit the refunds of the unlocated customers, and the property should be held for the benefit of the unlocated customers and for the use of the state in accordance with the Unclaimed Property Law.

.03 UUPA 1981

Act Sec. 9 of UUPA 1981 expressly applies to refunds ordered to be made by a court or administrative agency. Act Sec. 9 states:

> Except to the extent otherwise ordered by the court or administrative agency any sum that a business association has been ordered to refund by a court or administrative agency which has remained unclaimed by the owner for more than one year after it became payable in accordance with the final determination or order providing for the refund, regardless of whether the final determination or order requires any person entitled to a refund to make a claim for it, is presumed abandoned.

Although Act Sec. 9 of UUPA 1981 begins by stating that it applies to unclaimed refunds "[e]xcept to the extent ordered by the court or administrative agency," it must be assumed that Act Sec. 9 was not intended to give a court or administrative agency power to provide for a disposition of unclaimed refunds different than that required under the unclaimed property statute, unless such authority is specifically conferred upon the court or administrative agency by other statutes or constitutional provisions. Otherwise, the holdings in *Boswell v. Whatley* and *Cory v. Public Utilities Commission,* discussed above, would be nullified because the administrative agency's decision could supersede the statutory requirements for disposition of unclaimed refunds.

> ***COMMENT:*** The comments of the National Conference of Commissioners on Uniform State Laws regarding Act Sec. 9 contain no hint that there was any intention to expand the powers of court or administrative agencies to order disposition of unclaimed refunds in any manner that would be inconsistent with the unclaimed property statutes.

PLANNING NOTE: Currently, the reported court decisions have involved amounts ordered to be repaid by utilities. However, it is likely that the provisions applicable to unclaimed refunds will also be applied to amounts originating from other sources, such as class action suits and the decisions of a variety of administrative agencies.

¶ 815 Mineral Interests and Oil and Gas Royalties

Oil, gas, and other mineral interests generate money for the owners when the interests are exploited. The producers or developers of the mineral interests often pay royalties to a large number of owners whose lands lie upon or within the oil, gas, or mineral deposit areas. These myriad mineral interests necessarily result in millions of royalty payments, many of which remain unclaimed by the owners.

.01 Oklahoma

In 1984 Oklahoma focused its attention on this type of unclaimed property and enacted a statute requiring the escrow of such proceeds generated by mineral interests located in Oklahoma, after the property remained unclaimed for one year, to transfer to the state. The constitutionality of the 1984 amendments to Oklahoma's version of the 1954 Uniform Disposition of Unclaimed Property Act was challenged in *American Petrofina Co. of Texas, et. al. v. Nance, et al.*[9] Plaintiffs, producers, and/or purchasers of oil and gas in Oklahoma filed suit against members of the Oklahoma Tax Commission contending that the 1984 amendments were contrary to the U.S. Supreme Court's ruling in *Texas v. New Jersey* and, therefore, violated the Supremacy Clause of the U.S. Constitution because the amendments conflicted with federal common law.

Plantiffs also alleged that because the state is not required under the law to defend and indemnify the company except to the extent of the value of the property paid or delivered to the state, Oklahoma's unclaimed property law contravenes the U. S. Supreme Court's proscription against multiple liability for unclaimed property.

The U.S. District Court agreed, and the U.S. Court of Appeals confirmed, that the 1984 amendments were unconstitutional. The court held that the amendments were invalid and unenforceable under the Supremacy Clause of the U.S. Constitution because they were inconsistent with the federal common law set forth in *Texas v. New Jersey* (see ¶ 510.04).

[9] 697 F.Supp. 1183 (1986). Affirmed, 859 F2d 840 (1988).

Under the *Texas v. New Jersey* rule, intangible property is subject to escheat or custodial taking by the state of the owner's last known address as shown on the records of the holder or if such state does not have an unclaimed property law pertaining to such property, then by the state of incorporation of the holder (see ¶ 510.04). Because the 1984 Oklahoma amendments purported to escheat proceeds of mineral interests located in Oklahoma, regardless of the state of the owner's last known address or state of incorporation of the holder, the statute conflicted with the law of the land as enunciated by the U.S. Supreme Court.

In *American Petrofina,* however, the trial court rejected the plaintiff's constitutional attack on the Oklahoma Uniform Act, finding that it was neither arbitrary nor unreasonable in its limited guarantee against multiple or further liability and noting its failure to require notice of transfers of property valued at less than $50.

.02 Texas

A similar suit was filed in Texas challenging a 1985 statute comparable to the 1984 Oklahoma Act. The Texas statute also required the reporting and payment of unclaimed proceeds of mineral interest located in Texas regardless of the state or last known address of the owners or state of incorporation of the holders (where the holders' records failed to show a last known address of the owner). This case was settled, however, with the principal element of the settlement providing that the holders did not have to report to Texas any mineral proceeds belonging to owners whose last known addresses were in other states. In short, holders need only comply with the *Texas v. New Jersey* rule when reporting such property to Texas.

.03 The Uniform Unclaimed Property Acts

The 1954, 1966, and 1981 Uniform Unclaimed Property Acts did not specifically address this category of property. Instead the various mineral-producing states relied upon their "omnibus" or "catch-all" provision.[10] The 1995 Uniform Unclaimed Property Act defined "mineral" and "mineral proceeds" as follows:

> (8) "Mineral" means gas; oil; coal; other gaseous, liquid, and solid hydrocarbons; oil shale; cement material; sand and gravel; road material; building stone; chemical substance; gemstone; fissionable and nonfissionable ores, colloidal and other clay; steam and other geothermal resource; or any other substance defined as a mineral by the law of this State . . .
>
> (9) "Mineral proceeds" means amounts payable for the extraction, production, or sale of minerals, or, upon the abandonment of those

[10] See *Citronelle-Mobile Gathering, Inc. v. Boswell,* 341 So. 2d 933 (1977).

payments, all payments that become payable thereafter. The term includes amounts payable:

(i) for the acquisition and retention of a mineral lease, including bonuses, royalties, compensatory royalties, shut in royalties, minimum royalties, and delay rentals;

(ii) for the extraction, production, or sale of minerals, including net revenue interests, royalties, overriding royalties, extraction payments, and production payments; and

(iii) resulting from an agreement or option, including a joint operating agreement, unit agreement, pooling agreement and farm-out agreement.

¶ 820 Gift Certificates

Gift certificates, merchandise certificates, scrip, or similarly denominated instruments represent a unique form of property right.

Generally, these instruments entitle the bearer to select from merchandise or services offered by the issuing retailer or a value equivalent to the amount indicated on the instrument. Apparently, many people purchase these instruments or receive them as gifts or for returned merchandise but never use them.

From the standpoint of the application of the unclaimed property laws to gift certificates and similar instruments, the first problem is in determining what type of property is involved: tangible or intangible. If tangible property, it may not be subject to the state's unclaimed property statute if the law is one that does not include general types of tangibles.

Also, under the principles relating to escheat jurisdiction, discussed in *Texas v. New Jersey,* tangible property would be subject to escheat only by the state in which the property is actually located. (See Chapter 5, regarding state power to escheat intangible property.)

In the principal case relating to escheat of gift certificates, *Callahan v. Marshall Field & Co.,*[11] it seemed to be presumed that the certificates represented intangible property. In that case, the court repeatedly referred to the property as intangible. This conclusion appears logical because it is not the certificate itself, e.g., the piece of paper, that is sought to be escheated nor is it any specific, identifiable item of merchandise, because none has been selected by the owner. The intangible property represented by the certificate is the right to select property or services that is the subject of the state's claim.

---

[11] 83 Ill. App. 3d 811, 404 NE3d 368, 38 Ill. Dec. 944 (1980).

It must also be determined what property escheats and if the property is cash, how much. In *Murdock v. Stetson Co.,*[12] the state sued for a "monetary award representing the approximate wholesale price of the [Stetson] hats for which the certificates were issued."

However, because the court denied the state's claim on other grounds, it did not decide whether the "wholesale price of the hats" was the appropriate measure of value. Likewise, in *Marshall Field,* discussed above, the court did not discuss the amount or nature of the property to be escheated, other than to refer to it as intangible personal property.

UUPA 1981 takes care of the problem by specifying that "the amount presumed abandoned is equal to the price paid by the purchaser," or in the case of credit memos, that the amount "is equal to the amount credited to the recipient." Under this approach, the purchase price, or face amount, would be subject to escheat, rather than the wholesale price or some discounted amount.

Escheat of property represented by gift certificates may also depend upon whether certain conditions to the holder's liability are applicable against the state. For example, in *Murdock v. Stetson,* the court held that the defendant's duty to perform (under the gift certificate contract) "was not to ripen unless and until the certificate was presented to it by the holder thereof. This condition precedent never having occurred, its obligation never became due at all."

The court went on to say that another reason why the amounts represented by the gift certificates would not escheat was the fact that a provision was printed on each certificate stating that it would be invalid one year from the date of issuance. "[E]ach certificate by its terms was invalid one year after sale and the Commonwealth is bound by this contractual term." However, in *Marshall Field,* similar provisions on the gift certificates and credit memoranda limiting the time within which the instruments would be honored were held invalid as an attempt to establish a "private escheat law."[13]

> ***COMMENT:*** Pursuit by the states of property represented by gift certificates and similar instruments is likely to increase in the years ahead. This should be especially true in those states adopting UUPA 1981 because it lays to rest some of the problems previously encountered by the states.

---

[12] 32 Pa. D. & C. 2d 300 (1963).

[13] See also *New Jersey v. Jefferson Lake Sulphur Co.,* 36 N.J. 577, 178 A2d 329 (1962). Cert. denied, 370 US 158, 82 SCt 1253 (1962).

.01 Gift Certificate as Intangible Personal Property

The most understandable definition of "intangible personal property" is personal property that is not tangible. Thus, it is property that is incapable of being seen, weighed, measured, felt, or touched, and it is not perceptible to the senses.[14]

Under these definitions, it is abundantly clear that the property evidenced by an unredeemed certificate is intangible in nature. The right to select merchandise, to acquire a service, or to apply a payment to a charge account certainly cannot be seen, weighed, measured, felt, or touched, and it is in no other way perceptible to the senses. It is an incorporeal right lacking in substance and body.

Again, it must be emphasized that the state is not escheating the certificate itself, the piece of paper, which is tangible. The only intrinsic value associated with the certificate is attributable to intangible elements rather than to any tangible embodiments.[15]

Additionally, the state is not considering the escheat of tangible merchandise that could be selected by the owner of a certificate. Therefore, we are only dealing with the unexercised right to select such property.

> ***COMMENT:*** It is interesting to note, in fact, that with respect to gift certificate rights that do escheat to the state, the state only acquires title to an unexercised right.

The only case located that refers to the nature of gift certificates is *Callahan v. Marshall Field & Company*.[16] That decision considered the application of the Illinois Uniform Disposition of Unclaimed Property Act to certificates issued by an Illinois corporation. The nature of the property represented by gift certificates was not in question. For purposes of this case, it was apparently accepted by the court without dispute that such property was intangible.

.02 The 1995 Uniform Unclaimed Property Act

The 1995 Uniform Unclaimed Property Act contains Act Sec. 2(a)(6), which addresses some perceived problems with the abandonment of gift certificates.

- When does a gift certificate become payable or distributable?
- If a certificate is redeemable only in merchandise, what is the monetary value that escheats?

---

[14] *Moeller, McPherrin & Judd v. Smith,* 255 N.W. 551, 127 Neb. 424 (1934).

[15] *Texas Instruments, Inc. v. U.S.,* 551 F2d 599 (1977).

[16] 83 Ill. App. 3d 811, 404 NE2d 368 (1980).

- Is the five-year dormancy period proposed in UUPA 1981 realistic for this category of property?

Act Sec. 2(a)(6) reads:

> Property is presumed abandoned if it is unclaimed by the apparent owner during the time set forth below for the particular property gift certificate, three years after December 31 of the year in which the certificate was sold, but if redeemable in merchandise only, the amount abandoned is deemed to be [60] percent of the certificate's face value.

.03 Gift Certificates: A New Trend in Exemptions

The mid-1990's saw the beginning of a new trend: the exclusion of gift certificates from the otherwise comprehensive scope of unclaimed property legislation. Although the most recent version of the Uniform Unclaimed Property Act—the 1995 Uniform Unclaimed Property Act—retained this property category, the retailer's lobby led a state-by-state approach in favor of exclusion.

The various exclusions took various forms. Some states simply omitted the statutory provision that had covered gift certificates. In 1996, Florida simply omitted former Fla. Stat. § 717.114. Maryland, on the other hand, amended its definition of "personal property" to exclude, among other property categories, gift certificates.[17] Some states excluded under a certain dollar value.[18] Two states tied the exclusion to the presence or absence of an expiration date: Idaho excluded gift certificates with "the expiration date prominently displayed on its face,"[19] while California included with its coverage only certificates that did contain an expiration date.[20]

A recent decision in New Jersey has re-examined the underlying contract contemplated by the parties at the time the certificate was sold. The certificates were issued by a hotel to be redeemed only for services and/or merchandise. The Supreme Court noted that all other categories of unclaimed property (including those gift certificates that are redeemable in cash) were essentially monetary claims; therefore, the Court held that these certificates were not escheatable because they were only redeemable for services and/or merchandise at the issuer.[21] Whether other courts will follow this important distinction remains to be seen.

Most issuers of gift certificates and like instruments do not maintain the name and last known address of the purchaser. Therefore,

---

[17] See Md. Code § 17-101(m)(1).

[18] See N.H. Rev. Stat. Ann. Ch. 471-C:16 (under $100), Utah Code Ann. Ann. § 67-4a-211, (under $25).

[19] Idaho Code § 14-502 (2)(b).

[20] Cal. Code of Civ. Proc. § 1520.5.

[21] *In re November 8, 1996, Determination of the State of New Jersey, Department of the Treasury, Unclaimed Property Office*, 309 N.J. Super. 272, 706 A2d 1177 (1998). Affirmed, 156 N.J. 599, 722 A2d 536 (1999).

under the backup rule contained in *Texas v. New Jersey* (see ¶ 510.04), all of the proceeds from unclaimed gift certificates are reportable to the holder's state of incorporation. If the state of incorporation has exempted, or provisionally exempted, gift certificates from its law, it appears that this property will remain with the holder indefinitely.

> ***PLANNING NOTE:*** Careful attention to the placement of this type of liability on the books of a multi-corporate holder may provide planning opportunities to seize on the exemptions contained in the states' laws.

¶ 825 Vendor-to-Vendor Checks and Credits

The gift certificate exclusion inspired another trend: the exclusion of payables owed from one business to another. The underlying rationale must be that businesses do not require as much consumer protection as individuals. In addition, unclaimed checks made payable to vendors and suppliers with whom regular contact is maintained may be evidence of errors or settlement processes in the accounting system.

> ***CAUTION:*** Careful analysis of unclaimed items due to current vendors or suppliers should be undertaken to ascertain their validity whether or not a particular state law exempts them, because they may not be "due and owing" as is contemplated in the state's statute.

Perhaps the most comprehensive business-to-business exclusions are found in Maryland's law, Md. Code § 17-101(m)(2)-(4):

> (2) Credits in connection with the sale of consumer goods to a wholesaler or retailer in the ordinary course of business;
>
> (3) Outstanding checks or credits issued to vendors or customers in the ordinary course of business (except banking and financial institutions);
>
> (4) Credit balances in vendor or commercial accounts that occur in the ordinary course of business (except banking and financial institutions).

Whether these business-to-business exclusions will become as widespread as those regarding gift certificates remains to be seen.

¶ 830 ERISA Property

The case law that has developed in the area of property generated under a benefit provided for by the Employee Retirement Income Security Act of 1974 (ERISA) has been problematic. Michigan sought payment of monies representing uncashed medical and hospital benefit checks issued by Blue Cross.[22] Although the insurer raised the issue of whether these checks truly represented liquidated amounts, Blue Cross argued that the ERISA required conflicting state legislation to bow to the federal regulatory scheme.

Specifically, the Michigan Court of Appeals found that:

1. The checks represented liquidated claims and
2. The Michigan Code of Escheats did not affect the administration of ERISA.

A similar argument was raised by Aetna Life Insurance Company in federal court in Connecticut.[23] Connecticut had sought the report and remittance of more than $2.5 million representing ERISA-covered benefits. The trial court found the Michigan *Blue Cross* decision to be unpersuasive.

Connecticut appealed. The U.S. Court of Appeals for the Second Circuit reversed, holding that the impact of the state's legislation upon the goal of ERISA—national uniformity in the supervision of benefit plans—to be too remote as to require preemption. The U.S. Supreme Court declined to hear Aetna's appeal, thereby foreclosing, for all practical purposes, an ERISA-based preemption argument.

Two recent cases have held that state unclaimed property laws interfere with the administration of ERISA plans: *Commonwealth Edison v. Vega* [24] and *Manufacturer's Life Insurance Co. v. East Bay Restaurant and Tavern Retirement Plan, et. al.*[25] Given the fact that two federal appellate circuits (Second and Seventh) had reached contrary results, it was anticipated that the U.S. Supreme Court would hear the *Commonwealth Edison v. Vega* case. However, that Court declined to resolve the issue. Therefore, whether or not holders of this category of property report is based upon geography.

CAUTION: It is recommend that holders review this issue with their advisors.

¶ 835 IRA Accounts

Funds in an individual retirement account (IRA), a retirement plan for self-employed individuals or similar account, or plan established pursuant to the Internal Revenue Code are not payable or distributable unless, under the terms of the account or plan, distribution of all or part of the funds would then be mandatory.

---

[22] *Attorney General v. Blue Cross*, 168 Mich. App. 372, 424 NW2d 54 (1988).

[23] *Aetna Life Insurance Co. v. Borges*, CA-2, 869 F2d 142 (1989).

[24] 174 F3d 870 (1999).

[25] 57 F.Supp. 2d 921 (1999).

Most states have applied a practical test to property rights that are held in the form of an IRA. The beginning of the holding period starts at the date for mandatory distribution of the property, not the earliest date on which the owner could withdraw the funds without a penalty. Therefore, the beginning of the holding period would be age 70 1/2.

> ***CAUTION:*** The types of property discussed in Chapter 8 seem to be problematic and will undoubtedly be the subject of future litigation. The amounts involved in these arenas are vast and the states' interest in these types of properties will soon awaken.

Chapter 9

STATES' ENFORCEMENT OF UNCLAIMED PROPERTY LAWS—AUDITS

¶ 901 Overview

Since the adoption of the initial model legislation, the Uniform Disposition of Unclaimed Property Act of 1954 (the 1954 Uniform Act), the states have been in the process of developing the compliance and enforcement arms of their unclaimed property programs to ensure that holders are made aware of their reporting responsibilities under the Act. Holders who are not in compliance with the Act are identified and brought into compliance by various actions undertaken by the states including audit, litigation, and self-assessment.

A brief historical perspective unclaimed property law compliance may be found at ¶ 905. A discussion of the examination authority of the states is at ¶ 910 and the right of a state treasurer to examine records if he has "reason to believe" that there has been a failure to report unclaimed property is discussed at ¶ 915. ¶ 920 describes current examination programs. The gathering and compilation of audit evidence is discussed at ¶ 925. The report of examination is discussed at ¶ 930. ¶ 935 discusses record retention and the use of estimates. Collection procedures are examined at ¶ 940, and ¶ 945 discusses penalties and other sanctions as well as waivers of interest and amnesty programs. Finally, ¶ 950 examines current compliance trends.

¶ 905 Historical Development

Although a few states enacted statutes relating to the disposition of unclaimed or abandoned property prior to the promulgation of the 1954 Uniform Act, the states did very little in the way of advising holders of their reporting responsibilities or determining compliance by selected holders until the late 1970s.

As a result of more and more states enacting the 1954 Uniform Act or the later versions, more holders became aware of the responsibilities that the Act imposed upon them. This was particularly true of public issuers of securities who had reporting responsibilities to many or all states.

The traditional scenario in most states upon enactment of this legislation was as follows. The state legislature designated a program administrator, usually the state treasurer, state comptroller, or the state revenue department. Thereafter, a mailing was made by the administrator to the banking community, the savings and loan community, the insurance community, and selected companies in the state. Upon receipt of the original reporting form, the institutions reviewed their records in varying degrees of detail and reported some, but usually not all, of the unclaimed property that was found in their financial books and records. Upon receipt of reports disclosing reportable property, the state proceeded to fulfill its statutory obligation of mailing notices to owners of unclaimed property and publishing their names in the newspaper. In many states this constituted the only effort to obtain compliance by holders with this legislation.

Thereafter, the state received remittance reports for owners who were not located as a result of the mailed notices or the newspaper notice published by the state. Truly, an environment of voluntary compliance existed for several years.

In the early 1970s, a few states began to closely examine the reporting practices of various holders and determined that there was a potential for recovering substantial amounts of unreported property by various types of holders. Some of the large states, such as California, New York, Pennsylvania, New Jersey, and Massachusetts, began field audit programs and sent examiners into the field to inspect the books and records of such holders as banks, life insurance companies, mutual funds, and issuers of securities. Based on preliminary results from these field audit programs, it was discovered that there was substantial noncompliance with the unclaimed property laws and that significant amounts of money awaited recovery by the states.

In addition, several practices were disclosed that resulted in the non-reporting or under-reporting of unclaimed items. Specifically, the practice of service-charging dormant accounts and written instruments at commercial banks became an issue. The lawfulness of service charges is discussed in length in Chapter 4.

Since the institution of various field audit programs in a number of states, several legal issues have been litigated and various decisions have been handed down that have helped to clarify the legal relationship between the holder, the owner, and the state. See Chapter 2 for a complete description of the legal issues in the field of unclaimed property law.

.01 Revisions to the 1954 Uniform Unclaimed Property Act

As a result of the compliance efforts of several states, an inherent weakness in enforcement remedies in the Uniform Disposition of Unclaimed Property Act of 1954 was noted and, therefore, the Uniform Law Commission made minor revisions in 1966 and substantial revisions to the Act in 1981. The revisions, in large part, dealt with various aspects of compliance administration and the drafting of new provisions to provide the state with the statutory enforcement tools necessary to collect unclaimed property that had remained unreported. Various fiscal disincentives were included, such as the assessment of interest and substantial penalties and the charging of examination fees. In addition, the 1981 Uniform Unclaimed Property Act (UUPA 1981) removed the "reason to believe" pre-condition for conducting audits by states (see ¶ 915).

¶ 910 Field Examinations—Examination Authority

The Uniform Unclaimed Property Act, in its various versions, has always contained a provision specifically authorizing the administrator of the unclaimed property law to examine the records of a holder to determine compliance with the provisions of the Uniform Unclaimed Property Act. All states currently have the statutory right to examine records of holders to determine compliance with the Act.

The authority of the state to inspect and examine records of holders to determine whether reportable property was present was upheld in the case of *Robert Q. Crane v. Federated Department Store.*[1] The store contended that any property that they may hold would be unclaimable by virtue of the running of the statute of limitations. They contended, therefore, that no examination of their records was permissible. The Massachusetts Appeals Court, however, upheld the validity of the lower court's order to permit the examination of the company's records.

In some cases, holders have raised questions as to whether the state, under its unclaimed property law, had sufficient authority to review records that were in possession of the holder. This issue seems to be relatively well settled in that most of the states currently examine holders on a routine basis to determine the level of compliance with this

[1] Mass. App. Ct. No. 79-0389CV (1981).

law, not only by specific holder but also by various industry classifications.

In *United States v. Alabama,*[2] the U.S. District Court upheld the right of the State of Alabama to examine the records of a federally chartered credit union for unclaimed property.

In *Clovis National Bank v. Callaway,*[3] the Court found that an unclaimed property examination "was not the exercise of visitorial powers and is not preempted by the federal statue."

.01 Issues of Sensitivity and Confidentiality

In many instances, records disclosing unclaimed property are sensitive even within the holder's own organization. Records such as dormant account registers, aged outstanding unclaimed insurance proceeds and unclaimed trust benefits in many cases provide a serious internal control problem for the holders of such property. It has been well recognized in accounting theory and practice that additional internal controls over such assets, which may be easily manipulated, is required. Therefore, many holders consider most of the records relating to unclaimed property as highly confidential and subject them to an extra level of control within the organization itself.

In reviewing such records, the unclaimed property examiners are aware of such sensitive restrictions and deal with such information on a routine basis. Consequently, the argument occasionally raised by holders as to the confidentiality of certain records is certainly not a barrier that prevents the examination of such records by the unclaimed property examiner.

.02 Examination Authority is not Supervisory or Regulatory

The Uniform Unclaimed Property Act, in its various versions, never contemplated that the examination authority conferred on the administrator any sort of supervisory or regulatory control. In disputes relating to the right of the administrator of the unclaimed property law to review records of holders, the argument has been advanced that such an examination would constitute the exercise of a supervisory or regulatory role.

Even though many of the holders, such as banks, insurance companies, and public utilities, who are examined for unclaimed property are regulated, the function of the unclaimed property examination is solely the discovery of unreported property and does not involve the supervision of operations or solvency of the holder being examined. This point was made clear in the Minnesota Supreme Court decision of *Minnesota*

[2] 434 F. Supp. 64 (1977).

[3] 69 N.M. 119, 364 P2d 748 (1961).

v. First National Bank of St. Paul,[4] wherein the court stated, "the potential evils of the treasurer's examination would amount at most to an occasional inconvenience."

12 U.S.C. 484(b) now specifically authorizes states to conduct audits of national banks to determine compliance with unclaimed property laws. However, a 1982 amendment to this statute required the state to articulate a "reasonable cause to believe" that the particular banking institution held presumptively abandoned property prior to the audit.[5] As further discussed in ¶ 915, the states have been successful in articulating such cause. The phenomenon of unclaimed property audits is no longer new. Most of the states that actively examine for unclaimed property have developed their programs over the past 10 or 20 years. Most states currently have active audit programs and, on a routine basis, examine the records of holders to determine whether or not they are properly reporting all of the unclaimed property that they hold. This situation is changing rapidly as more and more states begin to tap the revenue potential of the unclaimed property reservoir. Coupled with the reduction in holding periods to five and three years, unclaimed property audits are now a serious source of new, nontax receipts for the states.

Occasionally a holder will attempt to forestall an audit by claiming that its property is exempt under state law. Illinois has exempted "active express trusts" from its unclaimed property legislation. Chicago Title & Trust claimed this exemption and refused access to its records. The Illinois Court of Appeals denied the claim, stating that to do otherwise would "allow the regulated to become the regulator."[6]

.03 Contract Auditors

Most, if not all, states contract with one or more private firms that recover unclaimed property from holders on a contingent fee basis. The states empower these private firms to examine holders' records and subsequently collect unreported unclaimed property. An audit by one of these private firms will encompass several or most states to spread the cost of the audit to those states that actually recover funds.

> ***CAUTION:*** Several holders have encountered what can be termed "excessively aggressive" tactics by these firms because of the contingent fee nature of their compensation and appearance of a conflict of interest.

---

[4] 313 NW2d 390 (1981).

[5] *Midlantic National Bank v. Berman*, Civ. No 90-4610 (D.N.J. 1991).

[6] *Fryzel v. Chicago Title & Trust Company*, 527 NE2d 1025 (Ill. App.1988).

.04 Whistle-Blowers and Informants

In a case that began with a whistle-blower's lawsuit, BankAmerica, California's largest bank, paid at least $187.5 million to settle claims that the state and several cities and counties brought for unreported unclaimed bond interest and principal that had accumulated for several decades.[7]

The suit, filed by a former bank executive and joined by the state, alleged that the bank lost control of bond proceeds starting in 1978 and engaged in a cover-up. The suit also said the bank kept inadequate records and an accurate audit of the bank was impossible. The state and the former executive attempted to persuade the court that an estimate based on the gross dollar value of all bond issues handled by the bank be employed. After an exhaustive reconstruction of records, the court found that the use of an estimate would be improper and that the bank's records could be used to determine the amount owed versus an estimate.

By the time the money was distributed, the total exceeded $200 million, including interest. The original plaintiff was a former vice president in the bank's trust department who left in 1990. He filed a "whistle-blower" claim under California's False Claims Act (a whistle-blower statute), accusing the bank of costing the state enormous amounts of money through illegal practices including, among other things, that the Bank failed to report unclaimed property to the state. This ex-employee of the bank and his attorneys will receive nearly 14 percent of the damages, or $25 million.

> ***CAUTION:*** The threat of an insider informing a state that a holder is holding unreported unclaimed property is an increasing trend and states actively follow up on all such allegations.

.05 Office Compliance Routines

As a result of increasing pressures on the states for revenue, the area of unclaimed property has been targeted as a potential source of additional revenue. In many states, very active office compliance routines are in place that are designed to determine whether holders are filing reports under the Uniform Unclaimed Property Act and further evaluating whether all of the types of property ordinarily held by a specific holder are indeed being reported.

In some states, office compliance is a very sophisticated process that involves a computerized database of information on holders that report. Reports that are filed are coded by types and amounts of property reported and compared to prior year reports and industry

[7] San Francisco Superior Court No. 968484.

norms. In some states, office compliance is a process that is a function of the time available by the staff in the unclaimed property division to review reports and question ones selected for further screening. Many holders selected for field audit are identified through this process. In addition, in most states the reports that have been filed are a public record and contract auditors mine these reports for potential audit candidates.

As holding periods have been reduced, the increase in activity in this area has been substantial. Several states have greatly augmented the size of the holder base that they administer in an attempt to reach holders throughout the United States that may have a reporting responsibility to the state.

¶ 915 Reason to Believe

The Uniform Unclaimed Property Acts of 1954, 1966, and 1981 contain a specific section relating to the examination of records. Act Sec. 23 of the 1966 Uniform Unclaimed Property Act reads as follows:

> The [state treasurer] may at reasonable times upon reasonable notices examine the records of any person *if he has reason to believe* [emphasis added] that such person has failed to report property that should have been reported pursuant to this Act.

Some threshold criteria have been applied as a basis to formulate the reason to believe. Specifically, they are as follows:

- The holder has filed no reports.
- The holder has filed reports disclosing no property reportable.
- Cutoff of amounts, i.e., nothing less than $10, $25, or $50 appears on the report, or nothing over $100.
- Omission of various classes of property ordinarily held by the subject holder.
- The disclosure of service charges or other reductions in the amount due the owner that are not supported by a valid and enforceable contract.

Act Sec. 30 of UUPA 1981 eliminated the "reason to believe" requirement. For the minority of states that have not yet adopted UUPA 1981, the decision of the Oklahoma Supreme Court in *Lincoln Bank & Trust Co. v. Oklahoma Tax Commission* [8] should be constructive. At the time the bank sought to enjoin the state's audit, the Oklahoma unclaimed property law still contained the "reason to believe" requirement. However, the state produced evidence that 75 other banks that had previously been audited all held unreported

[8] 1992 OK 22, 827 P2d 1314 (1992).

abandoned property. Thus, the Oklahoma Tax Commission was able to convince the court that it did indeed have "reason to believe."

The above criteria for establishing a reason to believe are subject to the application of judgment by the individual making the determination. The determination is founded on an evaluation that is based on the reporting history of other similar organizations and experience with holders of unclaimed property.

Maryland law also retains the "reason to believe" requirement. When the state filed suit to examine the holder's records, PHH Corporation argued that the state erred by formulating its rationale improperly after the audit had begun.[9] The Maryland Court of Special Appeals denied the holder's request for relief, noting that the state could develop its rationale as the audit progressed.

¶ 920 Examination Programs

Nearly all of the states that examine for unclaimed property utilize a standardized examination program. The purpose of the examination program is to make uniform the application of standards and procedures in the conduct of each unclaimed property examination and to provide consistency in the application of the law by unclaimed property examiners. However, the unclaimed property examiner has wide discretion as to how far back in time to go in an audit and what categories of property to include in the scope of the audit.

As a basis for determining the extent and scope of any particular examination, the unclaimed property examiner evaluates the nature of the holder's operations and determines what types of properties the holder may generate. Through an interview process and through discussions with holder personnel, the examiner inquires as to the nature of unclaimed items that may be generated by the holder, together with the accounting treatment afforded such items. In addition, the examiner inquires as to the holder's prior reporting of such unclaimed items and whether any service charges or fees are imposed while holding any property in an inactive status. If it is disclosed that any sort of service charge or fee is imposed, the examiner will automatically prepare tests to determine whether it is a policy or practice of the holder to waive such service charges or fees if the owner makes claim for the property prior to its transfer to the state. (See Chapter 4 regarding the lawfulness of charges.)

[9] *Comptroller of the Treasury v. PHH Corporation*, 123 Md. App 214 (1998).

.01 Internal Controls and Documentation of Accounting Error

Once the auditor has gained an adequate understanding of the entity's internal control, that understanding is documented in the work papers. Methods of documentation include the preparation of flowcharts, internal control questionnaires, and narrative descriptions. The auditor will use professional judgment to determine which method(s) should be used to document the understanding. It is important to review the auditor's work papers for how internal controls were evaluated for potential accounting error and the adjustments that the auditor is proposing for such errors.

Flowcharts. A flowchart is a symbolic diagram of a specific part of an internal accounting control system indicating the sequential flow of data and/or authority. A properly prepared flowchart should reflect all operations, movements, delays, and filing procedures associated with whatever is being charted, and it should also indicate the conversion of source documents into accounting information—for example, ledgers, journals, or computer-generated documents. Flowcharting is a method for the auditor to collect the necessary information for the study and review of controls and their subsequent evaluation. Flowcharting is also an effective method of visual communication and can bring to the attention of the auditor the absence of necessary controls.

Internal control questionnaire. The second tool used in the documentation of the auditor's understanding of the internal control is the internal control questionnaire.

Most internal control questionnaires are designed to yield affirmative or negative answers to the questions. An affirmative answer generally indicates a satisfactory degree of internal control; a negative answer indicates a possible weakness in control or at least indicates that further investigation is required. An internal control questionnaire should be supported with a written supplemental statement explaining the circumstances of accounting error and how adjustments are being made for such error.

Narrative descriptions. An auditor may document his or her understanding of the internal controls over unclaimed items by preparing a narrative description of the system. Following the auditor's discussion with appropriate company personnel, a written description of the system is prepared.

> ***PLANNING NOTE:*** Flexibility is the primary advantage of the memorandum, because all systems can be described verbally. However, the success of this technique depends on the writing proficiency of the auditor. A poorly written internal control narrative

can lead to a misunderstanding of the system, resulting in the improper design and application of tests of controls that can lead to improper conclusions about the extent of accounting error present in an unclaimed property item population.

All of these documentation methods have a bearing on adjustments as the result of accounting error related to unclaimed items. The amount of detail in the auditor's analysis of internal controls provides some opportunities to evaluate the validity of the audit findings. These internal control reviews will determine how far the auditor might go in testing transaction data and designing substantive tests.

¶ 925 Gathering and Compilation of Audit Evidence

In every unclaimed property audit the auditor will obtain audit evidence to support the final amounts that may be claimed as due and owing to a state under its unclaimed property statute. "Evidence" can be defined as any information that has an impact on determining the examination objective. A variety of professional standards have been promulgated to provide guidance in the collection and evaluation of evidential matter. Furthermore, numerous nonpromulgated examination procedures are an integral part of an examination engagement. Irrespective of the examination rules and procedures, both promulgated and nonpromulgated, judgment by the examiner is the key ingredient in the examination process.

Although a variety of information may have some impact on the examiner's decision process, it is well recognized that both the quality and quantity of evidence must be evaluated. The third standard of fieldwork refers to these two characteristics as competent (quality) and sufficient (quantity). Thus, the examiner must collect competent evidential matter in a sufficient quantity. Evidential matter is competent when it is both valid and relevant.

Generalizing about what constitutes reliable evidence is difficult, because the particular examination circumstances must be considered. However, recognizing the possibility that exceptions do exist, the following generalizations are accepted:

- Evidence is more reliable if it is obtained from an independent source.
- The stronger the system of internal control, the more reliable the evidence.
- Evidence obtained directly by the examiner through physical examination, observation, computation, and inspection is more persuasive than information obtained indirectly.

Unlike the definitional problem associated with the term "competent," it is easy to define "sufficient," because the term refers simply to the amount of evidence collected. However, examination judgment is concerned in determining when sufficiency has been achieved, as it is in determining the competency of evidential matter. The concept of sufficiency recognizes that the examiner can never reduce examination risk to zero, and the accumulation of evidence should be persuasive rather than convincing. This concept is consistent with the idea that examiners are not free to collect unlimited amounts of evidence, because they must work within economic limits. Cost cannot, however, be the sole basis for the quantity or quality of examination procedures.

Evidential matter can be classified as "underlying accounting data" and "corroborating evidence." Underlying accounting data consists of general and specialized journals, ledgers, manuals, and supporting worksheets and other analyses. Generally, underlying accounting data are tested by retracing transactions through the accounting system, recomputing amounts, and performing other mathematical calculations. Although underlying accounting data are an important part of evidential matter, such data may not be sufficient to meet the burden of proof. It has been established by *Blue Cross of Northern California v. Cory* [10] and *Employer's Insurance of Wausau v. Smith* [11] that the state has the burden of proving that unclaimed property exists and the amounts of that property.

The collection and evaluation of sufficient competent evidential matter can be described, and should be applied, as a logical process. Conceptually, the examiner should design a substantive test by relating assertions made by the holder to specific examination procedures that are designed to test the validity of the assertions. This would include assertions that all unclaimed property items had been reported or that certain categories of property are not generated by the holder.

The four basic types of evidence that are collected during an unclaimed property examination are as follows:

1. **Documentary evidence.** This consists of document type records or "writings." This is the primary type of evidence gathered by the auditor and constitutes the work papers that the auditor prepares.
2. **Oral evidence or testimonial evidence.** This consists of interviews with holder personnel that are reduced to narrative summaries.
3. **Computational evidence.** Examples of this type of evidence would include recomputing service charge totals, making esti-

[10] 174 Cal. Rptr. 901 (Cal. App. 1981).

[11] 453 NW2nd 856 (1990).

mates, or analyzing ratios or trends in data. Many unclaimed property audits are completed by the use of estimates, and the methods used by the auditor must be carefully scrutinized for reasonableness and accuracy. If a statistical model is used, the underlying statistical methods must be sound and properly executed.

4. **Physical evidence.** This would involve the auditor's observance of physical assets of property, such as verifying the existence of safe deposit box contents.

PLANNING NOTE: A review of the auditor's work papers is essential in formulating an audit defense strategy. Many unclaimed property audits are conducted that give rise to several adjustments based on law and fact, if a holder took the time to review them carefully.

.01 Burden of Proof and "Accounting Errors" Defenses

The issue of "accounting error" is ever present in the factual analysis of unclaimed property liabilities. As records become older, they lose integrity and completeness. Frequent accounting system changes can greatly compound this problem. Systems conversions are points in time where old and unreconciled differences are written off or adjusted to income/expense. It is well recognized by the states that appropriate adjustments must be taken into consideration for such accounting error when compiling audit findings.

CAUTION: However, the mere assertion that accounting errors existed within the accounting system will not provide an adequate defense against paying unclaimed property to a state. A careful review of all the facts and circumstances will be necessary for this defense to be valid.

In recent years an active community of "audit defense" representatives from CPA firms and law firms has changed the face of unclaimed property audit programs. Holders, through their defense representatives, are focusing on the details of the evidence obtained in audits rather than arguing the basic validity of the law.

PLANNING NOTE: The typical defense strategy is to claim that all or a major portion of the auditor's findings are not really unclaimed property but rather are "accounting errors" that should be eliminated from a state's claim. Holders and their defense representatives also attempt to refute written evidence obtained from their records as unreliable or not specific enough to be claimed as unclaimed property by the state. They assert that a statement from a corporate officer that the findings are erroneous should be sufficient to make the claim disappear. Evidence obtained from a holder's records must be viewed in light of the internal controls that were in place during the audit period. Any defense of audit findings based on accounting error must be based on the internal controls, or lack thereof, that can be documented or reconstructed.

Holders should be familiar with two cases that clearly recite what has been the audit policy of the states for many years regarding "accounting error" and burden of proof defenses raised by holders. In the following two cases the courts held that once the state auditor has identified unclaimed property, it is the duty of the holder to provide evidence to prove that they are accounting errors or that they represent something other than unclaimed property. In 1998, Arizona Superior Court rejected a company's argument that "the State has to show that Defendant has not previously paid the property to the apparent owner. Defendant argues that the State of Arizona's audit cannot show this."[12] Instead the court ruled that "[t]he Defendant's argument is a "catch-22." No documents were kept by the defendant that would show whether a replacement check was issued. Therefore, the defendant reasoned, the state could not prove its case.

If this were the law, a defendant could benefit from simply destroying its records. The court construed the statute in a more commonsense fashion. If an audit of the books cannot demonstrate that replacement checks were issued, then the state has met its burden of proof under (the statute). If a corporation fails to keep adequate records of what it did with the proceeds of voided checks, the risk of loss falls on the corporation not the state. This logic seems well reasoned and is consistent with how states have applied this policy for the past three decades.

In an earlier case from the Utah Supreme Court, the issue of the validity of several outstanding checks that were over seven years old was challenged by a credit union.[13] The auditor identified these checks that were described as:

> checks that are highly likely to represent unclaimed property because;
>
> a) they were described in the Credit Union's records as outstanding bank items,
>
> b) the checks were not cleared through routine payment by the holder's bank but were added to the account's bank balance and the offsetting entry was subtracted from a Credit Union expense account and,

[12] *State of Arizona v. Magee-Walpole Consolidated, Inc.*, Super. Ct., Maricopa County, AZ., No. CV-97-20223 (Nov. 20, 1998) (unreported).

[13] *Division of Unclaimed Property v. McKay Dee Credit Union*, 958 P2d 234 (1998).

> c) the Credit Union had a reporting history dating back to 1974 and had never reported this type of property, and it would be very unusual for any financial institution doing the type of business Defendant does not to have some checks reportable in this time period.

The Credit Union claimed that because they did not keep the records necessary to refute the claim, they should not be required to pay these checks to the state as unclaimed property. The Credit Union argued:

> that there are a myriad of possible scenarios in which [Credit Union] could have been the 'owner' of the checks, in which case the property could not be considered unclaimed. [Credit Union] further argues that there was insufficient evidence to support a presumption of abandonment.

The Utah Supreme Court disagreed with this argument, holding that this defense tactic was being used regularly as the "lack of records to disprove the state" defense. Here the holders argued, as did Magee and Walpole in Arizona, that because they did not maintain the records that provided evidence that certain amounts were not owed, there could be no basis for the state to make a claim. In *Magee* and *McKay Dee Credit Union* the court rejected such arguments.

The Court in *McKay Dee Credit Union* went on to say:

> The Act does not require the State to rebut every possible scenario that favors McKay Dee's position. To the contrary, it simply requires the State to meet the statutory presumption of abandonment.

If holders do not maintain adequate records to identify specific items of unclaimed property, auditors have traditionally used estimation techniques to calculate the amount of unreported unclaimed property. When estimates are used, there are no identifiable owners that can be recognized with last known addresses. Therefore, only the holder's state of incorporation has the right to claim the property from the holder.[14] Nevertheless, several holders and their defense representatives attempt to use the rules of jurisdiction to minimize their liability when estimates are used. The use of estimates is discussed in more detail at ¶ 935.

If the state of incorporation is claiming the property, the holder may claim that some statistical distribution of the property should be used to minimize the amount payable to that state. The U.S. Supreme Court specifically rejected an "Allocation Theory" or "Site of Transaction Test" when they decided *Delaware v. New York* (see ¶ 515.01). If a state that is not the domiciliary of the holder is making the claim on estimated property, the holder may invoke a strict construction of the backup rule of "no address" property and may refuse to pay a portion of the estimated property to the nondomiciliary state.

---

[14] See *Texas v. New Jersey* (¶ 510.04) and *Delaware v. New York* (¶ 515.01).

CAUTION: Recently, holders and their representatives have turned the rules of jurisdiction in unclaimed property law on their head in an attempt to minimize their reporting obligation for unclaimed property. This tactic may well leave a holder exposed to a claim based on the proper application of the rules of jurisdiction (see Chapter 2).

¶ 930 The Report of Examination

The result of an examination performed by the unclaimed property examiner is a "Report of Examination" that is the basis for further collection action by the state.

The report will contain three basic sections. First, the report will indicate the scope of the examination, i.e., the type of properties covered and the cutoff dates for the examination. The report ordinarily covers property that is five years old or older (if the holding period is five years) that should have been reported and/or remitted in prior years. In some states, the report also discloses items that have been written off the books and are no longer reflected as liabilities but that the holder would have to report as unclaimed property if not claimed by the owner in future years.

This type of property is classified as "reinstatable property" in most of these reports. Reinstatable property findings place the holder on notice that amounts that have been written off will be due in future years. Once written off, these items may not be subjected to adequate accounting control, such that they can be adequately identified for future reporting. Many states do not audit for property that is due in future years.

The second section of the report of examination describes the procedures that were performed in the conduct of the examination. It is in this section that the detailed procedures that were utilized by the unclaimed property examiners are set forth.

The third and final section of the report of examination is the one that presents the findings made pursuant to the procedures performed by the examiners. In most cases, this section is presented in schedule form and lists, by category or property, the past due amount that should have been reported in prior years. The report also contains footnotes that describe in detail certain aspects of the holder's treatment of various categories of unclaimed items or legal positions taken by the holder relating to the reportability of items.

A draft of the report, or at least a schedule of the findings, is normally presented to the holder after the examiner completes the fieldwork part of the examination. This preliminary report draft and set of examination findings will eventually become the final amounts due unless the holder proposes adjustments.

> ***CAUTION:*** It is critical for holders to take the time to fully and completely review the methods utilized by the examiner and understand how the findings were derived. This is especially true if the examination was based fully or partially on estimates.

After any adjustments are made to the preliminary findings, a final report will be issued and a collection letter from the state will follow.

A few states, such as California and New York, have formal audit appeal procedures. In California these procedures constitute an informal hearing at which time a holder may present evidence to rebut examination findings.

¶ 935 Records Retention, Missing Records, and Use of Estimates

As a result of the long-term nature of unclaimed property, problems are continually encountered in relation to the availability of records or the lack of certain types of records. Most holders do not maintain all of their records intact for periods in excess of six or seven years. In many cases, supporting detail to entries in the general ledger, such as journal vouchers, journal sheets, etc., are discarded after a period of three to seven years. The unclaimed property examiner is frequently confronted with a lack of supporting detail, especially when nonreporting of a certain category of property is discovered and the task at hand requires that the examiner document the amount of such property.

Many organizations have adopted polices and procedures relating to the time period that certain records are retained. These time periods vary widely due to the nature of the holder's operations and the type of business. For instance, a depository institution maintains records relating to deposit accounts for a much longer period than an industrial firm would keep supporting documents relating to the financial transactions on its own account.

Certain state unclaimed property statutes impose record retention requirements. Act Sec. 31 of UUPA 1981 specifically provides that holders must retain records of their reports (and presumably the underlying detail) for a period of 10 years, except that a three-year period is provided for issuers of traveler's checks and money orders.

PLANNING NOTE: Retaining adequate records to support previously filed unclaimed property reports is highly recommended. Evidence that unclaimed property has already been reported is the best defense against a possible double claim by a state or states.

When searching for records that are ten, twenty, or thirty years old, a challenge is presented to the holder or to the unclaimed property examiner.

In many cases, extensive interviews must be held to determine what record retention procedures were in effect in prior years. In addition, the identification of locations where certain old records are stored is critical to the process of uncovering reportable unclaimed property. The inventorying of old records has only in recent years become a refined process. In prior years, many holders did not perceive a need for the retention of old records with substantial retrieval capabilities for such records. In many cases, representations must be obtained that certain records were diligently searched for but could not be located.

.01 Address Availability—Applying the Rules of Jurisdiction

The unclaimed property examiner is always concerned with the availability of name and address information. The primary basis of claim by the state is governed by the rules in *Texas v. New Jersey* (see ¶ 510). Therefore, the state can only make a claim to property due a resident with a last known address in that state or to property for which there is no last known address, if the holder is incorporated in that state. (See Chapter 5 for the rules of jurisdiction in unclaimed property law.)

What constitutes an "address"? Is a computer code of "01" sufficient to mean Alabama? Most, if not all, states do not consider a computer code to be an address. UUPA 1981 defines "address" as a description of location sufficient for the delivery and receipt of mail.

The auditor is confronted with issues of what constitutes an "address" all the time. The availability of addresses without a practical or cost efficient way of obtaining them is an ever-present problem. Here, a generally accepted approach is the use of an allocation or apportionment by statistical methods.

Audit resources and time are scarce. Looking up hundreds or thousands of addresses through the use of microfiche or manual ledger cards is hardly an effective use of an auditor's time. Therefore, such data is sampled and percentages are derived that provide the basis of the state's claim.

The use of an allocation or apportionment rests upon the verified assumption that records of addresses exist but the time and cost of research does not justify enormous audit time. However, the auditor must conduct sufficient address testing in order to ascertain the availability of addresses. In some cases, testing may reveal that only a certain percentage of addresses exist. In this situation, the auditor must conclude that the verified percentage of unknown addresses would be due to the state of incorporation of the holder. The resolution of these types of factual situations is a matter of audit judgment and negotiation with each holder.

.02 Estimation Techniques

The problem of locating old records containing information complete enough to properly document the existence of unclaimed property that may have been written off or otherwise not reported is an ever-present one. Because of record retention policies, it is ordinarily the case that part or all of the records necessary to document the amounts of unclaimed property that have been held by a holder are no longer in existence. This situation does not prevent the unclaimed property examiner from determining such amounts on the basis of certain estimation techniques.

To provide a holder with immunity against reporting unclaimed property because of a lack of records would create a substantial inequity and wrongfully enrich noncompliant holders. Therefore, in the field of unclaimed property auditing, estimation techniques have been used for decades. It should be pointed out, however, that estimation techniques are used in several areas of auditing other than unclaimed property auditing, such as when records have been lost due to fire, flood, or other natural catastrophes. Also, the reconstruction of amounts embezzled over a long period of time may require the use of estimates. Sales and use tax auditors regularly use estimates to produce collectable audit findings.

The issue of the state's right to estimate the amount of unclaimed property that has not been reported by a holder has been the subject of litigation.[15] There are no definite prohibitions against the use of estimates in the field of unclaimed property and, indeed, many unclaimed property examinations are completed by the use of estimates.

Act Sec. 30(e) of UUPA 1981 specifically provides for the use of estimates where records are not available.

---

[15] *New Jersey v. The Chubb Corp.*, 239 N.J. Super. 257, 570 A2d 1313 (1989).

When performing various routine tests, the unclaimed property examiner may discover that certain items have been written off or otherwise removed from the books by the holder. The specific methodology utilized in making estimates varies, depending upon each factual circumstance that is encountered by the unclaimed property examiner. Ordinarily, the use of estimates is considered only when all other avenues have been exhausted as to the location or existence of records.

A holder may also confirm that certain records have, indeed, been destroyed. The examiner is then confronted with the task of attempting to ascertain the dollar amount of such property by making projections or estimates of such amounts from current available records. Standard statistical and mathematical tools and models have been used over the years to make such projections and estimates. They include such methods as regression analysis, ratio analysis, and curve-fitting techniques. The use of projection methodology is widespread in the area of making estimates when known data is available for part of an overall period and an estimate must be made for the remainder of the audit period. In *New Jersey v. The Chubb Corp.,*[16] the court recognized the validity of the use of statistical methods for purposes of estimating abandoned property but cautioned that the method must be properly grounded.

In some states, unclaimed property examiners have been trained in the use of estimation techniques and have employed such methodology in the field for many years.

> ***CAUTION:*** Many unclaimed property examiners have little or no training in how to perform estimates that can withstand careful scrutiny or meet the standards of burden of proof required in a collection action. The lack of training can lead to outrageous audit findings that would not meet any audit or legal standard of burden of proof. A careful review of any estimate made by an unclaimed property auditor is essential in properly defending an audit claim.

Again, each factual situation dictates the specific methodology to be used and the procedures to be performed. Today, most unclaimed property audit controversies between states and holders involve the determination of the amount owed, not the legal underpinnings of the claim for the property itself.

Contract auditors who work on a contingent fee basis are regularly challenged on estimation methods that they employ because of the conflict of interest inherent in their receiving a percentage of the estimated amount.

---

[16] *Id.*

¶ 940 Collection Procedures

Unlike tax statutes, the states' unclaimed property laws do not provide for routine nonjudicial administrative collection procedures, such as those that are available in income, sales, or excise tax statutes.

In a few rare cases, the state does have the power to collect unclaimed property in a manner similar to that of collecting taxes. The Uniform Disposition of Unclaimed Property Acts of 1954 and 1966 basically provide that "if any person refuses to deliver property to the [state treasurer] as required under this Act, he shall bring an action in the court of appropriate jurisdiction to enforce such delivery." The basic remedy available to the administrator is the commencement of a suit in a court of competent jurisdiction for the collection of such amounts by judicial proceeding. This is a cumbersome and expensive procedure for both the holder and the state. Several suits have been brought for the collection of unclaimed property over the past several years, and they are the basis of most of the more current case law in the field of unclaimed property.

Currently, most contested audits result in some form of settlement between the holder and the state. State guidelines for settlements vary drastically and change frequently.

.01 Enforcement Actions Provided in the Statutes

Types of actions. The methods available to the state to encourage or enforce compliance with their unclaimed property laws generally fall within two main categories:

1. Civil actions to compel holders to report and/or pay or deliver unclaimed property to the state and
2. Criminal or civil penalties, or economic sanctions to encourage compliance or punishment for noncompliance.

As an adjunct of the enforcement power, states are empowered to examine the records of holders in order to determine whether a holder has failed to report unclaimed property to the state.

Civil actions. Act Sec. 32 of UUPA 1981 allows the state administrator (treasurer, controller, etc.) to bring an action in a court of appropriate jurisdiction against a holder who refuses to deliver to the state property that has escheated or been presumed abandoned. Whether a court would be an "appropriate jurisdiction" to render a personal judgment against the holder would be determined under the state law and established principles of jurisdiction, such as whether the holder had certain minimum contacts with the forum state so that maintenance of the suit would not offend "traditional notions of fair play and substantial justice."[17]

UUPA 1981 authorizes the state administrator to join with other states to seek enforcement of the Act. UUPA 1981 allows the enacting state to bring enforcement actions on behalf of another state, provided the other state agrees to pay the expenses incurred in bringing such action. Likewise, the administrator could request the attorney general, or other person, of another state to bring an enforcement action on its behalf. Some states already have such reciprocal enforcement provisions. See www.unclaimed.org for the most recent information.

There is also authority for a state to pursue legal action to protect its future or expectant interest. In the California case *In re Mercantile Guarantee Co.,*[18] the state intervened in a corporate dissolution proceeding, objecting to a plan of dissolution that would extinguish the rights of shareholders who did appear to claim their distributive shares within a certain period of time. The court held that because there was a probability of abandonment of some distributive shares, the state had an inchoate right to appear in the proceedings to ensure that the interests of the non-appearing shareholders would not be taken from them before the time for abandonment arrived. Thus, the state was allowed to intervene to protect its "future" rights. This future rights principle is the basis for the concept of "reinstatable property."

¶ 945 Penalties and Sanctions

Aside from authorizing the pursuit of civil enforcement actions, the primary approach of UUPA 1981 in encouraging compliance is the threat of imposition of fines and/or imprisonment for "willful" failure of a holder to report or pay unclaimed property to the state or perform other duties required by the Act. The obvious difficulty of utilizing this provision as an enforcement tool is in establishing that the noncompliance was willful, which is required under the burden of proof applicable to criminal cases.

UUPA 1981 requires the holder to pay a substantial rate of interest on the property or the value thereof from the date the property should have been paid or delivered to the state. Additionally, UUPA 1981 imposes civil penalties for willful refusal to pay or deliver unclaimed property to the state after a written demand has been made by the state.

---

[17] *International Shoe Co. v. Washington,* SCt, 326 US 310, 66 SCt 154 (1945).

[18] 238 Cal. App. 2d 426, 48 Cal. Rptr. 589 (1965).

California has adopted a statute that imposes interest at the rate of 12 percent per annum, from the date the property should have been paid or delivered, upon any person who fails to report or to pay or deliver unclaimed property to the state.[19] In *Blue Cross of Northern California v. Cory,*[20] the court held that the controller was entitled to receive prejudgment interest at the rate of seven percent per annum under California's general prejudgment interest provision up to the effective date of the unclaimed property interest section (January 1, 1977) and at the 12-percent rate thereafter. California has applied the 12-percent rate on all past due property since 1995 and will not consider waivers or releases from such interest.

The Massachusetts Abandoned Property Law provides for 12 percent per annum interest or the Internal Revenue Code (the "Code") rate for unpaid taxes,[21] whichever is higher, on property that the holder has not paid or delivered on the due date.[22]

New York law, in addition to imposing 10 percent per annum interest from the date the property was due the state, also allows the state comptroller to make a determination of the amount due from a holder who has failed to fully and completely report and pay or deliver unclaimed property. Such determination is served upon the holder and becomes presumptive evidence of the amount due. If, after an administrative hearing, the comptroller "certifies" the amount due from the holder, the comptroller may file a special proceeding in court based upon such certification and the "certification by him shall be conclusive proof thereof."[23]

.01 Amnesty Programs and Waiver of Interest and Penalties

Over the years some states have established "amnesty programs" in an effort to encourage holders to voluntarily come forward and report previously unreported property. Most of these programs were implemented without legislative mandate or approval. In 1999, California enacted legislation to create a formal amnesty program. The California amnesty program provides a mechanism for holders to report unclaimed property that was due in report years 1999 and prior without the imposition of interest on such amounts.[24] Several requirements of Assembly Bill 1888 must be met and a checklist evidencing that such requirements have been met must accompany the amnesty report (see ¶ 11,015).

In most states, a first-time filer of unclaimed property can request that interest or penalties not be imposed. The administrative practice

[19] Cal. Code of Civ. Proc. § 1577.
[20] 120 Cal. App. 3d 723, 174 Cal. Rptr. 901 (1981).
[21] Code Sec. 6621.
[22] 200A GLC § 12(e).
[23] N.Y. APL. § 1412.
[24] Assembly Bill 1888, Chapter 267, Laws 2000.

in most states has been to forgive past interest if a holder voluntarily comes forward to report past-due property. However, this practice changes from time to time and it is essential to determine the current status of a state's amnesty program before filing.

¶ 950 Current Compliance Trends

The vast nontax revenue potential in unclaimed property collections has resulted in a much greater emphasis on enforcement by the states in the past few years. Increasing the dollar volume reported by holders of unclaimed property is a high priority in virtually every state.

Over the past several years, the trend has been overwhelmingly toward a reduction in time periods to three years or less from the prior five- or seven-year period. Most states have reduced time periods on most types of property to three years, and in some cases, one year. Part of the rationale behind the reduction of the holding periods has been that the state has a much greater chance of reuniting the property with its rightful owner after a shorter holding period than a very lengthy one. This fact has been demonstrated in the many states that have recently reduced their holding periods. The amounts of unclaimed money claimed by owners have gone up drastically in recent years, confirming the rationale for shorter abandonment periods.

The trend towards reducing the holding periods brings more and more holders under the scrutiny of the states in anticipation of additional revenue.

Chapter 10

CLAIMS FOR PROPERTY REPORTED TO STATES BY OWNERS AND HOLDERS

¶ 1001 Overview

Owners, holders, and other states may claim property after it has been reported to a state. ¶ 1005 discusses the requirements of due process before an owner can be deprived of his or her property. Claims by owners are discussed at ¶ 1010; claims by holders at ¶ 1015. Claims by other states are discussed at ¶ 1020. ¶ 1025 examines restrictions on "investigator" fees. Finally, the states' national database and the National Association of Unclaimed Property Administrators' (NAUPA's) website may be found at ¶ 1030 and ¶ 1035, respectively.

¶ 1005 Due Process Requirements

Under all versions of the Uniform Unclaimed Property Act (1954, 1966, 1981, and 1995), the property remains subject to claim by the rightful owner at any time. This is an important feature of unclaimed property laws because, under the Due Process Clause of the U.S. Constitution, the owner must have notice and an opportunity to be heard before he or she is permanently deprived of his or her property.[1] See Chapter 2 for a thorough discussion of the constitutionality of unclaimed property statutes.

¶ 1010 Claims by Owners

Act Sec. 24 of the 1981 Uniform Unclaimed Property Act (UUPA 1981) allows any person who claims an interest in abandoned or escheated property delivered to the state to file a claim for recovery of the property with the state. Generally, only claims by the owner or the

[1] *Anderson National Bank v. Luckett*, SCt, 321 US 233, 64 SCt 599 (1944).

legal representative of the owner will be honored, and claims by creditors of the owner will not be recognized. An unsecured creditor is not considered to have an "interest" in the property because the creditor is merely owed a debt by the owner and has no ownership interest in the particular abandoned property.

State laws providing for garnishment of a judgment debtor's property held by a third party ordinarily require that the property be owed or distributable to the debtor as a condition to garnishment.[2] Unless the owner files a valid claim to recover the property, nothing is owing or distributable to the owner/debtor by the state and, thus, there is no property subject to garnishment.

Act Sec. 24 of UUPA 1981 requires the state unclaimed property administrator to consider any claim filed to recover unclaimed property and permits the administrator to hold a hearing and receive evidence concerning the claim. If the claimant disagrees with the determination made by the administrator, an action to establish the claim may be filed in court within a specified period of time.

Under Act Sec. 21 of UUPA 1981, an owner is entitled to any income or increments accruing to the property. However, a number of states had previously modified their laws to provide for payment of interest to owners. Act Sec. 24 of UUPA 1981 would also require payment of interest by the state to owners and would permit holders to pay owners and add interest. The state would then be required to reimburse the holder for such payment.

¶ 1015 Claims by Holders

Under Act Sec. 20(b) of UUPA 1981, a holder that has paid monies to the state under the Act may pay a person who appears to be entitled to such property and, upon proof of such payment, obtain reimbursement from the state. This situation frequently occurs with bank deposits or written instruments such as money orders and travelers checks. Holders involved in these types of businesses, for convenience or public relations purposes, find it preferable to honor the written instruments or requests for withdrawal of deposits when customers appear or present escheated instruments for payment. In such cases, the holder merely submits a claim to the state unclaimed property administrator along with some form of evidence of payment and the identity of the owner to whom the holder has made payment.

> ***CAUTION:*** In making payment to owners of property turned over to the state, holders would be wise to check first with the state

[2] *Boisseau v. Bass*, 100 Va. 207, 40 SE647 (1902).

to determine if the property has been claimed from the state. It is not unheard of for an owner to claim property both from the state and from the holder, thereby doubling his money and leaving the holder with an unreimbursable claim.

Not all states provide for the reimbursement of a claim paid by a holder. Before paying a claim, a holder should consult the unclaimed property law of the state from which reimbursement will be sought.

The National Association of Unclaimed Property Administrators (NAUPA) has developed a standard form for holders who are claiming property back from a state. This form is available online at www.unclaimed.org (also, see ¶ 11,020).

¶ 1020 Claims by Other States

The Uniform Unclaimed Property Acts of 1954 and 1966 do not contain a specific section allowing another state to claim property paid or delivered to a state. Some states had previously provided by statute for claims to be made by other states. Such claims would usually arise when the other state adopted an applicable unclaimed property law after the property was paid or delivered to the custodial state and, under the *Texas v. New Jersey* decision (see ¶ 510.04), had a superior right to the property, or when the property had been erroneously paid or delivered to the custodial state. UUPA 1981 added Act Sec. 25, under which a state could claim unclaimed property from another state.

¶ 1025 Restrictions on "Investigators" Fees

There are many persons in the United States engaged in the business of locating owners of abandoned or escheated property and assisting the owners in recovering their property for a fee or percentage of the recovered property. These individuals are sometimes referred to variously as "heir hunters," "heir finders," "investigators," or "locators." A growing number of states, concerned with actual or potential "gouging" of owners, have enacted laws limiting the fees that may be charged or imposing other restrictions on agreements between investigators and owners.

Neither the 1954 nor the 1966 Uniform Unclaimed Property Acts contained any provisions restricting investigators' fees or activities. UUPA 1981, however, rendered unenforceable any agreement to pay compensation to recover or assist in the recovery of unclaimed property if the agreement is made within 24 months after the date the property was paid or delivered to the state. Apparently, this is intended to allow states and holders, through their notices, publications, and other efforts, to first attempt to locate owners, thereby leaving the more-difficult-to-find owners to the investigators after the 24-month period has expired.

In *Goodman v. Cory,*[3] a licensed private investigator challenged the constitutionality of a provision of California's Unclaimed Property Law, which restricted to 10 percent the fee that could be charged to assist an owner in locating or recovering property reported to the state and placed other restrictions on agreements between such investigators or "locators" and owners. The California Court of Appeal upheld the validity of the statute, stating:

> there is no fundamental vested right to conduct business entirely free of reasonable governmental rules and regulations . . . [T]he statute on its face neither precludes appellant from pursuing his occupation nor imposes unreasonable limitations in the performance of his business activities.

The court also held that the investigator was not denied equal protection of the laws under the statute.

The *Goodman* case is the first reported decision dealing with statutory restrictions on investigators' fees or activities relating to state unclaimed property laws. The language of the court's opinion emphasizes the view that statutory limitations on investigators are, in large part, consumer protection laws and will be treated as such by the courts.

In addition to these statutory restrictions, several states have sought, by regulation or otherwise, to limit the access of "investigators" to the states' files containing owner information (e.g., address, dollar amount of property, etc.).

In Alabama, for example, two detectives unsuccessfully sued for the right to inspect the administrator's records. The state trial court held that only persons "possessing an interest" in the property had the right to inspect. However, the court did rule that Alabama must include last known addresses of the owners in its newspaper publications.[4]

In Pennsylvania, an investigator was more successful in arguing that the records of unclaimed property held by the Department of Revenue were subject to that state's Right to Know Act. Such legislation, sometimes known as "sunshine" or freedom of information acts, provides that governmental records, subject to certain exceptions, are

[3] 142 Cal. App. 3d 737, 191 Cal. Rptr. 272 (1983).

[4] *Trantham v. White,* Montgomery County Circuit Court No. CV86-1239-R (1989).

open to the public. The Pennsylvania court specifically rejected the requirement of having a demonstrable interest in the property.[5]

The issue of the owner's right to privacy in regard to his or her financial information was discussed in a pair of recent decisions of the Supreme Court of Oklahoma. In the first case, *Lincoln Bank & Trust Co. v. Oklahoma Tax Commission,*[6] the holder sought to prevent the state's audit, citing Oklahoma's Financial Privacy Act. The bank argued that the privacy of their depositors would be compromised by an unclaimed property audit. Oklahoma's highest court rejected that argument by noting:

- The public policy underlying the unclaimed property legislation, and
- That the financial information would retain its confidential nature in the hand of the state.

Having acknowledged the privacy of information held by banking and financial institutions in *Lincoln Bank,* the same court extended protection to information in the hands of other holders.[7] Merrill, an "heirfinder," filed suit under the state's Open Records Act. The court found that items, such as social security and federal identification numbers and names of estate administrators and heirs, established privacy claims and concerns that compelled confidentiality.

A decision by the West Virginia Supreme Court examined that state's abandoned property legislation in light of its Freedom of Information Act (FOIA). In *Keegan v. Bailey,*[8] the state's version of the Uniform Unclaimed Property Act provided that the abandoned property reports were available for inspection and copying "only by an owner of such property as to the particular property he owns." Thus an heirfinder would be excluded by this provision, despite the West Virginia FOIA.

Here the heirfinder argued that the information he sought—lists of state warrants that had not been cashed within the requisite six months from issuance—did not relate to presumptively abandoned property and, thus, was not excluded from the FOIA.

The trial court found in favor of the heirfinder; the Treasurer appealed. The West Virginia Supreme Court affirmed the trial court's ruling. It noted that the records of these uncashed state warrants were provided to the Treasurer long before the expiration of the dormancy period. Because the monies representing these uncashed warrants had not aged sufficiently to create the presumption of abandonment, the

---

[5] *Breinig v. Meyers,* 523 A2d 1211, 105 Pa. Commw. 250 (1987).

[6] 1992 OK 22, 827 P2d 1314.

[7] *Merrill v. Oklahoma Tax Commission,* 1992 OK 53, 831 P2d 634 (1992).

[8] 191 W. Va. 145, 443 SE2d 826 (1994).

report of such property did not relate to abandoned property and, therefore, was not exempt under the abandoned property legislation.

COMMENT: Given the increasing amounts of unclaimed property, the interest of such investigators should continue to rise.

¶ 1030 State's National Database

Over half of the states have provided their owner databases to a private vendor who operates www.missingmoney.com. This web site can be accessed by anyone who has an interest in finding unclaimed property.

¶ 1035 NAUPA Web Site

The National Association of Unclaimed Property Administrators (NAUPA) web site links to all states' web sites at www.unclaimed.org, which provides information on filing claims and downloading many of the states' claim forms.

PLANNING NOTE: All states have custodial laws that permit an owner, or heir of an owner, to reclaim their property. To accomplish this, a claim form must be submitted that contains sufficient evidence that the claimant is the actual owner. Claim processing standards vary widely from state to state and the length of time required to approve and pay claims also varies widely.

Appendix A

CASE SUMMARIES

¶ 10,001 Overview—Importance of Case Law Foundation

The law of unclaimed property has developed in two branches. The first branch involves the statutory law that has been enacted in the various states, especially the Uniform Unclaimed Property Act. The second branch of law is the case law that has developed over the past century.

The importance of the case law cannot be overemphasized. In Chapter 2, the concepts from many of these cases are explained in detail.

This appendix contains the most relevant and foundational cases that have been handed down by the courts since 1911. These case summaries provide greater insight into the law that has developed in the field of unclaimed property. Please note that not all of the cases discussed in ¶ 10,010 and ¶ 10,025 are discussed in the book.

¶ 10,005 How to Use This Appendix

To find a case on point, use the "Table of Cases Analyzed by Legal Issues and Unclaimed Property Categories" (¶ 10,010) that is an alphabetical listing of all of the cases. The issues and property categories discussed in each case are key coded.

Refer to the "Key to the Legal Issues" (¶ 10,015) and the "Key to the Property Categories" (¶ 10,020) to identify the particular issues and property category of interest to you.

¶ 10,010 Table of Cases Analyzed by Legal Issues and Unclaimed Property Categories

Case Name	Legal Issues	Property Category
Aetna Life Insurance Co. v. Borges	11	CC
Anderson National Bank v. Luckett	4,7,11,22	B
Bank of America v. Cory	6, 26, 27, 28, 29	B, N
Bank of America v. Cranston	5, 6, 12, 26, 29, 30, 32	A, B, D, E, Q
Blue Cross of Northern California v. Cory	1, 5, 6, 12, 20, 24, 26, 28	H, S
Borges v. Westport Bank & Trust Company	32	N
Callahan v. Marshall Field & Company	3, 13, 24, 26	F
Citronelle-Mobile Gathering, Inc. v. Boswell	5, 29, 30	Z
Commonwealth Edison Company v. Vega	11	CC
Connecticut Mutual Life Insurance Co. v. Moore	3, 7, 18, 19, 21, 25, 26	G
In re Continental Airlines, Inc.	11	C
Cory v. Golden State Bank	6, 13, 32	I, N
Cory v. Public Utilities Commission	24, 26	R
Delaware v. New York	19	D
Douglas Aircraft Company, Inc. v. Cranston	5, 6, 26, 29, 30	T
Employers Insurance of Wausau v. Smith	29, 30	H
Fahner v. Chicago Transit Authority	24	T
Fryzel v. Chicago Title & Trust Co.	9	E
Goodman v. Cory	4, 7, 35	35
Insurance Co. of North America v. Knight	1, 4, 5	K, S
Kane v. Insurance Co. of North America	1, 5	K, S
Lincoln Bank & Trust Co. v. Oklahoma Tax Commission	9	A, B
Metropolitan Life Insurance Co. v. Office of the State Comptroller	26	G
Minnesota v. First National Bank of St. Paul	9, 11, 22	B
In re the Monks Club Inc.	23, 26	C
Murdock v. John B Stetson Company	5, 6, 13	F
Nellius v. Tampax, Inc.		19, 31
New Jersey v. Chubb Corp.	37	K
New Jersey v. Elsinore Shore Associates	26	J
New Jersey v. Jefferson Lake Sulphur Co.	2, 24, 26	D
New Jersey v. Sperry & Hutchinson Co.	1, 5, 6	P
In re November 8, 1996, Determination of the State of New Jersey, Department of the Treasury, Unclaimed Property Office	18,24	F
Oregon ex rel. Mallicoat v. Coe	18	O

Case Name	Legal Issues	Property Category
Pennsylvania v. New York	19, 31	I
Presley v. County of Nassau	5, 12	L, EE
Provident Institution for Savings v. Malone	3, 7, 18, 26	B
Riggs National Bank v. District of Columbia	13, 27, 30, 31	A, B, N
Rose's Stores, Inc. v. Boyles	32	S, N, F
Screen Actors Guild, Inc. v. Cory	2, 6, 14, 24, 26	M
Security Savings Bank v. California	7, 18, 21	B
Sennett v. Insurance Co. of North America	1, 6, 28, 29	K, S, T
South Carolina Tax Commission v. Metropolitan Life Insurance Co.	6, 29, 30, 33	G
Standard Oil Co. v. New Jersey	4, 7, 15, 18, 19, 21	D, O
Texas v. New Jersey	19, 21, 31	S
Travelers Express Co. v. Cory	28, 29	I
Treasurer of Massachusetts v. John Hancock Mutual Life Insurance Co.	5, 28, 29	G, H,
Western Union Telegraph Co. v. Pennsylvania	4, 5, 19, 21	I

¶ 10,015 Key to the Legal Issues

1 Burden of Proof
2 Bylaw & Article Provisions
3 Conservator Concept
4 Constitutionality
5 Debtor-Creditor Relationships
6 Derivative Rights Doctrine
7 Due Process
8 Erroneous Payments
9 Examination Authority
10 Federal Credit Unions
11 Federal Pre-emption
12 Fiduciary Relationships
13 Fine Print Provisions
14 Foreign Funds
15 Full Faith & Credit Clause
16 Future Rights to Property
17 Immunity & Indemnity
18 Impairment of Contract

19 Jurisdiction to Escheat
20 Laches & Estoppel
21 Multiple Liability
22 National Banks
23 Non-Profit Organizations
24 Private Escheat Law
25 Proof of Death
26 Purpose of Unclaimed Property Law
27 Statute of Limitations
28 Against State to Bring Action
29 Between Holder and Owner
30 Prior to Enactment of the Law
31 Superior Right to Escheat
32 Waiver of Contractual Provisions
33 Waiver of Statute of Limitations
34 Reimbursement to Holder for Costs
35 Privacy Act, Heirfinders
36 Reporting Requirements
37 Audit Findings, Accuracy of
38 Owner Claims

¶ 10,020 Key to the Unclaimed Property Categories

A Bank Checks
B Bank Deposits
C Dissolution Distributions
D Dividends
E Fiduciary Property
F Gift Certificates & Scrip & Layaways
G Life Insurance Funds
H Medical Insurance Claims, Worker's Comp. Checks
I Money Orders
J Pari-mutuel Tickets, Gambling Tokens
K Property & Casualty Claims
L Property Held by Courts & Public Agencies
M Residuals

N Service Charges
O Stock
P Trading Stamps
Q Travelers Checks
R Utility Deposits & Refunds
S Vendor & Expense Checks—Payables
T Wages & Salaries
Z Oil Royalties—Mineral Interests
AA Credits Overpayments, etc.
BB Drug Transaction Property
CC ERISA Benefits
DD Income Tax Refunds
EE Concert Tickets

¶ 10,025 Alphabetical Listing of Cases

The most significant cases discussed in Chapters 1–10 are listed below alphabetically along with the paragraph number(s) at which the case is discussed.

.01 *Aetna Life Insurance Co. v. Borges* (¶ 830)

CA-2, 869 F2d 142 (1989). Cert. denied, 493 US 811, 110 SCt 57

Authors' Summary:

The State of Connecticut initiated proceedings in state court to recover more than $2.5 million in the form of unpresented drafts arising out of ERISA-covered benefits. Aetna Life Insurance Co. removed the case to federal court and argued that the preemption provision of ERISA (which supersedes any state law that might "relate to" the employee benefit plan) required that Connecticut's claim be dismissed. The magistrate distinguished *Attorney General v. Blue Cross & Blue Shield* [1] to uphold the preemption clause. The district court summarily agreed.

Connecticut appealed to the Second Circuit where the three-judge panel analyzed both the purposes of ERISA and the limits of a federal preemption clause upon the states' police powers. Noting that ERISA was intended to promote and protect the interest of employees and their beneficiaries in employee benefit plans, the panel found that this comprehensive statute did not address unpresented benefits or any

[1] 424 N.W.2d 54 (Michigan 1988).

time limit for honoring a benefit claim. After analyzing the economic impact of abandoned property legislation upon ERISA's goal of "naturally uniform supervision" of benefit plans, the panel found that the impact was "too tenuous."

.02 *Anderson National Bank v. Luckett* (¶ 205.05 and ¶ 1005)

SCt, 321 US 233, 64 SCt 599 (1944)

Authors' Summary:

Appellant, a national banking organization, brought suit in Kentucky court to enjoin state officials from enforcing a state statute providing for the presumption of abandonment of bank deposits. The holders of such deposits were required under the law to report the deposits to the state Department of Revenue after which a copy of the report would be sent to the sheriff of the appropriate county for posting on the courthouse door or bulletin board. Deposits turned over to the state remained indefinitely subject to claim by the owner unless the state obtained a judicial determination that the property had been actually abandoned. The bank contended that:

1. The statute, by not requiring a judicial proceeding, deprived the depositors and the bank of property without due process of law, and
2. The statute infringed upon the national banking laws and was an unconstitutional interference with the function of national banks as instrumentalities of the federal government. The state Court of Appeals sustained the statute in its entirety.

The U.S. Supreme Court held that the procedural provisions of the statute adequately met constitutional requirements and did not deprive the bank or its depositors of property without due process of law. The Court said, "it is no longer open to doubt that a state, by a procedure satisfying constitutional requirements, may compel surrender to it of deposit balances, when there is substantial ground for belief that they have been abandoned or forgotten . . . certainly when the state acquires them subject to all lawful demands of the deposits."

.03 *Bank of America v. Cory* (¶ 210.02)

164 Cal. App. 3d 66, 210 Cal. Rptr. 351 (1985)

Authors' Summary:

Action between Bank of America (Bank) and the State Controller (Controller) regarding Bank's right to assess service charges and discontinue payment of interest on various deposits subject to escheat to the State was consolidated with the taxpayers' suit to compel the Controller to enforce the Unclaimed Property Law (UPL) against certain banking practices. Following trial, Bank appealed the trial court's decision in favor of the Controller on the basis that a portion of the Controller's claim was barred by the statute of limitations. Bank also appealed the trial court's award of 25 percent damages. The Controller cross-appealed on the grounds that the trial court:

1. Refused to award 12 percent per annum interest on amounts due the State prior to January 1,1977,
2. Determined that enforcement of the UPL prior to the filing of the taxpayers' suit was ineffective, and
3. Found that taxpayers' were entitled to an award of attorney fees for their participation in the actions.

The Court of Appeals rejected Bank's statute of limitations argument on two grounds. First, under California law, there is no time limit on a depositor to bring an action against a bank with respect to a deposit. Because the Controller's rights under the UPL are derivative of the owners and he or she succeeds to whatever rights the owners may have, the Controller is likewise not barred by a statute of limitations from suing Bank to recover unlawfully withheld service charges and interest that escheated to the state. Second, even apart from the derivative rights theory, under California Code of Civil Procedure § 1570, there is no time limit on an action by the Controller to enforce the UPL.

However, the Court held that the trial court improperly awarded 25 percent damages to the Controller. On the Controller's cross-appeal, the Court agreed that the Controller should have been awarded 12 percent per annum interest on amounts owing as of January 1, 1977, and thereafter. The Court affirmed the trial court's judgment as to the taxpayers' suit except that it held attorney fees could only be awarded under the "common fund" doctrine and not pursuant to a California statute relating to attorney fees.

Judgment affirmed and modified.

.04 *Bank of America v. Cranston* (¶ 210 and ¶ 405)

252 Cal. App. 2d 208, 60 Cal. Rptr. 336 (1967)

Authors' Summary:

Bank of America brought an action seeking a declaratory judgment that sums payable on certain bank drafts, cashier's checks, certified checks, money orders, Christmas Club checks, traveler's checks, and corporate dividends that were issued or became payable more than four years prior to the effective date of California's unclaimed property act were not subject to the act. With respect to traveler's checks, the bank also argued that it should be presumed that any such check not presented for payment within four years was lost or stolen and that the customers should be deemed to have breached the agreement to notify the bank of any loss by theft.

The court held that there was no basis to adopt the presumption urged by the bank with respect to traveler's checks. Further, since the bank advertised that its traveler's checks could be presented without any time limit, it waived any right to repudiate the obligation. As to the sums payable on the other written instruments, the court held that the sums constituted "deposits," which are not subject to any statute of limitations. The unclaimed dividends also were not subject to a statute of limitations because, by segregating the dividend moneys, a trust was created.

The law is settled that the statute of limitations does not begin to run in favor of a trustee until the trustee repudiates the trust.

Judgment affirmed.

.05 *Blue Cross of Northern California v. Cory* (¶ 115.06, ¶ 215.02, ¶ 315.02, ¶ 320.02, ¶ 805, and ¶ 945)

120 Cal. App. 3d 723, 174 Cal. Rptr. 901 (1981)

Authors' Summary:

Blue Cross brought an action seeking a declaration that funds represented by unnegotiated and unreturned checks, including checks issued under its medical benefits policies, were not subject to California's unclaimed property act.

The court held:

- The evidence supported the finding that the amounts represented by outstanding benefit checks were not offers to pay unliquidated claims;
- There was no evidence to support the contention that a portion of the unclaimed funds were the product of duplications or erroneous payments;
- The amount represented by the checks constituted intangible personal property held or owing in the ordinary course of Blue Cross' business, within the meaning of the unclaimed property statute;
- The Controller did not need to show delivery of the checks because he was seeking money, not the checks;
- The moneys were not "trust funds" exempted under the provisions of Code of Civil Procedure § 1410;
- The provision in certain Blue Cross contracts that deemed a benefit claim withdrawn if the check thereon was not cashed

within six months of its issuance was contrary to the policy of the unclaimed property statute and, therefore, an invalid "private escheat law";

- The Controller's enforcement action was not barred by the statute of limitations as to any part of the property because the statute did not begin to run on the Controller's action until the property became payable to the state, e.g., six months following the report of the property (Blue Cross had never reported the property, as required by the statute);
- The Controller's claim was not barred by latches; and
- The trial court erred in only awarding seven-percent per annum interest instead of 12 percent per annum following the effective date of the 12-percent interest statute.

Judgment of the trial court affirmed and modified.

.06 *Borges v. The Westport Bank & Trust Company*

651 A2d 1358, 43 Conn. Supp. 278 (1993)

Authors' Summary:

This state-chartered bank remitted dormant accounts to the state but withheld approximately $29,000 representing service charges on those accounts. The state administrator filed suit to recover those funds in view of the fact that the bank did not enforce the service charge when a customer made the request.

The bank moved to dismiss the litigation. The trial court refused and upheld the common law doctrine of waiver. This doctrine, which has been applied in numerous other unclaimed property decisions, acknowledges that the state's rights are derivative of the missing owner and prohibits a holder from treating the state administrator less favorably than an owner who presents his passbook in person.

.07 *Callahan v. Marshall Field & Company* (¶ 320.10, ¶ 820, and ¶ 820.01)

83 Ill. App. 3d 811, 404 NE2d 368, 38 Ill. Dec. 944 (1980)

Authors' Summary:

The Director of the Department of Financial Institutions brought an action for declaratory judgment seeking a determination that the Illinois Uniform Disposition of Unclaimed Property Act, as originally enacted in 1961, applied to all unclaimed intangible property held by business associations and, specifically, to unredeemed gift certificates and credit memoranda issued by Marshall Field, and unclaimed wages owing by Marshall Field to its employees.

The court held that contrary to Marshall Field's contention, it is not necessary that the holder be one of those mentioned in the specific sections of the Act in order to be covered under the "catch-all" provision. The court also rejected the argument that certain provisions printed on its gift certificates and credit memoranda limiting the period during which they could be presented for redemption extinguished Marshall Field's liability to report the items as unclaimed property. The court stated that Marshall Field's theory, if upheld, would result in a "private escheat law" under which the holder, rather than the state, would enjoy the benefit of the unclaimed property. Such a result would be contrary to the purpose and policy of the Act.

Judgment for State affirmed.

.08 *Citronelle-Mobile Gathering, Inc. v. Boswell* (¶ 815.03)

341 So.2d 933 (1977)

Authors' Summary:

Citronelle-Mobile filed an action seeking a declaratory judgment that certain funds generally represented money held for unknown owners of oil in an oil field, to which title to the mineral interests had not been established. In a prior decision, the Alabama Supreme Court had held that the funds were subject to the unclaimed property act.

The Alabama Supreme Court reaffirmed its earlier decision that the funds were subject to the act. The court also held that moneys owing more than six years prior to the effective date of the act were not covered by the act because the six-year statute of limitations had run as between the owner and the holder, and there was no intent to retroactively remove the bar of the statute of limitations.

Judgment affirmed.

.09 *Commonwealth Edison Company v. Vega* (¶ 825)

174 F3d 870 (1999)

Authors' Summary:

The company and its pension plan sought a declaratory judgment that ERISA preempted Illinois' version of the Uniform Unclaimed Property Act. The property at issue consisted of approximately $125,000 of uncashed plan benefit checks. The federal trial court agreed with ComEd's contention that the Illinois Act "related to" ERISA to such an extent that it interfered with the administration of the plan.

The appellate court agreed that the Illinois Act related to the plan "directly and substantially" and found that the unclaimed property legislation was preempted.

Illinois filed a writ of certiorari with the U.S. Supreme Court. Although ComEd did not oppose the issuance of this writ, the Supreme Court declined to hear the matter.

.10 *Connecticut Mutual Life Insurance Co. v. Moore* (¶ 115.03, ¶ 205.06, ¶ 210.01, and ¶ 510.01)

SCt, 333 US 541, 68 SCt 682 (1948)

Authors' Summary:

Nine insurance companies, incorporated in states other than New York, brought an action for a declaration of the invalidity of the New York Abandoned Property Law, as applied to them, and for injunctive relief. The insurance companies argued that the New York law impaired the obligation of contracts, contrary to Art. I, Sec. 10 of the U.S. Constitution, by transforming conditional obligations into liquidated ones and that the statute deprived them of property without due process of law, because the state lacked power to sequester funds of the companies to meet obligations on insurance policies issued on New York residents for delivery in that state.

The U.S. Supreme Court affirmed the decision of the New York Court of Appeals and held:

1. The provisions of New York law requiring the presumption of abandonment of sums payable on life insurance policies when the insured would have reached the limiting age under the mortality table on which the reserve is based, and dispensing with the requirement of surrender of the policy upon making a claim did not impair the obligation of contracts. "When the state undertakes the protection of abandoned claims, it would be beyond a reasonable requirement to compel the state to comply with conditions that may be quite proper as between the contracting parties."
2. New York had sufficient contacts with the transactions in question to confer power on the state to seize the abandoned moneys due its residents.

.11 *In re Continental Airlines, Inc.*

161 B.R. 101 (Bankr. D. Del. 1993)

Authors' Summary:

Continental Airlines, a Chapter 11 debtor, objected to the claims filed on behalf of the state unclaimed property administrators. The Bankruptcy Court, following prior precedent, found that:

- Property for which the dormancy period had expired prior to the filing of the bankruptcy petition was escheatable, but

- Property that became presumptively abandoned after the filing was not.

.12 *Cory v. Golden State Bank* (¶ 405)

95 Cal. App. 3d 360, 157 Cal. Rptr. 538 (1979)

Authors' Summary:

The State Controller brought an action to recover funds from the bank as unclaimed property. The funds consisted of "service charges" withheld by the bank from sums payable on uncashed money orders. The bank contended that the charges were "lawfully withheld" because they were authorized by contract between the bank and the purchasers of money orders. Alternatively, the bank argued that it was entitled to deduct the charges under a warehouseman's or banker's lien.

The court held that the bank's contract argument failed because the purported contractual language was inconspicuous, in small print, and not called to the customer's attention. "Under these circumstances, it must be concluded the bank's money order purchasers are not chargeable with either actual or constructive notice of the service charge provision, and therefore cannot be deemed to have consented to the provision . . ." The court held the bank's argument that it had a warehouseman's or a banker's lien to be without merit. The court also held that even if the bank had a legal right to impose the charges, it could not do so against the state because of its practice of not imposing the charges on its customers when money orders were presented for payment.

Judgment affirmed.

.13 *Cory v. Public Utilities Commission* (¶ 320.05 and ¶ 810.02)

33 Cal. 3d 522, 658 P2d 749, 189 Cal. Rptr. 386 (1983)

Authors' Summary:

After a series of decisions, the Public Utilities Commission (PUC) ordered Pacific Telephone and Telegraph Company to refund ratepayers over-collections of approximately $381 million. Approximately $6 million of the refunds were unclaimed, either because the refund checks were returned as undeliverable or because the checks were not cashed. The PUC ordered the funds represented by the undeliverable checks be credited to the accounts of current customers on a pro rata basis. The State Controller contended that such amounts would be subject to the Unclaimed Property Law if not claimed by the owners for seven years and, consequently, the PUC had no authority to redistribute the funds to current customers.

The California Supreme Court held that the unclaimed refunds could not be redistributed to current customers of Pacific but must be preserved and eventually reported to the state under the Unclaimed Property Law. The Court stated that there is nothing in the law indicating that the PUC "having ordered the refunds, is authorized to subsequently repudiate the property rights of unlocated former customers, declare a forfeiture, and provide a windfall for current customers who have already received the full refund to which they are entitled."

.14 *Delaware v. New York* (¶ 510 and ¶ 515.01)

SCt, 507 US 490, 113 SCt 1550 (1993)

Authors' Summary:

Delaware obtained leave from the U.S. Supreme Court to file an action against New York. The basis of Delaware's claim was that New York had wrongfully escheated monies representing unclaimed security-related distributions held by brokerage houses whose trading addresses were in New York City. Delaware argued that these distributions, all of which lacked owner information, should be remitted to Delaware pursuant to *Texas v. New Jersey* because it was the state of incorporation of the brokerages.

New York argued that monies were in fact owed to the brokerages and therefore the monies were properly remitted because these brokerages' last known addresses were in New York. Texas and 40 other jurisdictions intervened in the proceedings and argued that the "holder" of the monies was the issuer of the security, not any particular brokerage house. California and five other jurisdictions also intervened and argued that the monies should be distributed in proportion to the various states' involvement in the security purchase and distribution process.

The Special Master appointed by the Supreme Court recommended that:

1. The issuer of the security be considered the "holder"; and
2. The "backup" rule of *Texas v. New Jersey* for "no address" property be modified in that such property would be reportable to the state of the issuer's "principal executive office" instead of the state of incorporation.

The Supreme Court flatly rejected the recommendation made by the Special Master that the backup rule be modified. The Court emphasized that its original rule for no-address property be retained, i.e., that the state of incorporation of the holder is entitled to the escheat of no-address property. This includes property not covered under the law of another state when the last known address of the apparent owner is located in such state. The "backup" rule also applies to all property with an owner's last known address in a foreign country.

.15 *Douglas Aircraft Company, Inc. v. Cranston* (¶ 215.01)

58 Cal. 2d 462, 374 P2d 819, 24 Cal. Rptr. 851 (1962)

Authors' Summary:

Douglas Aircraft Company brought an action against the State Controller seeking a declaration that certain unclaimed wage claims were not subject to California's unclaimed property act. Douglas contended that the wage claims were barred by the statute of limitations, which had run prior to the effective date of the Unclaimed Property Law (Sept. 18, 1959).

The California Supreme Court held that it need not resolve Douglas' constitutional arguments because it appeared that the legislature did not intend to retroactively abrogate the defense of the statute of limitations when the period of limitations had run prior to the effective date of the act.

Judgment of the trial court affirmed.

.16 *Employers Insurance of Wausau v. Smith* (¶ 805)

154 Wis. 2d 199, 453 NW2d 856 (1990)

Authors' Summary:

The trial court had ruled that:

1. Uncashed worker's compensation checks which had been issued in uncontested cases were not subject to Wisconsin's Unclaimed Property Act, and
2. The shorter abandonment period enacted after the issuance of these checks applied prospectively only.

On appeal, the Supreme Court of Wisconsin reversed. It held that the uncashed benefit checks constituted a liquidated debt and that the shorter abandonment period could be applied retroactively.

.17 *Fahner v. The Chicago Transit Authority*

127 Ill. App. 3d 405, 468 NE2d 1316, 82 Ill. Dec. 536 (1984)

Authors' Summary:

The Chicago Transit Authority (CTA) passed an ordinance declaring that all checks representing general payroll, vacation, sick leave, and bonuses that had remained unclaimed for four years would revert to the CTA. The state filed a claim to these funds. The trial court found that the monies were subject to the Illinois Unclaimed Property Act and that the conflicting municipal ordinance was invalid. The CTA sought relief in the Illinois Court of Appeals.

The Appellate Court also rejected the CTA's claims. It found that the CTA was a public corporation and, thus, was subject to the applicable provision of the Illinois Act. The court also found the ordinance invalid, noting that "municipal authorities cannot, however, under a general grant of power, adopt ordinances which infringe on the spirit of a state law or are repugnant to the general policy of the state."

Judgment in favor of the state affirmed.

.18 *Fryzel v. Chicago Title & Trust Co.*

173 Ill. App. 3d 788, 527 NE2d 1025, 123 Ill. Dec. 387 (1988)

Authors' Summary:

In 1981, the Department of Financial Institutions (DFI), acting upon a report from the Commissioner of Banks and Trusts, notified Chicago Title & Trust Company (CT&T) that it planned an examination of the company's records. CT&T refused the examination of that portion of its records that related to accounts it alleged were "active express trusts" noting that Act Sec. 7a of the Illinois Unclaimed Property Act exempts such a trust. (The 1981 Uniform Unclaimed Property Act (UUPA 1981) does not contain such an exemption.)

DFI sought a declaratory judgment, insisting that its right to examine pursuant to Act Sec. 23 of the Illinois Unclaimed Property Act (Act Sec. 30 of UUPA 1981) should not be thwarted by CT&T's own conclusion that such accounts qualified for the statutory exemption. The trial court disagreed.

The appellate court agreed with Illinois' contention and ordered CT&T to allow examination, noting that the examination per se imposed no limitations on either the trust or the trustees. In reversing the trial court, the appellate court stated: "[b]arring a proper investigation by the Director here would remove a holder of property from the scope of the Act solely on the basis of his own assertions and thereby allow the regulated to become the regulator."

Judgement reversed.

.19 *Goldstein v. PHH Corporation*

123 Md. App. 214, 717 A2d 950 (1998)

Authors' Summary:

PHH refused the Comptroller's agent access to its records, alleging that the Comptroller lacked the requisite "reason to believe" that the business (which had reported dividends) had failed to report wage and vendor checks. The trial court held that the Comptroller had not alleged sufficient evidence of noncompliance prior to the commencement of this audit.

The Court of Special Appeals reversed, holding that the Comptroller:

- In fact had sufficient "reason to believe" and
- In any event, such "reason to believe" need not be formulated prior to the selection of the audit candidate.

The court emphasized that the evidentiary showing necessary for the "reason to believe" standard was considerably less stringent than the showing for "probable cause."

.20 *Goodman v. Cory* (¶ 1025)

142 Cal. App. 3d 737, 191 Cal. Rptr. 272 (1983)

Authors' Summary:

Plaintiff, a licensed private investigator, sought a declaration that a California statute limiting the amount and circumstances under which a fee could be charged for assisting in the recovery of unclaimed property from the state was unconstitutional. The trial court upheld the validity of the statute.

The Court of Appeal agreed with the trial court stating, "there is no fundamental vested right to conduct business entirely free of reasonable governmental rules and regulations . . . [T]he statute on its face neither precludes appellant from pursuing his occupation nor imposes unreasonable limitations in the performance of his business activities." The court also held that appellant was not denied equal protection of the laws.

Judgment affirmed.

.21 *Insurance Co. of North America v. Knight* (¶ 805)

8 Ill. App. 3d 871, 291 NE2d 40 (1972)

Authors' Summary:

Plaintiff brought an action seeking a declaratory judgment that the Illinois Unclaimed Property Act was unconstitutional insofar as it required the Insurance Company of North America (INA) to report certain checks, drafts, and credit memoranda to the state and to declare that INA was not required under the statute to report such items. INA argued that the Act created an unconstitutional delegation of power because there was no definition of "intangible personal property," leaving the definition of such term to an administrative agency.

INA also argued that various facts negated the presumption of abandonment.

The court held that looking at the statute as a whole, it could not be said that there was such a want of definition of "intangible personal property" as to render the statute unconstitutional. As to INA's contention that various items were not subject to the Act, for example, because they were issued as mere offers of settlement, the court affirmed the trial court's conclusion that issuance of drafts or checks to third parties under circumstances that would normally indicate delivery creates prima facie evidence of intangible property that may be presumed abandoned. However, such evidence is subject to rebuttal either by the maker as holder or the payee as owner.

Judgment affirmed.

.22 *Kane v. Insurance Co. of North America* (¶ 805)

38 Pa. Commw. 42, 392 A2d 325 (1978)

Authors' Summary:

The State of Pennsylvania brought an action against Insurance Company of North America (INA) and several of its subsidiaries to escheat proceeds of uncashed checks and drafts issued by INA and "deposits" paid for the purchase of certain policies of perpetual fire insurance. The appeal in this case followed the remand by the Pennsylvania Supreme Court in *Sennett v. Insurance Company of North America.*[2]

The court held that the deposits relating to policies when the insured property had been sold were not escheatable because the policies provided that the deposits would be considered "sunk" for the benefit of the company if refunds were not claimed within a specified period. As to the policies on property that had been destroyed, such deposits remained subject to claim by the insureds. The state's claim regarding proceeds of uncashed checks, drafts, and credit memoranda failed because it did not prove that the persons to whom the instruments were payable were unqualifiedly entitled to them. The state failed to make out a prima facie case for escheat and failed to meet its burden of proof.

Judgment affirmed.

---

[2] 432 Pa. 525, 247 A.2d 774 (1968).

.23 *Lincoln Bank & Trust Co. v. Oklahoma Tax Commission* (¶ 915 and ¶ 1025)

1992 OK 22, 827 P2d 1314 (1992)

Authors' Summary:

The Tax Commission had attempted to audit various financial records to determine the bank's compliance. The bank sought injunctive relief, citing Oklahoma's financial privacy act, which was based upon the 1978 federal legislation, 12 U.S.C. 3401. The trial court granted a preliminary and later, a permanent injunction.

Upon the Commission's appeal, the bank argued that the financial privacy act was a later, more specific and, thus, controlling enactment. The Supreme Court disagreed and dissolved the injunction. The court cited several reasons for its holding:

- The Tax Commission was a "supervisory agency" and thus was unrestricted by the privacy act;
- The privacy act expressly permitted a bank to notify a governmental entity of a violation of statute, which was construed to include the unclaimed property legislation;
- The unclaimed property legislation expressly mandated that information so received remain confidential; and
- "[N]o privacy interest exists on property that is presumed abandoned by law."

Additionally, this decision shed further light on the showing the state administrator must make prior to inspection of a holder's records. Oklahoma's legislation, based upon the 1954 Uniform Disposition of Unclaimed Property Act, required that the administrator must first have a "reason to believe" that the holder is noncompliant. (UUPA 1981 omitted this "reason to believe" requirement, see Act Sec. 30(b).) The bank had argued that this required a showing of probable cause. The court found from the Commission's evidence, particularly that all 75 banks that had been examined were found to hold unreported property, that a "neutral nondiscriminatory pattern of enforcement" had been met.

.24 *Metropolitan Life Insurance Co. v. Office of the State Comptroller*

120 A.D. 2d 140, 508 N.Y.S. 2d 307 (1986)

Authors' Summary:

Appellant sought review of the Comptroller's determination that interest that insurers must compute on the unpaid proceeds of life insurance policies, annuity contracts, or endowment contracts pursuant to the Insurance Law is abandoned property and must be reported and remitted under the Abandoned Property Law. Appellant contended that the legislature did not intend the Abandoned Property Law to apply to the interest and that the Comptroller's ruling would give an unintended retroactive effect to the interest provision. The trial court agreed with the Comptroller.

The appellate court held that the Abandoned Property Law is to be liberally construed to accomplish its purposes and that the Comptroller's interpretation is clearly in accord with this legislative goal. Also, the court found no attempted retroactive application. The Comptroller required only that interest be paid from the effective date of the Insurance Law provision and, as such, it was a purely prospective application of the statute.

Judgment affirmed.

.25 *Midlantic National Bank v. Berman*

Civ No. 90-4610 (D. N.J. 1991) (unreported)

Authors' Summary:

Midlantic National Bank filed for a declaration that New Jersey had no right to examine the records of a national bank unless the state could articulate a "reasonable cause to believe" that such a bank was holding unclaimed property. Midlantic cited a 1982 amendment to the National Bank Act that had added such language.

New Jersey relied upon its examination statute, which did not require any showing of cause. New Jersey further argued that an examination was not an exercise of the "visitorial power" contemplated by that amendment to the National Bank Act.

The trial court agreed with Midlantic's interpretation of the conflicting federal and state statutes and granted the relief sought by the bank. Subsequently, New Jersey filed affidavits demonstrating "reasonable cause to believe" and conducted the examination.

.26 *Minnesota v. The First National Bank of St. Paul* (¶ 910.02)

313 NW2d 390 (1981)

Authors' Summary:

The state treasurer brought an action for declaratory and injunctive relief contending that Minnesota's Uniform Disposition of Unclaimed Property Act authorized the treasurer to examine the records of the bank. The bank argued that pursuant to 12 U.S.C. § 484, only the U.S. Comptroller of the Currency had the authority to examine such records. The trial court agreed with the bank and granted its motion for summary judgment.

The Minnesota Supreme Court held:

- Compliance with both the federal and the state provisions was not a physical impossibility; thus, there was no preemption on that basis;
- The state treasurer's examination was not the exercise of "visitorial powers" within the meaning of 12 U.S.C. § 484, and, therefore, there was no express federal preemption;
- There was no implied intent by Congress to bar the proposed examination by the state treasurer.

The court further stated that its holding did not leave the bank powerless against abuse of examination procedures. The courts have the power to issue protective orders to "prevent demonstrable undue interference or public disclosure that goes beyond the objectives of the unclaimed property law."

Judgment reversed.

.27 *In re Monks Club, Inc.*

64 Wn.2d 845, 394 P2d 804 (1964)

Authors' Summary:

Receivers in a proceeding to dissolve the Monks Club sought an order barring the Tax Commission from asserting any claim to unclaimed assets of the Monks Club under the state's unclaimed property act. The trial court issued an order barring the state from claiming any of the unclaimed funds.

The Washington Supreme Court held that the definition of "business association" contained in the act was broad enough to include nonprofit corporations such as the Monks Club. The court stated that "to hold that nonprofit corporations are subject to (the act) is in harmony with the purpose of the act, which is to place all abandoned intangible personal property in the custody of the state . . . " Also, the unclaimed shares of stockholders in funds resulting from liquidation are not available for distribution to other stockholders.

Order of trial court quashed and cause remanded.

.28 *Murdock v. John B. Stetson Co.*

32 Pa. D&C 2d 300 (1963)

Authors' Summary:

Plaintiffs filed a petition to escheat alleging that the value of certain merchandise represented by unredeemed gift certificates sold by respondent had escheated to the state. Gift certificates issued by respondent contained a provision which stated, "This certificate is invalid one year from the date of issue." Plaintiffs sought a monetary award representing the approximate wholesale price of the merchandise for which the certificates were issued plus interest.

The court denied the escheat petition on the basis that, under the terms of the certificate, respondent's duty to perform did not ripen unless and until the certificate was presented to it by the holder thereof. In addition, "each certificate by its terms was invalid one year after sale and the Commonwealth is bound by this contractual term."

.29 *Nellius v. Tampax, Inc.* (¶ 115.05 and ¶ 510.04)

394 A2d 233 (1978)

Authors' Summary:

The State Escheator filed suit to escheat certain stock, stock dividends, and cash dividends held by the defendant, a Delaware corporation. The records of the defendant showed that the address of the owner of the stock was in Massachusetts. Other evidence indicated that the registered owner transferred the stock to someone else, whose identity and address could not be determined with certainty.

The court held that the State Escheator lacked standing to maintain the action under the guidelines established in *Texas v. New Jersey* (see ¶ 10,025.46). Under those guidelines, Delaware, as the domicile state of the holder, could not escheat because the owner's last known address, as shown on the holder's records, was in another state and such other state had abandonment property statutes.

The defendant's motion for summary judgment was granted.

.30 *New Jersey v. The Chubb Corp.* (¶ 935.02)

239 N.J. Super. 257, 570 A2d 1313 (1989)

Authors' Summary:

New Jersey obtained a partial summary judgment enabling it to utilize estimation techniques to claim monies represented by uncashed insurance drafts. These drafts were issued by a property and casualty insurer that had not previously reported the funds and had not retained most of the claim files. The trial court ruled that insurance drafts were covered by New Jersey's "omnibus" provision but cautioned the state that the estimation and extrapolation techniques must be scientifically reliable.

.31 *New Jersey v. Elsinore Shore Associates*

249 N.J. Super. 403, 592 A2d 604 (1991)

Authors' Summary:

The Casino Control Commission ordered that this casino cease operation and that a conservator should hold in trust $875,000 for payment of unredeemed gaming chips and tokens. The casino petitioned to have the funds returned in order that it could pay a reappearing owner.

The Appellate Division ruled that these funds were subject to New Jersey's version of UUPA 1981, citing the "omnibus" clause. The court further noted that the state's earlier change from an absolute escheat to a custodial escheat law meant that the law no longer had to be narrowly construed.

.32 *New Jersey v. Jefferson Lake Sulphur Co.* (¶ 115.06 and ¶ 820)

36 N.J. 577, 178 A2d 329. Cert. denied, 370 US 158, 82 SCt 1253 (1962)

Authors' Summary:

The State of New Jersey filed an action to obtain possession, pursuant to its escheat law, of dividends on defendant's stock unclaimed for at least five years. The defendant admitted that it had sought to circumvent the escheat law by amending its certificate of incorporation to provide that funds set aside for payment of dividends would revert to the corporation if not claimed within three years from the date the dividend became payable. The trial court found the charter amendment to be invalid.

The Supreme Court of New Jersey held that the amendment was an effort to establish a private escheat law. The statute represents the public policy of the state and it manifests the legislative will that such unclaimed moneys be used for the good of all our citizens ". . . [D]efendant's private escheat law is clearly opposed to the spirit and essence of the public custodial escheat law and to the broad public policy represented thereby. In such a conflict the private law cannot survive."

Judgment affirmed.

.33 *New Jersey v. Sperry & Hutchinson Co.*

31 N.J. 385, 157 A2d 505 (1960)

Authors' Summary:

The state brought actions to require escheat of the cash value of unredeemed trading stamps. Sperry & Hutchinson Co. (S&H) argued that because the state's rights can be no greater than the right of the owner of unclaimed property, there was no property to escheat because the right of redemption did not arise until a prescribed number of stamps had been accumulated by a collector. The trial court dismissed the state's actions.

The court held that the state could not aggregate rights that do not exist to establish a right unto itself; it succeeds only to individual, non-aggregated claims. Because the state did not prove that any individual had collected a sufficient number of stamps to be entitled to redeem the stamps, the liability of S & H remained contingent and not subject to escheat.

Judgment affirmed.

.34 *In re November 8, 1996, Determination of the State of New Jersey, Department of the Treasury, Unclaimed Property Office* (¶ 820.03)

156 N.J. 599, 722 A2d 536 (1999)

Authors' Summary:

The Hilton at Short Hills issued gift certificates redeemable in either merchandise or services at the hotel. The state treasurer concluded that the value of these certificates were escheatable. Hilton appealed.

The trial court concluded that the purchasers intended to receive merchandise or services, not a cash redemption. Based upon the parties' intentions, the court held that the Unclaimed Property Act did not cover this property.

The state appealed to the Supreme Court of New Jersey, which upheld the trial court.

.35 *Oregon ex rel. Mallicoat v. Coe* (¶ 320.06)

254 Ore. 365, 460 P2d 357 (1969)

Authors' Summary:

The state administrator claimed funds held by a county treasurer for the redemption of a school bond that had been issued in 1935 and had matured in 1946. Oregon adopted unclaimed property legislation in 1957 and subsequently demanded the funds. The county refused.

The trial court sustained the county's demurrer and the state administrator appealed. The Supreme Court of Oregon reversed, finding that the unclaimed property legislation prevailed over the specific legislation governing redemption of school bonds.

.36 *Pennsylvania v. New York* (¶ 115.05, ¶ 320.03, ¶ 510.05, and ¶ 710.07)

SCt, 407 US 206, 92 SCt 2075. Rehearing denied, 409 US 897, 93 SCt 91 (1972)

Authors' Summary:

The State of Pennsylvania brought an original action in the U.S. Supreme Court against New York regarding the authority of the states to escheat, or take custody of, unclaimed funds paid for the purchase of money orders. Pennsylvania proposed that the state in which the money order was purchased be permitted to take the funds, and that such state should be presumed to be the state of the purchaser's residence. New York argued that the rule established in *Texas v. New Jersey* (see ¶ 10,025.46) should be strictly applied.

The Court adopted the Special Master's recommendation that the *Texas v. New Jersey* rule should be sustained and applied to this case. Thus, the unclaimed amounts owing on the money orders were subject to escheat by the state of the last known address of the creditor as shown on the holder's records. If no address of the creditor is shown on such records or if the state of last known address has no applicable escheat law, the right to escheat or take custody would be in the domiciliary state of the debtor, in this case, New York. As to Pennsylvania's protest that a windfall would result to New York because most money order sellers did not retain records of addresses of obligees on money orders, the Court stated that ". . . nothing we say here prohibits the States from requiring Western Union (the debtor) to keep adequate address records."

In 1974, Congress enacted P.L. 95-495, which established a new rule of jurisdiction for traveler's checks, money orders, and other similar written instruments. P.L. 95-495 created a "place of sale" or place of purchase rule that requires the reporting of such items to the state in which the records of the holder indicate its sale. This is the only exception to the rules of jurisdiction set forth in Texas v. New Jersey that have ever been the subject of federal legislation.

.37 *Presley v. County of Nassau*

148 Misc. 2d 125, 560 N.Y.S.2d 173 (1990). Affirmed, 188 A.D.2d 594, 591 N.Y.S.2d 72 (1992)

Authors' Summary:

Elvis died prior to a scheduled concert in 1977. Six years later, approximately $86,000 representing unredeemed concert tickets remained unclaimed. Elvis' estate filed suit for these monies. The estate argued that the ticket holders should not be entitled to have the "memorabilia" value of the ticket plus the opportunity to receive a refund. The trial court reasoned that intent of the parties at the time of the contract governed and ruled the ticket purchasers bargained for a concert, not a memento. Because the purchasers did not receive the benefits of the bargain, they were entitled to a refund. Therefore the monies representing the unredeemed tickets were subject to New York's law. The decision was affirmed on appeal.[3]

.38 *Provident Institution for Savings v. Malone* (¶ 205.01)

SCt, 221 US 660, 31 SCt 661 (1911)

Authors' Summary:

The state filed a petition in probate court seeking custody of deposits that had been inactive and unclaimed for 30 years. The bank argued that this recent enactment (1907) deprived its depositors of their property without due process of law and also impaired the obligations of the contract between the bank and its depositors.

The probate court granted the state's petition. The bank appealed to the Supreme Judicial Court of Massachusetts. That court affirmed the probate court's decision. The bank then appealed to the U.S. Supreme Court.

That Court noted that this legislation was analogous to the "appointment of custodians for the real and personal property of an absentee." As for the bank's insistence that there had been no abandonment and that the "money is in safe hands," the Court stated "while there was a possibility that the money might so remain the bank had no right to require that it should be so left."

In response to the bank's argument that the legislation was applicable only to savings banks and was therefore discriminatory, the Court stated:

> Deposits in savings banks are made in expectation that they may remain much longer uncalled for than is usual in deposits in other banks. This fact makes savings deposits all the more likely to be forgotten and abandoned. And as the depositors are often wage-earners, moving from place to place, there is special reason for intervening to protect their interest in this class of property in banks to which the State's supervisory power is constantly exercised.

The Supreme Court affirmed the judgment in favor of the state.

---

[3] The New York court considered the two prior decisions concerning Presley concert tickets and followed the rationale of the Tennessee Court (which in turn had rejected the reasoning of the North Carolina Court), see Presley v. City of Memphis, 769 S.W.2d 221 (Tenn.App. 1988) and *North Carolina Treas. V. Asheville,* 300 S.E.2d 283 (N.C.App. 1983).

.39 *Riggs National Bank v. District of Columbia*

581 A2d 1229 (1990)

Authors' Summary:

The trial court had ruled that the District of Columbia was entitled to claim monies representing:

- Official checks and deposit accounts which belonged to residents of the District and of those states with which the District had a reciprocal agreement,
- Deposit accounts belonging to owners with an address in other nonreciprocal states, and
- Service charges assessed and the interest which would have accrued had these charges not been assessed.

The District's request for an assessment of interest and penalties was denied. Both parties appealed. The appellate court affirmed the trial court's ruling with regard to the monies in category 1 (official checks and deposits) but reversed the ruling with regard to category 2 (deposits held for residents of states other than the District and its reciprocal states) and category 3 (service charges and interest). The appellate court also reversed the trial court and held the District was entitled to interest and penalties.

.40 *Rose's Stores, Inc. v. Boyles*

106 N.C. App. 263, 416 SE2d 200 (1992)

Authors' Summary:

The Treasurer demanded that Rose's Stores, Inc. report and remit monies representing unclaimed layaway deposits and payments. Rose's filed a declaratory judgement action arguing that the monies were not subject to escheat.

North Carolina's "omnibus" clause specifically included accounts payable. Additionally, Rose's policy provided that such monies were refundable, less a $200 service charge, upon customer request. Nonetheless the trial court found that Rose's was not a "holder" and therefore not required to report and remit the property.

The Treasurer appealed and the Court of Appeals reversed the trial court. The court found that Rose's refund policy made it clear that the retailer was the holder, not the owner, of the monies. The court also rejected Rose's alternate argument that the monies constituted liquidated damages for the purchaser's breach of the installment sales contract, ruling that Rose's had failed to insert such a provision in the contract.

Finally, the Court of Appeals distinguished this case from North Carolina's only other appellate decision regarding unclaimed property,

Treasurer v. City of Asheville,[4] (unclaimed refunds from Elvis concert not escheatable) by noting that "there is no inherent value, either sentimental or pecuniary in a layaway deposit slip."

On September 30, 1992, the Supreme Court of North Carolina agreed to review the case. Currently, no further action has been taken.

.41 *Screen Actors Guild, Inc. v. Cory* (¶ 115.06)

91 Cal. App. 3d 111, 154 Cal. Rptr. 77, Cal. App. 2d Dist. (1979)

Authors' Summary:

The Screen Actors Guild brought an action seeking a declaratory judgment that unclaimed "residuals" paid to it for distribution to its members were not subject to California's Unclaimed Property Law. The Guild contended that the residuals were not escheatable because:

1. They were expressly exempt from the Law because the funds were deposited in a foreign bank,
2. The funds were exempt "employee benefit trust" distributions, and
3. The Guild's bylaws provided for forfeiture to the Guild of any residuals unclaimed after six years.

The court held that the funds deposited in the foreign bank were in the Guild's constructive possession and were held by it as trustee. Thus, they were not "funds held only in a foreign country" within the meaning of the law. The unclaimed residuals did not constitute employee benefit trust distributions; they were nothing more than the payment of deferred compensation. Further, the Guild did not enforce the forfeiture in practice. The Guild's bylaw providing for forfeiture of the residuals after six years was contrary to the policy of the Unclaimed Property Law. "In short, a private escheat law cannot circumvent the effect of a public one."

Judgment affirmed.

.42 *Security Savings Bank v. California* (¶ 205.03)

SCt, 263 US 282, 44 SCt 108 (1923)

Authors' Summary:

The state sought to escheat savings deposits that had been unclaimed for more than 20 years. Both the trial court and the Supreme Court of California found in favor of the state. The U.S. Supreme Court awarded a writ of error to consider the bank's argument that the underlying legislation was "obnoxious to both the contract clause and the due process clause."

---

[4] 300 S.E. 2d 283 (1983).

The Supreme Court noted that the contract of deposit did not give the bank a right to retain the money in the event that it was not called for by the depositor.

The bank also argued that the service of process upon the depositors by publications in a newspaper was so defective that the depositors would not be bound by the judgment, which could expose the bank to liability.

The Supreme Court found that the publication requirement was not so reasonable as to be a denial of due process.

> Deposits in savings banks are made in expectation that they may remain much longer uncalled for than is usual in deposits in other banks. This fact makes savings deposits all the more likely to be forgotten and abandoned. And as the depositors are often wage-earners, moving from place to place, there is special reason for intervening to protect their interest in this class of property in banks to which the State's supervisory power is constantly exercised.

The Supreme Court affirmed the judgment in favor of the state.

.43 *Sennett v. Insurance Co. of North America* (¶ 215.02)

432 Pa. 525, 247 A2d 774 (1968)

Authors' Summary:

The State of Pennsylvania brought an action to compel Insurance Co. of North America (INA) to pay to the state, as escheatable property, uncollected wages, proceeds of uncashed checks and drafts, and "deposits" on perpetual fire insurance policies. With respect to the perpetual fire insurance policies, the insured would be entitled to a partial refund if the insured cancelled the policy or transferred the insured property. These policies provided, however, that if the insured, following sale of the property, did not demand the refund within a specified time period, the deposit money would be considered as "sunk for the benefit of the company." INA also contended that the state's escheat action was barred by the statute of limitations.

The Supreme Court of Pennsylvania held:

- As to perpetual fire insurance policies, there was no evidence of sale; thus, the moneys had to remain in the company's reserves and were not escheatable unless there was a showing that there were refunds payable;
- The statute of limitations did not begin to run until the property was reported to the state. The Court stated:

  "INA simply has to take a stand: if it reports the holding of these funds (as a precautionary measure), the statute will run; if it does not, the Commonwealth is not precluded thereafter from initiating an action even if the fifteen year period has expired"; and

- INA's argument that because the state's rights are derivative, its claim would be barred by the six-year statute of limitations applicable between the company and owners without merit.

Affirmed in part; reversed in part.[5]

.44 *South Carolina Tax Commission v. Metropolitan Life Insurance Co.* (¶ 210.03)

266 S.C. 34, 221 SE2d 522 (1975)

Authors' Summary:

The South Carolina Tax Commission brought an action to collect the maturity value of certain life insurance policies as abandoned property. Metropolitan Life Insurance Co. contended that it was not obligated to pay amounts on policies when the six-year statute of limitations had run prior to the effective date of the Uniform Unclaimed Property Act. The Commission argued that Metropolitan had waived the defense because it admitted that it would not refuse to pay policyholders and beneficiaries as a result of the lapse of time.

The court stated that the derivative nature of the state's rights must be considered.

> Metropolitan may not waive its contractual rights as to these policies against the policyholders, and then enforce those same rights against the Tax Commission.

Thus, Metropolitan had waived the defense of the statute of limitations.

Judgment of the trial court in favor of Metropolitan reversed.

.45 *Standard Oil Co. v. New Jersey* (¶ 510.02)

SCt, 341 US 428, 71 SCt 822 (1951)

Authors' Summary:

The State of New Jersey filed a petition seeking a decree escheating certain property held by the Standard Oil Co. The property at issue was comprised of unpaid dividends declared upon the stock of Standard Oil and 12 shares of common stock of the company. Standard Oil contended that the escheat judgment of the New Jersey court denied it of its property without due process of law because the judgment did not protect the company from later liability to the stockholder-owners because:

[5] See *Kane v. Insurance Company of North America*, above.

1. The notice to claimants was inadequate,
2. The statute and judgment thereunder impaired the obligation of contracts, and
3. The New Jersey court lacked jurisdiction to escheat the property.

The Supreme Court held:

- The notice by publication was adequate.

  "If the state has the responsibility of looking after abandoned property subject to its sovereign power, these publications are adequate to affect the owner's rights";
- There was no impairment of contract by the New Jersey statute, "but only the exercise of a regulatory power over abandoned property";
- The state court had jurisdiction to escheat the property because the court had jurisdiction to seize the property by virtue of the publication of notice and service of summons on the company. Also, the stock certificates and dividends may be abandoned property subject to the disposition of the domiciliary state of the corporation when the whereabouts of the owners are unknown for such lengths of time and under such circumstances as permit the declaration of abandonment; and
- The company would be protected from future claims by owners because the state court had jurisdiction to escheat, and the Full Faith and Credit Clause of the Constitution bars escheat by any other state.

Judgment affirmed.

.46 *Texas v. New Jersey* (¶ 115.05, ¶ 320.03, ¶ 505, ¶ 510, and ¶ 510.04)

SCt, 379 US 674, 85 SCt 626 (1965)

Authors' Summary:

The State of Texas brought an original action in the U.S. Supreme Court against New Jersey, Pennsylvania, and the Sun Oil Co. seeking an injunction and declaration of rights as to which state had jurisdiction to escheat various small debts owing by Sun to creditors. Texas claimed power to escheat because the debts were evidenced on the books of Sun's two Texas offices situated in that state or were owing to persons with last known addresses in Texas, or both. New Jersey argued for the right to escheat on the basis that it was the state of Sun's incorporation. Pennsylvania claimed power to escheat because it was the state of Sun's principal business offices. Florida intervened claiming the right to escheat obligations owing to persons whose last known addresses were in that state.

The Court, adopting the recommendation of a special master, held that the state whose claim to escheat is superior to all others is the state of the last known address of the owner, or creditor, as shown by the debtor's (holder's) books and records. If the last known address is in a state not providing for escheat of the property, or if no last known address were shown on the debtor's records, the property would be escheatable by the state of corporate domicile of the debtor. However, in such case, the state of domicile could retain the property only until some other state came forward with proof of its superior right, e.g., proof that the last known address was in such state or enactment of appropriate escheat law. The Court noted that the decision could have been resolved otherwise and was not controlled by statutory or constitutional provisions nor by past decisions, nor was it entirely one of logic. "It is fundamentally a question of ease of administration and of equity."

.47 *Travelers Express Co., Inc. v. Cory* (¶ 215.02)

CA-9, 664 F2d 763 (1981)

Authors' Summary:

Travelers Express Co., Inc. brought a declaratory relief action in federal district court (based on diversity of citizenship) after the California State Controller demanded payment of escheated property withheld from the state as a result of the deduction of "service charges" from sums payable on uncashed money orders. The district court held that Travelers Express was not entitled to withhold the service charges from the state.

Travelers Express appealed on two issues:

1. That the statute of limitations barred the Controller's suit on property escheated before February 8, 1974 (three years before his 1977 demand letter), and
2. Traveler's claim that the Controller was equitably estopped from asserting any claims to amounts deducted in service charges from money orders escheated before August 1978.

Relying on *Blue Cross v. Cory* (see above), the Ninth Circuit Court of Appeals held that although the statute of limitations on an enforcement action by the Controller will commence running six months after the holder has reported the property in compliance with the Unclaimed Property Law, the statute did not start to run in this case because Travelers Express did not report the property as required. Travelers Express reported only the net amounts remaining after deduction of the service charges. The court stated that "Travelers must have filed a report of the entire amount of unclaimed money orders pursuant to California Code of Civil Procedure § 1530. This Travelers did not do. The report should have been followed with a written explanation of why the service-charged portion was not subject to escheat. This travelers also did not do." As to Travelers Express' estoppel argument, the court upheld the district court's determination that Travelers Express did not detrimentally rely on the Controller's alleged acquiescence in its service charge practices.

.48 *Treasurer of Massachusetts v. John Hancock Mutual Life Insurance Co.* (¶ 215)

388 Mass. 410, 446 NE2d 1376 (1983)

Authors' Summary:

The State Treasurer claimed funds represented by uncashed checks issued by John Hancock Mutual Life Insurance Co. for such items as accident and health insurance payments, life insurance proceeds, agent commissions, salaries, and vendor payments. The trial court ruled that the Treasurer had standing to bring this action and that John Hancock was not required to report and remit funds under G.L.C. 200A.

The Supreme Judicial Court affirmed the trial court's decision on the standing and statute of limitations issues, but held that John Hancock was subject to the reporting and payment requirements of G.L.C. 200A § 7. With respect to the statute of limitations, the court said that the unclaimed property is not due the Commonwealth until the report is filed. "Until the property is owed to the Commonwealth, the statute of limitations does not begin to run." The court also held that John Hancock's contractual obligations, which gave rise to issuance of the uncashed checks, constituted "intangible personal property" and were subject G.L.C. 200A § 5.

.49 *Western Union Telegraph Co. v. Pennsylvania* (¶ 510.03)

SCt, 368 US 71, 82 SCt 199 (1961)

Authors' Summary:

Pennsylvania brought an action in state court to escheat certain unclaimed obligations (sums owing on telegraphic money orders) of Western Union, which were alleged to be property within the state. Western Union sold money orders from its offices in Pennsylvania and other states. The State Supreme Court held that the obligations escheated to Pennsylvania.

The U.S. Supreme Court held that Pennsylvania lacked power to escheat the obligations because its courts could not protect Western

Union from claims by other states to escheat the same property. The Court said,

> . . . Western Union was not protected by the Pennsylvania judgment, for a state court judgment need not be given full faith and credit by other states as to parties or property not subject to the jurisdiction of the court that rendered it.

Judgment of the Supreme Court of Pennsylvania reversed.

Appendix B

PRACTICE TOOLS

¶ 11,001 Overview

This appendix contains forms and instructions that may be useful in reporting unclaimed property.

¶ 11,005 Annual Report of Unclaimed Personal Property

STATE OF CALIFORNIA
CONTROLLER'S OFFICE

ALL INFORMATION MUST BE TYPED

THIS FORM MUST BE COMPLETED AND ATTACHED TO THE REPORT

EFT DEBIT REF. NO:______________ HOLDER TYPE CODE:______________ [SCO USE ONLY] REMITTANCE TYPE:______________

ANNUAL REPORT OF UNCLAIMED PERSONAL PROPERTY
BUSINESS YEAR END ___/___/______

REPORT DUE BEFORE: 11/01/1999

A. EMPLOYER IDENTIFICATION NO. __ __ - __ __ __ __ __ __ __ BRANCH NO. __ __ __ __ __ __

B. NAME OF HOLDER: ______________________________
STREET ADDRESS: ______________________________
P.O. BOX NUMBER: ______________________________
CITY: ______________ STATE: ______ ZIP: _ _ _ _ _ - _ _ _ _ COUNTRY: ________

ADDRESS INQUIRIES ON THIS REPORT TO:
NAME: ______________ TITLE: __________ PHONE NO. _ _ _ - _ _ _ - _ _ _ _ EXT. ______

C. THE FOREGOING ADDRESS IS THAT OF: MAIN OFFICE # _______ BRANCH # __________
IF INCORPORATION, STATE OF INC: ______________ DATE OF INC.: ___/___/______

D. TOTAL FOR ACCOUNTS:

$50.00 AND OVER	$______________.____
$50.00 AND OVER WITHOUT NAMES	$______________.____
$49.99 AND UNDER	$______________.____
GRAND TOTAL	$______________.____
TOTAL SHARES	______________

E. TYPE OF ORGANIZATION SIC CODE: _________
(FINANCIAL INSTITUTIONS, CHECK ONE AND PLEASE SUPPLY THE CHARTER DATE)
FEDERAL: _____ DATE: ___/___/______ STATE: _____ DATE ___/___/______

F. IF YOU ARE THE SUCCESSOR TO A PREVIOUS HOLDER OF PROPERTY, OR IF YOU HAVE CHANGED YOUR NAME, PLEASE LIST SUCH PRIOR NAME BELOW:
____

G. IF YOU ARE REPORTING FOR A HOLDER OF UNCLAIMED PROPERTY, PLEASE PROVIDE THE FOLLOWING INFORMATION:
REPORTING AGENCY: ______________________________
STREET ADDRESS: ______________________________
CITY: ______________ STATE: ________ ZIP _ _ _ _ _ - _ _ _ _ COUNTRY: ________

H. VERIFICATION: If made by an individual, shall be verified by the individual; if made by a partnership, by a partner; if made by an unincorporated association or private corporation, by an officer; if made by a public corporation, by its chief fiscal officer or other employee authorized by the holder (Section 1530 (e) CCP).

The undersigned, ______________________________ declares, under penalty of perjury, that, to the best of (his) (her) knowledge and belief, the following sheets contain a full, true and complete report of unclaimed property which is presumed unclaimed under the provisions of Part 3, Title 10, Chapter 7, Code of Civil Procedures -- commencing with Section 1500, and Title 2, California Administrative Code, Sections 1150 et seq.

SIGNATURE: ______________________________ TITLE: ______________ DATE: ______________

(UFS-1 06/1999)

Kathleen Connell
Controller of California

Annual Report of Unclaimed Personal Property

ALL INFORMATION MUST BE TYPED

Unclaimed Property
State of California

(List accounts of $50.00 or more separately — use for Cash-Only Reports or Safe-Deposit-Only Reports)

Holder:______ City:______ Branch:______ Page:____ of____

MULTIPLE OWNERS NUMBER ____ OF ____			
LAST NAME ______	TITLE ____	DATE OF LAST CONTACT ____	
FIRST NAME ______	M.I. ____	SOC. SEC./TAX I.D. NO. ____	
OWNER CODE ____	OWNER DATE / /	REFERENCE NO. ____	
BUS. NAME ______		PROPERTY TYPE ____	
ADDRESS ______		TOTAL AMT. DUE OWNER ____	
CITY ______		LAWFUL CHARGES ____	
STATE ____ ZIP ____	COUNTRY ____	SAFE DEPOSIT BOX NO. ____	
IN CARE OF ______		LIEN AMOUNT ____	

MULTIPLE OWNERS NUMBER ____ OF ____			
LAST NAME ______	TITLE ____	DATE OF LAST CONTACT ____	
FIRST NAME ______	M.I. ____	SOC. SEC./TAX I.D. NO. ____	
OWNER CODE ____	OWNER DATE / /	REFERENCE NO. ____	
BUS. NAME ______		PROPERTY TYPE ____	
ADDRESS ______		TOTAL AMT. DUE OWNER ____	
CITY ______		LAWFUL CHARGES ____	
STATE ____ ZIP ____	COUNTRY ____	SAFE DEPOSIT BOX NO. ____	
IN CARE OF ______		LIEN AMOUNT ____	

MULTIPLE OWNERS NUMBER ____ OF ____			
LAST NAME ______	TITLE ____	DATE OF LAST CONTACT ____	
FIRST NAME ______	M.I. ____	SOC. SEC./TAX I.D. NO. ____	
OWNER CODE ____	OWNER DATE / /	REFERENCE NO. ____	
BUS. NAME ______		PROPERTY TYPE ____	
ADDRESS ______		TOTAL AMT. DUE OWNER ____	
CITY ______		LAWFUL CHARGES ____	
STATE ____ ZIP ____	COUNTRY ____	SAFE DEPOSIT BOX NO. ____	
IN CARE OF ______		LIEN AMOUNT ____	

MULTIPLE OWNERS NUMBER ____ OF ____			
LAST NAME ______	TITLE ____	DATE OF LAST CONTACT ____	
FIRST NAME ______	M.I. ____	SOC. SEC./TAX I.D. NO. ____	
OWNER CODE ____	OWNER DATE / /	REFERENCE NO. ____	
BUS. NAME ______		PROPERTY TYPE ____	
ADDRESS ______		TOTAL AMT. DUE OWNER ____	
CITY ______		LAWFUL CHARGES ____	
STATE ____ ZIP ____	COUNTRY ____	SAFE DEPOSIT BOX NO. ____	
IN CARE OF ______		LIEN AMOUNT ____	

(UDS -1A REV. 4/98)

KATHLEEN CONNELL
CONTROLLER OF CALIFORNIA

THIS FORM MUST BE COMPLETED WHEN REPORTING SECURITIES AND ATTACHED TO THE REPORT

ALL INFORMATION MUST BE TYPED

ANNUAL REPORT OF UNCLAIMED PERSONAL PROPERTY
SECURITIES SUMMARY *(SUMMARY OF REPORTED ISSUES)*

REPORT ID
SCO USE ONLY

HOLDER NAME ______________________________

****

CUSIP No: ____________ Security Name: ______________________________

Security Type: ______ Security Series: ____________ Total No. Shares/Units/Bonds etc. reported this issue: ______.______
(extend to third decimal place)

****

CUSIP No: ____________ Security Name: ______________________________

Security Type: ______ Security Series: ____________ Total No. Shares/Units/Bonds etc. reported this issue: ______.______
(extend to third decimal place)

****

CUSIP No: ____________ Security Name: ______________________________

Security Type: ______ Security Series: ____________ Total No. Shares/Units/Bonds etc. reported this issue: ______.______
(extend to third decimal place)

****

CUSIP No: ____________ Security Name: ______________________________

Security Type: ______ Security Series: ____________ Total No. Shares/Units/Bonds etc. reported this issue: ______.______
(extend to third decimal place)

****

CUSIP No: ____________ Security Name: ______________________________

Security Type: ______ Security Series: ____________ Total No. Shares/Units/Bonds etc. reported this issue: ______.______
(extend to third decimal place)

****

CUSIP No: ____________ Security Name: ______________________________

Security Type: ______ Security Series: ____________ Total No. Shares/Units/Bonds etc. reported this issue: ______.______
(extend to third decimal place)

****

CUSIP No: ____________ Security Name: ______________________________

Security Type: ______ Security Series: ____________ Total No. Shares/Units/Bonds etc. reported this issue: ______.______
(extend to third decimal place)

****

CUSIP No: ____________ Security Name: ______________________________

Security Type: ______ Security Series: ____________ Total No. Shares/Units/Bonds etc. reported this issue: ______.______
(extend to third decimal place)

(SS-1 4/98)

KATHLEEN CONNELL
CONTROLLER OF CALIFORNIA

ANNUAL REPORT OF UNCLAIMED PERSONAL PROPERTY

ALL INFORMATION MUST BE TYPED

USE FOR STOCK PROPERTY WITH OR WITHOUT CASH

UNCLAIMED PROPERTY
STATE OF CALIFORNIA

HOLDER: ______ CITY: ______ BRANCH: ____ PAGE: ____ OF ____

MULTIPLE	LAST NAME	TITLE	DATE OF LAST CONTACT	SECURITY REPORTED	SHARES REPORTED *
OWNERS	FIRST NAME	M.I.	SOC. SEC./TAX I.D. NO.	SECURITY TYPE CUSIP NUMBER	SECURITY SERIES
NUMBER	OWNER CODE OWNER DATE / /		REFERENCE NO.	TOTAL BOND/DEB RPTD	MATURITY DATE / /
____	BUS. NAME		PROPERTY TYPE	BOND/DEB INTEREST *	NO. OF UNITS RPTD *
OF	ADDRESS		TOTAL AMT. DUE OWNER	BEG & END DIV/INT DATE / / TO / /	NO. OF WARRANTS *
____	CITY		LAWFUL CHARGES	CASH IN LIEU FRAC SHRS	
	STATE ZIP COUNTRY		SAFE DEPOSIT BOX NO.	ORIGINAL SECURITY	ORIGINAL SHARES *
	IN CARE OF		LIEN AMOUNT	SHARES REDEEMED AMT	* (Extend to the third decimal place)

MULTIPLE	LAST NAME	TITLE	DATE OF LAST CONTACT	SECURITY REPORTED	SHARES REPORTED *
OWNERS	FIRST NAME	M.I.	SOC. SEC./TAX I.D. NO.	SECURITY TYPE CUSIP NUMBER	SECURITY SERIES
NUMBER	OWNER CODE OWNER DATE / /		REFERENCE NO.	TOTAL BOND/DEB RPTD	MATURITY DATE / /
____	BUS. NAME		PROPERTY TYPE	BOND/DEB INTEREST *	NO. OF UNITS RPTD *
OF	ADDRESS		TOTAL AMT. DUE OWNER	BEG & END DIV/INT DATE / / TO / /	NO. OF WARRANTS *
____	CITY		LAWFUL CHARGES	CASH IN LIEU FRAC SHRS	
	STATE ZIP COUNTRY		SAFE DEPOSIT BOX NO.	ORIGINAL SECURITY	ORIGINAL SHARES *
	IN CARE OF		LIEN AMOUNT	SHARES REDEEMED AMT	* (Extend to the third decimal place)

MULTIPLE	LAST NAME	TITLE	DATE OF LAST CONTACT	SECURITY REPORTED	SHARES REPORTED *
OWNERS	FIRST NAME	M.I.	SOC. SEC./TAX I.D. NO.	SECURITY TYPE CUSIP NUMBER	SECURITY SERIES
NUMBER	OWNER CODE OWNER DATE / /		REFERENCE NO.	TOTAL BOND/DEB RPTD	MATURITY DATE / /
____	BUS. NAME		PROPERTY TYPE	BOND/DEB INTEREST *	NO. OF UNITS RPTD *
OF	ADDRESS		TOTAL AMT. DUE OWNER	BEG & END DIV/INT DATE / / TO / /	NO. OF WARRANTS *
____	CITY		LAWFUL CHARGES	CASH IN LIEU FRAC SHRS	
	STATE ZIP COUNTRY		SAFE DEPOSIT BOX NO.	ORIGINAL SECURITY	ORIGINAL SHARES *
	IN CARE OF		LIEN AMOUNT	SHARES REDEEMED AMT	* (Extend to the third decimal place)

(UDS -1 REV. 4/98)

¶ 11,010 Reporting Instructions for Holders of Unclaimed Property

Reporting Instructions for Holders of Unclaimed Property

KATHLEEN CONNELL
California State Controller

January 2001

Contents

Reporting Instructions for Holders of Unclaimed Property

Introduction

The State of California's Unclaimed Property Law (Code of Civil Procedures, Section 1500 et seq.) requires business associations, banking and financial organizations, life insurance corporations, and others to review their records each year to determine whether they hold any funds, securities, or other property that has been unclaimed for the required dormancy period. The law requires these "holders" to annually report such unclaimed property to the State Controller's Office.

Reporting Instructions for Holders of Unclaimed Property is designed to assist holders in preparing these annual reports. At the same time, this guide is not intended to be the sole source of information regarding the holder's legal obligations under the Unclaimed Property Law. Each organization should review the entire law to ensure that all reporting requirements are met. Review of the law should be ongoing, as revisions to the statute may cause changes in reporting requirements.

To ensure complete, accurate, and timely reporting of unclaimed property, these guidelines and all other related materials should be forwarded to the person(s) in the organization responsible for the preparation of the unclaimed property reports.

It should be noted that, when the reports are prepared by a reporting service, quality and accuracy remain the responsibility of the organization for whom the report is prepared.

This guide should be retained for ongoing reference. A new edition will not be published unless and until there are changes in the law that significantly affect reporting requirements.

Holder Assistance

Directory

Filing Unclaimed Property Reports (General Information)	(916) 323-2845
Diskette Program Reporting	(916) 323-2845
Magnetic Media Reporting	(916) 323-2845
Reciprocal Reporting	(916) 323-4674
Claims Research	(916) 323-2827
Securities Reporting	(916) 323-2858

Amnesty

Simply submit all reports and deliveries before December 31, 2001. To obtain information on Unclaimed Property Amnesty, visit the State Controller's Web site at www.sco.ca.gov.

Amnesty Reporting	(916) 445-9978
State Controller's Amnesty E-mail	ucpamnesty@sco.ca.gov
Facsimile	(916) 323-6986

The amnesty unclaimed property report must be mailed at the time of remittance to:

Office of the State Controller
Division of Collections
Bureau of Unclaimed Property
Amnesty Reporting Services
P.O. Box 997188
Sacramento, CA 95899-7188

Reimbursement Requests

If reimbursements to the owners are made by the holder, use the following instructions.

- If any reimbursements are made before the check is remitted, remove the paid accounts from the reports; adjust the check amount to balance with the report.

- If any reimbursements are made after the check is remitted, do not change or remove the data on the report; send a written request for reimbursement of the paid accounts to:

Office of State Controller Kathleen Connell
Division of Collections
Bureau of Unclaimed Property
Consumer Services
P.O. Box 942850
Sacramento, CA 94250-5873

Reimbursements will be processed only when a workable report is received and uploaded.

Format Approval Requests

All format approval requests must be mailed or faxed to:

Office of State Controller Kathleen Connell
Division of Collections
Bureau of Unclaimed Property
Reporting Services
P.O. Box 942850
Sacramento, CA 94250-5873
Fax: (916) 322-4239

General Instructions for Reporting Unclaimed Property

Who Must Report

Reports must be filed by any business entity holding property that belongs to another person, when the owner has not claimed it or, in certain cases, corresponded with the holder or otherwise indicated an interest in the property within the time limits specified in the Unclaimed Property Law, Part 3, Title 10, Chapter 7, Code of Civil Procedure (CCP) Section 1500.

"Holders" and "owners of unclaimed property," as well as other related terms, are defined in CCP Section 1501.

Property must be reported and remitted to California if the conditions for escheat stated in CCP Sections 1513 through 1521 exist, and if:

- The last known address of the owner is in California; or
- There is no address of the owner in the records of the holder or the owner is unknown, and the holder is domiciled in California.
- The last known address of the owner is in a state that does not provide by law for escheat of such property; or
- The last known address of the owner is in a foreign country; and
- The holder is domiciled in California; or the holder is a government subdivision or agency of California.

What Must Be Reported

Unclaimed property that must be reported includes life insurance policy proceeds, money orders, travelers checks, safe deposit box contents, intangible interest (stock), dividends, bond principal and interest, and a variety of intangible personal property. These and other examples are discussed in further detail in this guide.

If the holder pays or delivers escheated property to the State Controller in compliance with the law and subsequently receives a claim on the property from the owner or from another state, the State Controller shall, upon written notice of such claim defend the holder against the claim and indemnify the holder against any liability on the claim. (CCP Section 1561(a))

In addition, CCP Section 1532(b) provides indemnity to a holder and its transfer agent for the delivery of a duplicate certificate to the State Controller.

Life Insurance Policy Proceeds

A holder must report all funds held and owing under any life or endowment insurance policy or annuity contract that has matured or terminated, when such funds have remained unclaimed for more than three consecutive years after becoming due and payable. A policy is deemed to be matured if the insured has attained, or would have attained if he or she were living, the limiting age under the mortality table on which the reserve is based. (CCP Section 1515) Interest, dividends, or other amounts earned must be reported and remitted along with the funds due on such policies.

Money Orders and Travelers Checks

Sums payable on money orders that have been outstanding for more than seven years must be reported. Sums payable on travelers checks issued by (not through) the organization and outstanding for more than 15 years must be reported. (CCP Section 1511)

Safe-Deposit or Safekeeping Repository

Reports on the contents of safe-deposit boxes and other safekeeping repositories shall be submitted separately. ***Do not include this report with reports containing other property types.*** The contents of a safe-deposit box or safekeeping repository that have been unclaimed by the owner for more than three years from the date on which the lease or rental period of the box or safekeeping repository expired, or from the date of termination of any agreement under which the box or safekeeping repository was provided to the owner without cost, whichever occurred last, must be reported. (CCP Section 1514)

While all of the contents must be reported, only the more important items, such as money, jewelry, tableware, stock certificates, bonds, deeds, and wills, need to be listed on the inventory. Unimportant documents may be listed as "miscellaneous papers of no apparent value." If the safe-deposit box or safekeeping repository is empty, do not report it.

What May Be Destroyed - Everything reported must be delivered to the State Controller's Office unless the Controller's Office determines that it is not in the interest of the State to take custody of the property. In such cases, the Controller's Office will authorize the holder in writing to dispose of the property. (CCP Section 1533)

Intangible Interest (Stock), Dividends, Bond Interest and Principal

Any dividend, profit, distribution, interest, payment on principal, or other sum held for or owed to a shareholder, certificate holder, bond holder, or other security holder, or a participating patron of a cooperative, who has not claimed it or corresponded in writing with the holder or the holder's transfer agent concerning that property within three years, escheats to this state.

Any intangible interest in a business association, as evidenced by the stock records or membership records of the association, escheats to this state if the interest is owned by another person who has neither claimed a dividend or other sum nor corresponded in writing with the holder within three years.

When stock or other security escheats, any dividend or other distribution attached to the stock or other security escheats at the same time.

In the case of unclaimed intangible interest (stock) or dividend, the issuing corporation is deemed to be the holder. The stocks referred to herein are those of record belonging to the shareholder, whether or not a certificate has been issued to, or is in the hands of, the shareholder or the holder.

Unexchanged stock, unclaimed cash in lieu of fractional shares, or unclaimed cash held for the redemption of stock resulting from the merger, consolidation, acquisition, or similar event escheats beginning with the date the prior corporation lost contact with the owner and not the date of merger, consolidation, acquisition, or similar event.

Liquidation

All tangible or intangible property distributable in the course of a voluntary or involuntary dissolution or liquidation of a business association that is unclaimed by the owner within six months after the date of final distribution or liquidation escheats to California. (CCP Section 1517)

Property Held by a Business Association

The following property held or owing by a business association escheats to this state.

- Demand, savings, and matured time deposits, and accounts subject to a negotiable order of withdrawal that are unclaimed for more than three years. No banking or financial institution may discontinue interest or dividends on any savings deposit because of inactivity. (CCP Section 1513(a)(b))

- Drafts, certified checks, cashier checks, and sums payable on any other written instrument for which a banking or financial organization is directly liable, when these instruments are outstanding for more than five consecutive years. (CCP Section 1513(d))

- Any funds held in an individual retirement account when the owner has not accepted payment of principal or income, increased or decreased the principal, or corresponded in writing or otherwise indicated an interest for more than three years after the funds became payable or distributable. (CCP Section 1513 (f))

- Wages, payments to vendors, refunds and/or credits due customers, and similar items held or owing in the ordinary course of the holder's business that remain unclaimed by the owner for more than three consecutive years after becoming payable or dispersible. (CCP Section 1520 (a))

Due Dates

Unclaimed property reports and remittances must be submitted to the State Controller's Office before ***November 1*** of each year. ***Exception:*** Life insurance companies must submit reports and remittances before ***May 1*** of each year. (CCP Section 1530(d))

It is the holder's responsibility to report and remit property before the applicable due date. CCP Section 1577, which became effective January 15, 1977, states:

> In addition to any damages, penalties, or fines for which a person may be liable under other provisions of law, any person who fails to report or pay or deliver unclaimed property within the time prescribed by this chapter, shall pay to the State Controller interest at the rate of 12 percent per annum on such property or value thereof from the date such property should have been paid or delivered.

Negative Reports

Organizations that neither hold nor owe unclaimed property are not required to submit a report. However, the State Controller can require the filing of such a report by sending notification to the holder.

Report Requirements

All holders reporting unclaimed property involving 50 owners or more are now required to submit unclaimed property reports using the State Controller's magnetic tape format or the diskette program. This is effective with unclaimed property reports due November 1, 1999. (CCP Section 1530)

Reports submitted on paper that contain 50 accounts or more will be returned to the holder, and the holder may be subject to penalties as described in CCP Section 1576.

Reports for less than 50 accounts that are filed on the State's paper reporting forms must be typed. Handwritten forms will be returned to the holder.

Note: Regardless of the method used for filing, all holders must complete and submit the Face Sheet (Form UFS-1) with the report.

When reporting securities, the Securities Summary (Form SS-1) must be completed and submitted as well.

Reports must include all property that has remained unclaimed for the required dormancy period as of June 30 (or the end of the holder's fiscal year).

It is imperative that holders file complete and accurate reports in accordance with the holder reporting instructions and the Unclaimed Property Law. Failure to follow these instructions may result in a report being returned to the holder for correction and may result in an assessment of penalties. (CCP Section 1576)

If a report is rejected, the funds will remain with the State Controller's Office. The holder will be responsible for paying any claims until an acceptable report is received by the State Controller's Office. (Once an acceptable report is received, the holder may request reimbursement for claims paid.)

Unclaimed property forms, reporting instructions, magnetic media specifications, diskette reporting program, and laws and regulations are available on the Internet at www.sco.ca.gov, listed under Unclaimed Property Publications. Prior to preparing unclaimed property reports, each organization should review the law and the reporting instructions to ensure that all requirements are understood. Questions regarding the reporting process may be directed to the Bureau of Unclaimed Property's Reporting Services at (916) 323-2845.

Notification Requirements

Equity companies and financial institutions are required to send notices to owners, prior to closure of the account(s), stating that the property will escheat to the State. The notice shall be sent not more than 12 months nor less than six months before the property becomes escheatable. The outside of the envelope should be clearly marked indicating to the owner that it is the Final Notice of Account Closure. (Holders should consult CCP Sections 1513.5, 1516(d), and 1520(b) for the complete requirements to be followed for notifying owners of unclaimed property.)

Failure to Report or Remit Property

Any person who willfully fails to render any report or perform other duties required under the Unclaimed Property Law and the holder reporting instructions, including use of the report format described in CCP Section 1530, shall be punished by a fine of $100 for each day such report is withheld or such duty is not performed, but not more than $10,000. (CCP Section 1576(a))

Any person who willfully refuses to pay or deliver escheated property to the State Controller as required under the Unclaimed Property Law shall be subject to a fine of not less than $5,000 nor more than $50,000. (CCP Section 1576(b))

Charges for Late Submissions

Any person who fails to report, make payment on, or deliver unclaimed property (cash and securities) within the time prescribed by the Unclaimed Property Law is subject to interest penalties of 12% per annum. Such interest, payable to the State Controller, accrues from the date such property or value thereof should have been paid or delivered. (CCP Section 1577)

Note: For detailed information on the application of CCP Section 1577 to securities, refer to the California Administrative Code, Title 2, Subchapter 8, Article 4.5, Sections 1172.20-1172.80, of the Unclaimed Property Regulations, effective January 30, 1998.

In addition, a holder who is late or negligent in filing may be liable for damages, penalties, or fines under other provisions of law.

Record Keeping

Holders are required to retain all records pertaining to unclaimed property for a period of seven years after such property is reported to the State Controller. (California Administrative Code, Title 2, Subchapter 8, Article 5, Section 1175, of the Unclaimed Property Regulations)

Blocked Accounts

In the case of blocked accounts, approval from the court of jurisdiction is required before they can escheat to the State Controller.

Statute of Limitations

A statute of limitations does not prevent the escheat of any property otherwise escheatable to the State. (CCP Section 1570)

Property Remittance

All escheated property specified in a report shall be paid or delivered to the Controller at the same time the report is filed. (CCP Section 1532 (a))

Remitting Money

Payment of unclaimed cash in the amount of $20,000 or more shall be made by electronic funds transfer, pursuant to CCP Section 1232. Effective October 1, 1999, holders may remit by Automated Clearinghouse (ACH) Debit, ACH Credit, and Fedwire. Holders remitting less than $20,000 are encouraged to voluntarily remit via ACH debit to take advantage of this cost-saving method of remitting unclaimed cash. The *Electronic Funds Transfer Information Guide* is available on the Internet at www.sco.ca.gov, or holders may obtain a copy from the Bureau of Unclaimed Property's EFT Unit at (916) 324-0360.

If checks are remitted for amounts under $20,000, they should be made payable to the Controller of the State of California.

Remitting Securities

When securities are escheated, the holder shall deliver a duplicate certificate registered to the Controller of the State of California. (CCP Section 1532)

If a holder is unable to deliver a duplicate certificate due to a bankruptcy or similar situation, and the intangible interest is held in book-entry form, the holder may request approval to electronically remit the securities through the

State's broker. To remit electronically, the holder must obtain written approval from the State Controller.

When requests are made to transfer stock certificates, include the State Controller's Federal Tax ID, 94-6001347, with the transfer instructions.

The only dividend reinvestment plan in which the State Controller's Office participates is for mutual funds. Earnings on non-mutual funds shall not be credited to a dividend reinvestment plan.

Remitting Mutual Funds

Open-end mutual fund shares shall be transferred to book-entry accounts registered to the Controller of the State of California.

When requests are made to transfer shares, include the State Controller's Federal Tax ID, 94-6001347, with the transfer instructions.

All earnings are to be reinvested.

Mutual fund statements and requests for consent should be mailed directly to:

> Office of State Controller Kathleen Connell
> Division of Collections, Bureau of Unclaimed Property
> P.O. Box 942850
> Sacramento California 94250-5873

Once the holder has filed the annual Unclaimed Property Report and the mutual fund shares have been transferred to an account registered to the Controller of the State of California, ***the holder is not allowed to transfer any shares from the State's account without prior written consent from the State Controller.*** (CCP Section 1540)

Reciprocal Reporting

The State of California has entered into reciprocal agreements and obtained letters of understanding to exchange and collect unclaimed property for other states. The purpose of these agreements and letters of understanding is to ease the holder's burden in complying with various states' laws and to reduce the number of report forms a holder may need to file with each individual state. ***In order to take advantage of reciprocal reporting, your principal place of business must be located within California.*** Reciprocal reporting is not a requirement. If your company chooses to report its unclaimed property for one or all reciprocal states through the State of California, the following guidelines must be followed.

Notify each reciprocal state in writing of your intent to file your unclaimed property report through the state in which you are located.

File, report, and remit in accordance with each reciprocal state's unclaimed property law.

Identify, list, and subtotal all accounts by state.

Identify aggregate amounts by state (i.e., Nevada aggregate — $234.78, Florida aggregate — $4567.98, etc.). Refer to page 18, Reciprocal Reporting — Aggregates, for direction.

Identify and remit all accounts with no known addresses to the state of corporate domicile. If the state of domicile is a reciprocal state, you may report this property through the agent state, providing you identify those accounts (with no known addresses) to the appropriate reciprocal state. The following is a list of reciprocal states for which California is currently acting as agent:

> Arkansas, Florida, Idaho, Illinois, Kansas, Kentucky, Louisiana, Maine, Maryland, Massachusetts, Minnesota, Mississippi, Missouri, Nebraska, Nevada, New Jersey, North Carolina, North Dakota, Ohio, Oklahoma, Oregon, Pennsylvania, Rhode Island, South Dakota, Utah, Virginia, Washington, Wisconsin, and Wyoming.

If you have further questions regarding reciprocal reporting or would like an updated list, please contact the Reciprocity Officer at (916) 323-4674.

Where to File

Send the report and remittance to:

> Office of State Controller Kathleen Connell
> Division of Collections, Bureau of Unclaimed Property
> P.O. Box 942850
> Sacramento, California 942850-5873

For express delivery services, use the following street address:

> Office of State Controller Kathleen Connell
> Division of Collections, Bureau of Unclaimed Property
> 3301 C Street, Suite 712
> Sacramento, California 95816

Instructions for Completing Report Forms

Please use only the authorized forms provided by the State Controller's Office to prepare the report. If additional copies are required, photocopies may be used.

Note: All forms must be typed; handwritten forms will not be accepted.

Face Sheet: Form UFS-1

Annual Report "As Of" Date

The "as of" date must be either June 30 or the date of the holder's business-year end. If the "as of" date falls between January 1 and June 30, the report is due November 1 of the same year. If the "as of" date falls between July 1 and December 31, the report is due November 1 (or May 1 if reporting life insurance) of the following year.

Example:	Report "as of" date:	06/30/1999
	Report due date:	11/01/1999
	Report "as of" date:	12/31/1999
	Report due date:	11/01/2000

Employer Identification Number

Enter the holder's federal employer identification number (FEIN). Do not use the holder's state identification number.

Name and Address

Enter the holder's name, street address, post office box, city, state, zip code, and country (foreign countries only). For state and country codes, refer to Appendices E and F.

Reporting Office

Enter the branch office number, if applicable. Enter the state and the date of incorporation.

Totals for Report

For accounts of $50 and over with names, enter the total dollar amount of all accounts.

For accounts of $50 and over without names, enter the total dollar amount of all accounts.

For accounts of $49.99 and under, enter the total dollar amount of all accounts.

Grand Total — Enter the total of the above three lines. (This total must match the total on the remittance check.)

Total Shares — Enter the total shares, units, bonds reported. This number must be extended to the third decimal place. (The total must match the total on Form SS-1.)

Type of Organization

Enter the Standard Industrial Classification (SIC) Code, if known.

Financial Institution — Enter a check mark in the type of charter field and enter the charter date.

Successor to Previous Holder

If the present holder is the successor to another which previously held the property, or if the holder has had a change of name, list the prior name.

Reporting Agent

If the report is filed by an agent, complete this section. For state and country codes, refer to Appendices E and F. If the address is in the United States, leave the country code blank.

Verification

The report must be signed by an authorized individual. The report does not have to be signed before a notary public.

Securities Summary: Form SS-1

This form must be completed and submitted when securities are reported. For each reported issue, enter the CUSIP number, security name, security type, security series, and total number of shares/units/bonds.

Holder Name

Enter the complete name of the reporting organization.

CUSIP Number

Enter the CUSIP number for the reported issue.

Security Name

Enter the exact issue name as traded.

Security Type

Enter "B" for bonds, "C" for common stock, "D" for debentures, "P" for preferred stock, "R" for rights, "U" for units, "W" for warrants, "I" for beneficial interest, or leave blank for mutual funds.

Security Series

Enter the security series, if applicable. Example: 2.75 preferred.

Total Number of Shares/Units/Bonds

Enter the sum of all shares for this issue. The number of shares must be extended to the third decimal place. Example: 3.134. If there is no fractional number, use three zeros. Example: 3.000.

Note: The sum of all shares, units, bonds, etc., listed on the SS-1 form(s) must match the totals on the UFS-1 form.

Detail Sheet: Form UDS-1

General Information

Read the instructions below prior to processing the report.

If a headquarters office is filing separate reports for one or more branch offices, use a separate detail sheet (Form UDS-1) for each branch.

Separate all property information by property type, dollar value, and the following criteria:

- Property $50 and over, with names.
- Property $50 and over, without names.
- Property $49.99 and under combined into one aggregate account, except for securities property types 02, 03, 05, 06, 07, 08, 10, 11, 13, and 14 (refer to page 17, Aggregate Records).

Note: An aggregate account is created by totaling all cash accounts that are, individually, $49.99 or less.

When reporting securities/mutual funds, sort in alpha-order by Issue/Fund, Type, and Series, starting a new detail page with each new Issue/Fund. Within each Issue/Fund group, sort in alpha-order by owner name. Complete Form SS-1, summarizing the total for each Issue/Fund.

Multiple owner accounts contain two or more owners. Each owner must be listed separately. When reporting "AKA" and "DBA" accounts, use separate owner records. (Refer to page 15, Owner Information.)

If an owner has two or more items of the same property type (e.g., two savings accounts), combine them into one entry, except for security property types 01 through 17.

Prepare the report in duplicate. The original is sent to the State Controller's Office; the duplicate should be retained by the holder for seven years. (California Administrative Code, Title 2, Subchapter 8, Section 1175)

Escrow accounts normally escheat under California Code of Civil Procedure, Section 1518, as being held in fiduciary capacity for the benefit of another. The escheat period commences when the property (money) "becomes payable or distributable." The property does not become payable or distributable if the escrow company is still deciding who is entitled to the property. Whether, and when, it becomes payable or distributable is a question that should be determined primarily by looking at the escrow instructions and other facts relating to the account, such as correspondence or documented telephone calls. Even if the property had become payable or distributable, the escheat period would be interrupted if the escrow company has received one or more of the types of communications from the owner as listed in CCP 1518(a):

> ....the owner has not, within a period of 3 years, increased or decreased the principal, accepted payment of principal or income, corresponded in writing concerning the property, or otherwise indicated an interest as evidenced by a memorandum or other record on file with the fiduciary.

The Unclaimed Property Law was not intended to be a means of arbitration by the State Controller's Office when disputes arise.

Escheatable contents of safe-deposit boxes and safe-keeping items must be submitted in a separate report. Do not include any other property type or any other report. (Refer to page 17, Safe-Deposit and Other Repositories.)

Holder Information

Fill in the following fields.

Holder — Enter the name of the holder. The holder name must be the same as on Form UFS-1, line B.

City — Enter the holder's location.

Branch — Enter the branch number.

Page — Enter the page number. Example: Page 1 of 10.

Owner Information

Fill in the following fields.

Multiple Owners Number — If there is only one owner named on the account, this field must be left blank.

If there is more than one owner per account, fill in "1 of 3," etc. The primary-owner information must be listed in the first-owner record. The second-owner and all subsequent owner information must be listed in consecutive records, beginning with the Multiple Owners Number field. There must be no more than one owner name per record.

Last Name — Enter the owner's last name. If the owner's name is unavailable, type "Unknown" in the Last Name field.

Title — Enter Mrs, Dr, Lt, etc., without punctuation.

First Name — Enter the owner's first name.

M.I. — Enter the owner's middle initial without punctuation.

Second and Successive Owners — Fill in only the following information: Last Name, Title, First Name, Middle Initial, Owner Code (refer to Appendix D, Ownership Codes), Owner Date, and Business Name, if applicable.

Note: If the owner code is "AKA" or "DBA," the second-owner name is considered a "Second Owner." Create a second-owner record. If an

individual and a business are both listed as owners of the same account, create a second-owner record for the business name.

Owner Code — Enter the ownership code, if applicable. For a complete listing of ownership codes, refer to Appendix D.

Owner Date — Enter the applicable date only when an ownership code is followed by a date.

Bus. Name — Enter the business name of the account owner. If the first word of the business name is "The," put "The" after the name.

Example:	**Correct**	**Incorrect**
	Adam Company The	The Adam Company

Address — Enter the owner's address. If the last known address is unknown, leave this field blank.

City — Enter the owner's city. Leave blank if unknown.

State — Enter the owner's state (refer to Appendix E, State Codes). Leave blank if unknown.

Zip — Enter the owner's zip code up to 9 digits. Leave blank if unknown.

Country — Enter the country code if the owner's last known address is in a foreign country (refer to Appendix F, Country Codes). If the owner's last known address was in the USA, leave this field blank.

In Care Of — Enter the name associated with the "in care of" mailing address. Leave blank if not applicable.

Date of Last Contact — Enter the date of last contact by the owner. This is defined as the date of last communication or activity initiated by the owner concerning the property.

Soc. Sec. No. — Enter the owner's Social Security number if the named owner is an individual, the taxpayer identification number (FEIN) if the named owner is a business. This field is required for all named owners. If the Social Security or taxpayer identification number is not in the holder's records, a written explanation must accompany the report.

Reference No. — Enter the account number used to identify the account, check, or other property.

Property Type — Enter the appropriate two-digit property type (refer to Appendix C, Property Type Codes).

Total Amt. Due — Enter the amount of cash remitted for the owner of the account. Include all interest or earnings accumulated through the date remitted. Deduct lawful charges, if applicable.

Lawful Charges — Enter the amount of lawful charges, if any, which were deducted from the Total Amt. Due field.

Aggregate Records

For aggregate records, use only the following fields.

Last Name — Enter the word "AGGREGATE."

Property Type — Enter property type 25.

Total Amt. Due — Enter the total dollar amount of the aggregate record, which is the sum of all accounts, without stock, that are under $49.99.

Reciprocal Reporting — Aggregates

To report an aggregate account for a reciprocal state, use only the following fields.

Bus. Name — Enter the state name as shown in the example below.

Example: Nevada State of Agg

Property Type — Enter the appropriate property type for the property being aggregated. Do not use property type 25.

Total Amt. Due — Enter the total dollar amount of the aggregate record.

Safe-Deposit and Other Repositories

Do not send money or other property with safe-deposit reports. The contents of safe-deposit boxes and safekeeping items must be reported separately from other property. If a safe-deposit box or any other safekeeping repository is empty, do not report it. Do not include it with any reports containing property types other than 41, 42, or 43 (refer to Appendix C, Property Type Codes).

List the contents of safe-deposit boxes and safekeeping repositories on the inventory sheet (for example, money, jewelry, tableware, stock certificates, bonds, deeds, and wills). Attach one copy of the inventory sheet to the detail sheet for each account reported. Mark the inventory sheet to correspond with the owner's name and the identifying number and/or safe-deposit box number. Legible reproductions of inventories already prepared are acceptable.

Note: Instructions concerning delivery of safe-deposit contents to the State Controller's Office will be given to the holder after the inventories have been reviewed.

Safe-deposit reports must be completed using the forms and procedures listed below.

Face Sheet — Form UFS-1

Use instructions on page 11. Exception: Do not complete Section D, Totals for Accounts.

Detail Sheet – Form UDS-1

Use instructions on page 13. Exception: Leave the Total Amt. Due and Lawful Charges fields blank.

Complete the following additional fields.

Safe-Deposit Box No. — Enter the safe-deposit box number. Use this field for property type 41 only (refer to Appendix C, Property Type Codes).

Lien Amount — Enter the amount due to the holder for any unpaid rent or storage charges and the cost of opening the safe-deposit box. (CCP Section 1530(b)(3))

Securities

The following instructions list the required and optional fields used for securities property types 01-17.

Securities Property Types — Cash Only

Property types listed in this section are for cash properties related to securities.

Property Type 01: Cash in Lieu of Fractional Shares — Use this property type when reporting cash for fractional shares, with or without cash dividends.

Enter data in the following required field:
TOTAL AMT. DUE

Enter data in the following fields if held in the holder's records:
BEG & END DIV/INT DATE
CASH IN LIEU FRAC SHRS
ORIGINAL SECURITY
ORIGINAL SHARE

Property Type 04: Dividends — Use this property type only when reporting cash dividends.

Enter data in the following required field:
TOTAL AMT. DUE

Enter data in the following fields if held in the holder's records:
BEG & END DIV/INT DATE

Property Type 09: Mutual Fund/Money Market Fund Earnings — Use this property type only when reporting cash earnings for mutual funds and/or money market funds.

Enter data in the following required field:
TOTAL AMT. DUE

Enter data in the following fields if held in the holder's records:
BEG & END DIV/INT DATE
ORIGINAL SECURITY
ORIGINAL SHARES

Property Type 12: Securities Exchanged for Cash — Use this property type only when reporting cash for any authorized securities that were exchanged for cash and/or security redemptions, with or without cash dividends.

Enter data in the following required field:
TOTAL AMT. DUE

Enter data in the following fields if held in the holder's records:
BEG & END DIV/INT DATE
CASH IN LIEU FRAC SHRS
ORIGINAL SECURITY
ORIGINAL SHARES
SHARES REDEEMED AMOUNT
MATURITY DATE

Property Type 15: Liquidating Fund Earnings — Use this property type only when reporting cash earnings on shares that were distributed as part of a business association's liquidation, with or without cash dividends.

Enter data in the following required field:
TOTAL AMT. DUE

Enter data in the following fields if held in the holder's records:
BEG & END DIV/INT DATE

CASH IN LIEU FRAC SHRS
ORIGINAL SECURITY
ORIGINAL SHARES

Property Type 16: Municipal Bond Earnings — Use this property type only when reporting cash earnings for municipal bonds, with or without cash interest.

Enter data in the following required field:
TOTAL AMT. DUE

Enter data in the following fields if held in the holder's records:
BEG & END DIV/INT DATE
CASH IN LIEU FRAC SHRS
ORIGINAL SECURITY
ORIGINAL SHARES
MATURITY DATE

Property Type 17: Bond Interest — Use this property type only when reporting cash bond interest.

Enter data in the following required field:
TOTAL AMT. DUE

Enter data in the following fields if held in the holder's records:
BEG & END DIV/INT DATE
CASH IN LIEU FRAC SHRS
ORIGINAL SECURITY
ORIGINAL SHARES
MATURITY DATE

Securities Property Types (With or Without Cash)

Property types listed in this section should be used only for properties containing securities, with or without cash. These property types require specific issue type codes. The following table defines each issue type code.

Issue Type	Description
B	Bonds
C	Common
D	Debentures
I	Beneficial Interest
P	Preferred
R	Rights
U	Units
W	Warrants
Leave Blank	Mutual Funds

Property Type 02: Units — Use this property type when reporting units.

Enter data in the following required fields:
SECURITY REPORTED
SECURITY TYPE — Valid Security Type is U
CUSIP NUMBER
NO. OF UNITS RPTD

Enter data in the following fields if held in the holder's records:
TOTAL AMT. DUE
BEG & END DIV/INT DATE
SECURITY SERIES

Property Type 03: Debentures/Bonds — Use this property type when reporting debentures or bonds.

Enter data in the following required fields:
SECURITY REPORTED
SECURITY TYPE — Valid Security Types are B or D
CUSIP NUMBER
TOTAL BOND/DEB RPT

Enter data in the following fields if held in the holder's records:
TOTAL AMT. DUE
BOND/DEB INTEREST
BEG & END DIV/INT DATE
SECURITY SERIES
CASH IN LIEU FRAC SHRS
MATURITY DATE

Property Type 05: IRAs – Securities — Use this property type when reporting securities classified and governed by the Internal Revenue Service Code as Individual Retirement Accounts.

Enter data in the following required fields:
SECURITY REPORTED
TOTAL BOND/DEB RPTD or SHARES REPORTED or NO. OF UNITS RPTD or NO. OF WARRANTS
SECURITY TYPE — Valid Security Types are C, P, B, D, R, U, W, I, or Blank
CUSIP NUMBER

Enter data in the following fields if held in the holder's records:
TOTAL AMT. DUE
BOND/DEB INTEREST
BEG & END DIV/INT DATE
CASH IN LIEU FRAC SHRS
ORIGINAL SECURITY

SECURITY SERIES
MATURITY DATE
ORIGINAL SHARES

Property Type 06: Liquidating Funds – Securities — Use this property type when reporting securities distributed as part of a business association's liquidation.

Enter data in the following required fields:
SECURITY REPORTED
TOTAL BOND/DEB RPTD or SHARES REPORTED or NO. OF UNITS RPTD or NO. OF WARRANTS
SECURITY TYPE — Valid Security Types are C, P, B, D, R, U, W, I, or Blank
CUSIP NUMBER

Enter data in the following fields if held in the holder's records:
TOTAL AMT. DUE
BOND/DEB INTEREST
BEG & END DIV/INT DATE
CASH IN LIEU FRAC SHRS
ORIGINAL SECURITY
SECURITY SERIES
MATURITY DATE
ORIGINAL SHARES

Property Type 07: Municipal Bonds — Use this property type when reporting municipal bonds.

Enter data in the following required fields:
SECURITY REPORTED
SECURITY TYPE — Valid Security Type is B
CUSIP NUMBER
TOTAL BOND/DEB RPTD

Enter data in the following fields if held in the holder's records:
TOTAL AMT. DUE
BOND/DEB INTEREST
BEG & END DIV/INT DATE
CASH IN LIEU FRAC SHRS
SECURITY SERIES
MATURITY DATE

Property Type 08: Mutual Funds/Money Market Funds — Use this property type when reporting mutual funds or money market funds. The Security Type field must always be blank when reporting mutual funds or money market funds.

Enter data in the following required fields:
- SECURITY REPORTED
- CUSIP NUMBER
- SHARES REPORTED

Enter data in the following fields if held in the holder's records:
- TOTAL AMT. DUE
- BEG & END DIV/INT DATE
- ORIGINAL SECURITY
- SECURITY SERIES
- ORIGINAL SHARE

Property Type 10: Shares Exchanged for Shares — Use this property type when reporting securities of one issue that were exchanged for another issue due to a merger, acquisition, or reorganization.

Enter data in the following required fields:
- SECURITY REPORTED
- TOTAL BOND/DEB RPTD or SHARES REPORTED or NO. OF UNITS RPTD or NO. OF WARRANTS
- SECURITY TYPE — Valid Security Types are C, P, B, D, R, U, W, I, or Blank
- CUSIP NUMBER
- ORIGINAL SECURITY
- ORIGINAL SHARES

Enter data in the following fields if held in the holder's records:
- TOTAL AMT. DUE
- BOND/DEB INTEREST
- BEG & END DIV/INT DATE
- CASH IN LIEU FRAC SHRS
- SECURITY SERIES
- MATURITY DATE

Property Type 11: Securities — Use this property type when reporting stock.

Enter data in the following required fields:
- SECURITY REPORTED
- SECURITY TYPE — Valid Security Types are C, P, or I
- CUSIP NUMBER
- SHARES REPORTED

Enter data in the following fields if held in the holder's records:
- TOTAL AMT. DUE
- BEG & END DIV/INT DATE
- CASH IN LIEU FRAC SHRS
- SECURITY SERIES

Property Type 13: Warrants — Use this property type when reporting warrants.

Enter data in the following required fields:
SECURITY REPORTED
SECURITY TYPE — Valid Security Type is W
CUSIP NUMBER
NO. OF WARRANTS

Enter data in the following fields if held in the holder's records:
TOTAL AMT. DUE
BEG & END DIV/INT DATE
CASH IN LIEU FRAC SHRS
SECURITY SERIES
MATURITY DATE

Property Type 14: Rights — Use this property type when reporting rights.

Enter data in the following required fields:
SECURITY REPORTED
SECURITY TYPE — Valid Security Type is R
CUSIP NUMBER
SHARES REPORTED

Enter data in the following fields if held in the holder's records:
TOTAL AMT. DUE
BEG & END DIV/INT DATE
CASH IN LIEU FRAC SHRS
SECURITY SERIES
MATURITY DATE

Appendices

Security Field Descriptions

Field Name	Field Length	Field Description
Security Reported	30	Enter the issue name related to the CUSIP number in the CUSIP number field.
Shares Reported	13	Enter the number of shares reported for the owner. The number of shares must be extended to the third decimal place. For example: 3.134. If there are no fractional number, use three zeros. For example: 3.000.
Security Type	1	Enter the issue type related to the CUSIP number entered in the CUSIP field.
CUSIP Number	11	Enter the CUSIP number for each reported issue.
Security Series	6	Enter the issue series description related to the CUSIP number entered in the CUSIP Number field, if applicable.
Total Bond/Deb Rptd	11	Enter the total dollar amount of the bond or debenture being reported.
Maturity Date	10	Enter the maturity date for the security being reported. Dates must be entered numerically. For example: 01/05/1988.
Bond/Deb Interest	6	Enter the interest rate for the bond or debenture being reported. The interest rate must be extended to the third decimal place. For example: 15.250. If there is no fractional number, use three zeros. For example: 15.000.
No. of Units Rptd	13	Enter the number of units being reported. The number of units must be extended to the third decimal place. For example: 3.3134. If there is no fractional number, use three zeros. For example: 3.000.

Security Field Description (cont.)

Field Name	Field Length	Field Description
Beg & End Div/Int Date	10	Enter the beginning and ending dividend or interest date for the security.
No. of Warrants	13	Enter the number of warrants being reported. The number of warrants must be extended to the third decimal place. For example: 3.134. If there is no fractional number, use three zeros. For example: 3.000.
Cash In Lieu Frac Shrs	7	Enter the cash amount being remitted in lieu of fractional shares. This amount must be included in the Total Amt. Due field.
Original Security	30	Enter the name of the original security if the security reported was exchanged for cash and/or another security.
Original Shares	11	Enter the number of original shares that were exchanged for cash or other shares. The number of shares must be extended to the third decimal place. For example: 3.134. If there is no fractional number, use three zeros. For example: 3.000.
Shares Redeemed Amt.	11	Enter the total dollar amount for securities exchanged for cash. For example: Five shares exchanged at $4.20 each for a total of $21.00. This amount must be included in the Total Amt. Due field.

Escheat Periods

California Unclaimed Property Law

Section	Description	Period
1513(a)(b)	Savings, Matured Time Deposits, Demand Deposits (Checking), NOW, plus Interest or Dividends	3 years
1513(c)	Travelers Checks	15 years
1513(d)	Written Instruments (Banking and Financial Assns.)	5 years
1513(e)	Money Orders	7 years
1513(f)	IRAs, Keogh Plans	3 years
1514	Safe-Deposit Boxes, Safekeeping Repositories	3 years
1515	Funds Held by Life Insurance Companies	3 years
1516	Stocks, Dividends, Profit Distributions, Interest	3 years
1517	Liquidating Distributions	6 months
1518	Funds Held by Fiduciaries, Agents	3 years
1519	Funds Held by Government or Governmental Agencies	3 years
1519.5	Ordered Refunds	1 year
1520	Misc. Property Held in Normal Course of Business (Wages, Vendor Checks, Credit Balances, Gift Certificates)	3 years
1521	Employee Benefit Trust Distributions	3 year

Property Type Codes

Property Code	Property Classification
01	Cash in lieu of fractional shares
02	Units
03	Debentures or bonds
04	Dividends
05	IRAs - securities
06	Liquidating fund - securities
07	Municipal bonds
08	Mutual funds, money market funds
09	Mutual funds earnings, money market funds earnings
10	Shares exchanged for shares
11	Securities
12	Securities exchanged for cash
13	Warrants
14	Rights
15	Liquidating fund earnings
16	Municipal bond earnings
17	Bond interest
25	Aggregate accounts
26	Money orders
27	Travelers checks
28	Cashier/certified checks
41	Safe-deposit box contents

Property Type Codes (cont.)

Property Code	Property Classification
42	Safekeeping items
43	Savings bonds
55	Annuities
56	Checking accounts, demand deposits
57	Christmas club accounts
58	Collections
59	Commissions
60	Court settlements
61	Credit balances
62	Death benefits
63	Endowments
64	Escrow checks/deposits
65	Garnishments
66	Gift certificates
67	Inmate trust funds
68	Insurance claims checks
69	Insurance premiums
70	Interest checks
71	IRAs
72	Layaway deposits
73	Liquidating funds
74	Matured/terminated policies
75	Mineral proceeds

Property Type Codes (cont.)

Property Code	Property Classification
76	Other
77	Patient trust funds
78	Pensions, retirement funds
79	Refunds
80	Royalties/residuals
81	Salaries/wages
82	Savings accounts/credit union share accounts
83	Time deposits, CD accounts
84	Trusts
85	Vendor payments

Ownership Code Table

Definition	Abbreviation
Administrator	ADMIN
Agent	AGENT
Also known as	AKA
Also known as deceased	AKA DECD
Also known as estate of	AKA EST
Also known as in trust for	AKA ITF
Also known as trustee	AKA TR
Annuitant	ANTNT
Assignee	ASSIGNEE
As trustee for	ATF
Attorney for	ATTY/F
Beneficiary	BENF
Borrower	BORROWER
Buyer	BUYER
Co-conservator	COCONS
Community property	CP
Conservator	CONS
Co-owner	CO-OWNER
Co-trustee	COTR
Court order dated 10/18/1989	CT/ORD (MM/DD/CCYY)
Court order guardian 10/18/1989	CT/OR GDN (MM/DD/CCYY)
Custodian	CUST
Debtor ad item	DEBT/AD

Ownership Code Table (cont.)

Definition	Abbreviation
Debtor for	DEBT/FOR
Debtor in	DEBT/IN
Debtor of	DEBT/OF
Deceased	DECD
Deceased insured	DECD INS
Deceased trustee	DECD/TR
Deceased trustee under will of 10/04/1980	DECD TUW (MM/DD/CCYY)
Dependant	DEPEND
Doing business as	DBA
Doing business as estate	DBA EST
Doing business as payee	DBA PAYEE
Employee pension trust 10/04/1980	EPT (MM/DD/CCYY)
Employee profit sharing plan 10/04/1980	EPSP MM/DD/CCYY)
Estate	EST
Estate beneficiary	EST BENF
Estate payee	EST PAYEE
Estate trustee	EST TR
Estate under agreement 10/04/1980	EUA (MM/DD/CCYY)
Executor	EXEC
Executor under the will of	EXEC UWEE
For benefit of	FBO
Guardian	GDN
Guardian ad litem	GDN AD LT
Guardian estate	GDN EST

Ownership Code Table (cont.)

Definition	Abbreviation
Guardian trustee	GDN TR
Heir	HEIR
Incompetent estate	INCPT EST
Insured	INS
In trust for	ITF
Joint tenant	JT
Joint tenant under agreement 10/04/1980	JTUA (MM/DD/CCYY)
Joint tenant writ of survivorship	JT WROS
Joint trustees	J/TR
Life tenant under the will of	LF/TN UW
Minor	MINOR
Minor estate	MINOR EST
Minor trustee	MINOR TR
More than one owner - "and"	OWN/AND
More than one owner - "or"	OWN/OR
Natural guardian	NAT GDN
Owner	OWNER
Patient	PATIENT
Payable on death	POD
Payee	PAYEE
Payee (1), Payee (2), etc. (use numbers only)	# PAYEE [1]
Pension fund 10/04/1980	PF (MM/DD/CCYY)
Pension & profit sharing plan 10/04/1980	PPSP (MM/DD/CCYY)

[1] Can be any number (1 payee, 2 payee, 3 payee)

Ownership Code Table (cont.)

Definition	Abbreviation
Pension plan & trust 10/04/1980	PPT (MM/DD/CCYY)
Power of attorney	P/ATTY
Profit sharing plan (trust) 10/04/1980	PSP (MM/DD/CCYY)
Purchaser	PURC
Receiver	REC
Retirement trust	RT
Retirement trust under agreement 10/04/1980	RTUA (MM/DD/CCYY)
Successor co-trustee	SUC COTR
Successor trustee	SUC TR
Tenants in common	TC
Trustee	TR
Trustee payee	TR PAYEE
Trustee under agreement 10/04/1980	TUA (MM/DD/CCYY)
Trustee under agreement for benefit of 10/04/1980	TUA FBO (MM/DD/CCYY)
Trustee under will of 10/04/1980	TUW (MM/DD/CCYY)
Uniform gift to minors act ca 10/04/1980	UGMA CA [1] (MM/DD/CCYY)
Writ of survivorship	WROS

[1] Can be blank or any of the 50 states two-character code

State Code Table

State	Initial	State	Initial
Alabama	AL	Montana	MT
Alaska	AK	Nebraska	NE
Arizona	AZ	Nevada	NV
Arkansas	AR	New Hampshire	NH
California	CA	New Jersey	NJ
Colorado	CO	New Mexico	NM
Connecticut	CT	New York	NY
Delaware	DE	North Carolina	NC
District Of Columbia	DC	North Dakota	ND
Florida	FL	Ohio	OH
Georgia	GA	Oklahoma	OK
Hawaii	HI	Oregon	OR
Idaho	ID	Pennsylvania	PA
Illinois	IL	Rhode Island	RI
Indiana	IN	South Carolina	SC
Iowa	IA	South Dakota	SD
Kansas	KS	Tennessee	TN
Kentucky	KY	Texas	TX
Louisiana	LA	Utah	UT
Maine	ME	Vermont	VT
Maryland	MD	Virginia	VA
Massachusetts	MA	Washington	WA
Michigan	MI	West Virginia	WV
Minnesota	MN	Wisconsin	WI
Mississippi	MS	Wyoming	WY
Missouri	MO		

Country Code Table

Country	Code	Country	Code
Afghanistan	AFG	Bhutan	BHU
Albania	ALB	Bolivia	BOL
Algeria	ALG	Borneo	BOR
American Samoa	AS	Botswana	BOT
Andorra	AND	Brazil	BRA
Angola	ANG	Brit. Solomon Isles	BSI
Anguilla	AGU	Brit. Virgin Islands	BVI
Antigua	ANT	Brunei	BRU
Argentina	ARG	Bulgaria	BUL
Ascension	ASC	Burkina	BUK
Australia	AUS	Burma	BUR
Austria	AUT	Burundi	BRN
Azores	AZO	Caicos Islands	CAI
Bahamas	BAH	Cambodia	KAM
Bahrain	BHR	Cameroon	CAM
Bangladesh	BAN	Canada	CAN
Barbados	BAR	Cape Verde	CAP
Barbuda	BRB	Cayman Islands	CAY
Belgium	BEL	Central African Rep	CAR
Belize	BLZ	Chad	CHA
Benin	BEN	Chili	CHI
Bermuda	BER	China	CHN

Country Code Table (cont.)

Country	Code	Country	Code
Colombia	COL	France	FRA
Comoros	COM	French Guiana	FGU
Congo	CON	French Polynesia	FPO
Corsica	FRA	Futuna Island	FUT
Costa Rica	COS	Fiji	FIJ
Cuba	CUB	Finland	FIN
Cyprus	CYP	Gabon	BAG
Czechoslovakia	CZE	Gambia	GAM
Dahomey	DAH	Germany (East)	DDR
Denmark	DEN	Germany (West)	DFR
Djibouti	DJI	Ghana	GHA
Dominica	DOM	Gibraltar	GIB
Dominican Rep	DOR	Great Britain	UK
East Timor	ETI	Greece	CRE
Ecuador	ECU	Greenland	GRL
Egypt	EGY	Grenada	GRN
El Salvador	ELS	Guadalcanal	BSI
England	UK	Guam	GU
Equatorial Guinea	EGI	Guatemala	GUA
Estonia	EST	Guinea	GUI
Ethiopia	ETH	Guadeloupe	GUD
Falkland Islands	FAL	Guinea-Bussau	GUB
Faroe Islands	FAR	Guyana	GUY

Country Code Table (cont.)

Country	Code	Country	Code
Haiti	HAI	Korea, Democratic Peoples Rep	NKO
Holland	HOL	Kuwait	KUW
Honduras	HON	Lesotho	LES
Hong Kong	KON	Liberia	LIB
Hungary	HUN	Libya	LBY
Iceland	ICE	Lichtenstein	LIC
India	IND	Lithuania	LIT
Indonesia	INA	Luxembourg	LUX
Iran	IRN	Laos	LAO
Iraq	IRQ	Latvia	LAT
Ireland	IRE	Lebanon	LEB
Israel	ISR	Leeward Islands	LEE
Italy	ITL	Macao	MAC
Ivory Coast	IVC	Madagascar	MAD
Jamaica	JAM	Madeira Islands	MDI
Japan	JAP	Maka-Ku-Yokohama	JAP
Jordan	JOR	Malagasy Republic	MRL
Kampuchea	KAM	Malawi	MLA
Kenya	KEN	Malaysia	MAL
Khmer Republic	KAM	Maldives	MLD
Kiribati	KIR	Mali	MLI
Korea	RKO	Malta	MLT

Country Code Table (cont.)

Country	Code	Country	Code
Mariana Islands	CM	Norway	NOR
Martinique	MRT	Nyasaland	NYA
Mauritania	MAU	Oman	OMA
Mauritius	MAR	Panama	PAN
Mexico	MEX	Poland	POL
Micronesia	TT	Portugal	POR
Midway Island	MID	Prince Island	PRI
Mongolia	MON	Puerto Rico	PR
Montserrat	MOT	Pakistan	PAK
Morocco	MOR	Papua New Guinea	PNG
Mozambique	MOZ	Paraguay	PAR
Namibia	NAM	Peru	PER
Naura	NAU	Philippines	PHI
Nepal	NEP	Pitcairn Islands	PIT
Neth. Antilles	NAN	Qatar	QAT
Netherlands	NET	Rwanda	RWA
Nevis	NEV	Reunion Island	REU
New Caledonia	NCA	Rhodesia	RHO
Nicaragua	NIC	Romania	ROM
New Zealand	NEW	Saint Christopher	STC
Niger	NGR	Saint Helena	STH
Nigeria	NIG	Saint Lucia	STL
Northern Ireland	UK	Seychelles	SEY

Country Code Table (cont.)

Country	Code	Country	Code
Sierra Leone	SRL	Tsumed	NAM
Singapore	SIN	Tunisia	TAN
Solomon Islands	SOL	Turkey	TUR
Somalia	SOM	Turks Island	TKI
South Africa	SAF	Tuvalu	TUV
Spain	SPA	USSR	URS
Sri Lanka	SRI	Uganda	UGA
Sudan	SUD	United Arab Emirates	UAE
Surinam	SUR	Uruguay	URU
Swaziland	SWA	Vanuata	VAN
Sweden	SWE	Vatican City	VAT
Switzerland	SWI	Venezuela	VEN
Syria	SYA	Vietnam	VIE
Tahiti	TAH	Wake Island	WKI
Taiwan	TAI	Wales	UK
Tanzania	TAN	Wallis Islands	WAL
Tasmania	TAS	Western Samoa	WSA
Thailand	THA	West Africa	WAF
Tobago	TRI	Yemen, Peoples	YPD
Togo	TOG	Virgin Islands	VI
Tonga	TON	Yeman, Arab Rep	YAR
Trinidad	TRI	Yokohama	JAP
Tristan Da Cunha	TOC	Yugoslavia	YUG

Country Code Table (cont.)

Country	Code	Country	Code
Zaire	ZAI	Zimbabwe	ZIM
Zambia	ZAM		

¶ 11,015 Amnesty Form

STATE OF CALIFORNIA
DIVISIONS OF COLLECTIONS

STATE CONTROLLER'S OFFICE
BUREAU OF UNCLAIMED PROPERTY

AMNESTY
CERTIFICATION OF ELIGIBILITY

The following certification must be submitted, along with your amnesty report and remittance, to:

STATE CONTROLLER'S OFFICE
AMNESTY REPORTING SERVICE
P.O. BOX 997188
SACRAMENTO, CA 95899-7188

The undersigned, ______________________________ declares, under penalty of perjury, that, to the best
(print or type name of officer)
of (his) (her) knowledge and belief, the following report contains a full, true and complete report of unclaimed property that is presumed unclaimed under the provisions of Part 3, Title 10, Chapter 7, Code of Civil Procedure (CCP) — commencing with Section 1500, Title 2, California Administrative Code, Sections 1150 et seq. Furthermore, as a duly authorized officer of

____,
(print or type name of entity)

I hereby affirm the following: Initial each provision

As of January 3, 2000, the above-named entity was not the subject of an investigation by the California Attorney General's Office or an audit by the California State Controller's Office relating to the property herein reported, or a party to litigation with the California State Controller's Office relating to the property herein reported — CCP 1577.5 (b) (1). ☐

All property reported and remitted as indicated in the attached report was required to be reported on or before November 1, 1999 — CCP 1577.5 (b) (2). ☐

All property (i.e., funds, cash, securities) indicated in the attached report is hereby attached or has been delivered to the State Controller's Office or its authorized agent — CCP 1577.5 (b) (3). ☐

The attached report is submitted in the format required by the State Controller's Office — CCP 1577.5 (b) (4). ☐

All property reported in this report represents property that was due on or before November 1, 1999. It does not include property due after this date. ☐

All property identified is hereby submitted with this report. If not, evidence of delivery (i.e., statement of EFT, book entry) is attached — CCP 1577.5 (b) (6). ☐

All securities, if any, have been remitted in accordance with the California Code of Civil Procedure, Section 1532 — CCP 1577.5 (b) (7). ☐

All records pertaining to this report have been maintained to permit verification and compliance audits — CCP 1577.5 (b) (8). ☐

All property pertaining to this report is for the report period beginning ______________
(i.e., November 1, 1959; November 1, 1965) and ending November 1, 1999. ☐

The above named entity ( ) has ( ) has not reported to the State Controller's Office in the past. ☐

SIGNED BY:

______________________________ ______________
(Name of Authorized Officer) (Date)

______________________________ ______________
(Title) (Telephone Number)

______________________________ ______________
(Address) (E-mail Address, If Applicable)

______________________________ ______ ______
(City) (State) (Zip)

¶ 11,020 NAUPA Form

NAUPA
National Association of Unclaimed Property Administrators

Holder Request for Reimbursement
Standardized Holder Claim Form

State of:
Name:________________________ For funds paid to the Department for Report Year
Address:______________________________ Please Print or Type ending ______ Date remitted :__________

PART I: HOLDER INFORMATION: *(See instructions on reverse side for claim completion)*

Name of Holder:	Address:	City:	State:	Zip:
Tax ID#:	Telephone No.: ( )	Contact:		

PART II: CLAIM INFORMATION – *Please Note: Use only one form per "owner"*

Property Code	Acct Reference No (If Aggregate – Specify)	Owner's Name exactly as on report	Owner's Address as listed on report	Claimant's Name & Address If different than Owner	Date Pd to Owner or Acct Reactivated	Amt Paid

If amount was remitted in error – please explain **Total Request for Reimbursement: $** ______________
____
____

PART III: HOLDER CERTIFICATION

Sworn to and subscribed before me this

_________day of __________ 20___

Notary:___________________________

My commission expires:______________

I, ______________________________ a duly authorized representative of the holder listed above, do hereby certify that the above listed funds, or other property which was listed in the Report filed by the holder have been paid to the rightful owner(s) or their appointed representative. I agree, upon payment of the above described property to indemnify the state and hold it harmless from all claims and loss, demands, costs, and other expenses which the State may sustain by reason of turning over property to the holder and by reason further of its refusal to pay the property to any other person or persons:

Name of Representative (type of print)______________________________________

Signature of Holder Representative ____________________________________ Date____________

INSTRUCTIONS FOR HOLDER REQUEST FOR REIMBURSEMENT

PURPOSE: A holder of unclaimed property must complete this form from the State for funds which were paid by the holder and the rightful owner (or his representative) has been paid for the property.

COMPLETION OF FORM: All information must be complete. A separate Holder Request for Reimbursement should be submitted for each report year and each claimant.

Part I. Holder Information: Enter the name, address, Federal Tax ID number, telephone number, and contact person of the holder.

Part II. Claim Information: Enter all data necessary to identify property for which the holder is seeking reimbursement. The identification data entered on this form must be identical to the information included on the Report of Abandoned and Unclaimed Property submitted to the State by that holder.

1) Property Code-the universal NAUPA codes for the property claimed as defined on the Summary Sheet of Reported Items or Property Codes.
2) Account/Reference Number-the identification number of the property which was entered.
3) Owner(s) name and Address-the full name(s) and address(es) of all the owner(s) as shown on the report. If "unknown" at the time of report, designate same.
4) If the account was reported in the aggregate, please indicate in the "Account/Reference Number" column.
5) Claimant(s)-Name and Address-the full name(s) and address(es) of the person(s) who filed the claim if different than the owner.
6) Date Paid to Claimant or Date Account Reactivated-the date the claim was paid to the owner (or his representative) or when the account was reactivated by the holder.
7) Amount Paid-the amount paid for the property transmitted by the holder to the State.
8) Total of Reimbursement0the amount expected to be reimbursed to the holder by the State.

Part III. Holder Certification: This notarized statement must be completed before the State will process the request for reimbursement and make payment. Proof that the claimant was paid and entitled to the property must be maintained and is subject to audit and review by the State.

Appendix C

UNIFORM UNCLAIMED PROPERTY ACTS OF 1981 AND 1995[1]

¶ 12,001 Uniform Unclaimed Property Act (1981)

Drafted by the National Conference of Commissioners on Uniform State Laws *and by it* approved and recommended for enactment in all the states *at its* annual conference meeting in its ninetieth year in New Orleans, Louisiana, July 31–August 7, 1981. With Prefatory Note and comments. Approved by the American Bar Association Chicago, Illinois, January 25, 1982.

Uniform Unclaimed Property Act

The Committee that acted for the National Conference of Commissioners on Uniform State Laws in preparing the Uniform Unclaimed Property Act was as follows:

Howard T. Rosen, Gateway I, Newark, NJ 07102, *Chairman*

Sandra Day, Suite 100, Legislative Services Wing, State Capitol, Phoenix, AZ 85007

Andrew W. Mcthenia, Jr., Washington and Lee University, School of Law, Lewis Hall, Lexington, VA 24450, *Reporter*

Charles O. Ragan, Jr., Suite 610, First Tennessee Bank Building, Chattanooga, TN 37402

William A. Robinson, 2920 Military Road, N.W., Washington, DC 20015

Howard J. Swibel, Suite 5800, 200 East Randolph Drive, Chicago, IL 60601

Charles M. Welling, 900 Law Building, Charlotte, NC 28202

David J. Epstein, Suite 2060, Two Century Plaza, 2049 Century Park East, Los Angeles, CA 90067, *Reporter*

---

[1] Reprinted with permission.

John C. Deacon, P.O. Box 1245, Jonesboro, AR 72401, *President (Member Ex Officio)*

M. King Hill, Jr., Sixth Floor, 100 Light Street, Baltimore, MD 21202, *Chairman, Executive Committee (Member Ex Officio)*

William J. Pierce, University of Michigan, School of Law, Ann Arbor, MI 48109, *Executive Director*

Edward I. Cutler, P.O. Box 3239, Tampa, FL 33601, *Chairman, Division H (Member Ex Officio)*

Review Committee

C. Ben Dutton, 710 Guaranty Building, Indianapolis, IN 46204, *Chairman*

Robert E. Sullivan, Legal Department, 40 East Broadway, Butte, MT 59701

Advisors to Special Committee on Uniform Unclaimed Property Act

Gary Bosco, American Bankers Association

Joy Cherian, American Council of Life Insurance

Earl J. Grimm, American Society of Corporate Secretaries

John T. Higginbotham, American Bar Association, Section of Taxation

Jim Lord, National Association of Unclaimed Property Administrators

Thomas E. Montgomery, American Bar Association

Stephen P. Norman, Issuers of Money Orders and Travelers Checks

William Roche, Edison Electric Institute

William M. Tartikoff, Investment Company Institute

Donald H. Weeks, United States League of Savings Associations

Copies of all Uniform and Model Acts and other printed matter issued by the Conference may be obtained from:

National Conference of Commissioners on Uniform State Laws
645 North Michigan Avenue, Suite 510
Chicago, Illinois 60611

Commissioner's Prefatory Note

Why Change Is Needed

Thirty-one states and the District of Columbia have enacted either the original 1954 version of the Uniform Disposition of Unclaimed Property Act, or the 1966 revision of that Act. Of the remaining 20 states, all but 2 have some form of escheat or abandoned property legislation. The 1954 Uniform Act was drafted as a response to conflicting legislation among the various states and in response to a series of Supreme Court decisions in the late 1940's and early 1950's. The 1954 and 1966 Acts served well as evidenced by their numerous adoptions. However, the era of stability was ended with the decision in Texas v. New Jersey, 379 U.S. 670 (1965). That decision established a set of priorities for claimant states which were, in some instances, inconsistent with those established by the Uniform Act. A few states which previously had enacted the Uniform Act have changed their legislation to reflect the holding in *Texas v. New Jersey.*

In the last decade states have become increasingly aware of the opportunities for collecting and returning to their residents unclaimed money and using the "windfall" unreturned funds as general fund receipts for the benefit of citizens of the state. Accordingly several states have sought to enforce their unclaimed property laws with enhanced vigor. They have found, however, that obtaining compliance with the law has been extremely difficult. In some instances the uncertain status of unclaimed property statutes in the wake of *Texas v. New Jersey* accounts for the high degree of noncompliance; many holders feel they do not know what is required of them. In addition the enforcement provisions of the Uniform Act are inadequate and have not served to encourage compliance with the Act.

The Uniform Act served its time. However, to conform the Uniform Act expressly to the Supreme Court ruling in *Texas v. New Jersey* a comprehensive revision is desirable.

The Impact of *Texas v. New Jersey*

The 1954 and 1966 Uniform Acts basically tied the enacting state's claim to abandoned property to the ability of that state's courts to assert personal jurisdiction over the holder. The basic jurisdictional test of Sections 2, 4, 5, 6, 7, 8 and 9 for a presumption of abandonment bears a direct relationship to events taking place within the state. The thrust of this "contacts" test generally is to allow any state with jurisdiction over the holder, i. e., the debtor, to take unclaimed property. In recognition of the potential for conflict among jurisdictions over the application of a contacts test, the Uniform Act contained a reciprocity clause in Section 10. Section 10 allowed another state to claim abandoned property if the last known address of the claimant was in that state and if other states with contacts would forego their claims. The success of this clause was dependent upon uniform enactment by competing states. However, this was never forthcoming, and the assertion of competing claims by states continued.

The Supreme Court decisions leading up to *Texas v. New Jersey* did little to clarify the law. The state of residence of the creditor could claim, Connecticut Mutual Life Insurance v. Moore, 333 U.S. 541 (1948), and the state of the holder's domicile could likewise escheat, Standard Oil Co. v. New Jersey, 347 U.S. 428 (1951).

Standard Oil also held that it was a denial of due process for more than one state to escheat the same property. This rule created a race of diligence among the states. In Western Union Telegraph Co. v. Pennsylvania, 368 U.S. 71 (1962), however, the court told the most diligent state (Pennsylvania) that it had to assure Western Union that no other state would claim the property. In *Western Union*, Pennsylvania sought to escheat uncashed money orders and drafts which were held by Western Union and unclaimed by either the senders or the payees. The court held that Western Union should not be embroiled in a race of diligence among New York, Pennsylvania and other states. The Supreme Court's opinion in effect admonished the states mutually to resolve which state was entitled to claim abandoned property or, absent agreement, to present their conflicting claims to the only judicial forum in which they could be resolved, the Supreme Court. Thus any state facing an actual or potential dispute by a sister state was forced to bring an original action in the Supreme Court for a declaration of its rights before it could take the property. This was the condition of the law when the Supreme Court decided *Texas v. New Jersey*.[2]

The problem in *Texas v. New Jersey* was which of several states was entitled to escheat intangible property consisting of debts owed by Sun Oil Company and left unclaimed by creditors. Four rules were proposed:

1. that the funds should go to the state having the most significant "contacts" with the debt;

2. that the funds should go to the state of the debtor company's incorporation;

3. that the funds should be paid to the state in which the company has its principal place of business; and

[2] While the court in Texas v. New Jersey set down rules applying to both escheat statutes and custodial type unclaimed property statutes (such as the Uniform Act), all but a few of the states have laws which are custodial and allow the lawful owner to claim the property at any time.

4. that the funds should be paid to the state of the creditor's last known address as shown by the debtor's books and records.

Rule 4 was adopted by the Supreme Court as a "simple and easy" standard to follow. The court pointed out that this rule tended to "distribute escheats among the states in proportion of the commercial activities of their residents". In addition to the holding that the state of the creditor's last known address is entitled to escheat or custodially claim the property owed to the creditor, the court held that, if the creditor's address does not appear on the debtor's books or is in a state that does not provide for the escheat of intangibles, then the state of the debtor's incorporation may take custody of the property until some other state comes forward with proof that it has a superior right to escheat or take custody.

The *Texas v. New Jersey* rule makes the Uniform Act inadequate because the Uniform Act is based on the claimant state's ability to assert jurisdiction over the holder. Under *Texas v. New Jersey* a Uniform Act state may not claim certain property held by persons subject to its jurisdiction (which the Uniform Act covers) but can assert custody to property held by persons not subject to its jurisdiction (which the Uniform Act does not cover).

A simple hypothetical illustrates the problem of meshing the rule of *Texas v. New Jersey* with the Uniform Act. Assume a corporate holder, incorporated in State A, holding unclaimed property (an uncashed dividend check) belonging to a claimant whose last known address was in State B. The holder does not do business in State B. Under the *Texas v. New Jersey* rule, State B is the first priority claimant. However, since the holder does not do business there the Uniform Act would not authorize State B to assert a claim to the property. State A, if it had enacted the Uniform Act, could claim the property under its abandoned property law in accordance with the second priority rule of *Texas v. New Jersey;* however, that frustrates the goal of equitable distribution of unclaimed property among creditor states.

Why Uniformity Is Necessary

The 1954 and 1966 Uniform Acts responded to the need for symmetry in the law for the benefit of persons doing business in more than one state. Widespread enactment of the Uniform Act by the States indicates their recognition of the need for uniformity.

Since the 1954 and 1966 Acts are inconsistent with *Texas v. New Jersey* and other cases, the Conference, after receiving the report of a Study Committee, decided to revise the Uniform Act once again.

What the Act Does to Conform With *Texas v. New Jersey*

Section 3 of the Act provides a statutory response which is consistent with the Court's pronouncement in *Texas v. New Jersey.* Basically, the Act provides that unclaimed intangible property is payable to the state of last known address of the owner. In those instances in which that information is unknown or the state of the owner's last known address does not assert a claim to the property, it is payable to the state of the holder's domicile.

There are other sections which shore up this scheme of priority, some of which are necessitated by the *Texas v. New Jersey* decision and some of which merely represent a statutory enactment of existing practices among states. One issue which has been raised by academic commentators concerns the reporting requirements of abandoned property legislation in light of the priority rules among claimant states enunciated by *Texas v. New Jersey.* Because the *Texas v. New Jersey* decision authorizes a state to claim abandoned property even though it cannot assert personal jurisdiction over the holder, the question has arisen as to whether a claimant state in that instance has the power to compel reporting from a holder to ascertain the existence of its claim. That is an important consideration, for the right given to the state of last known address by *Texas v. New Jersey* is a hollow one if the state is without sufficient information to assert its claim to abandoned property.[3]

The state acts as a conservator of the lost owner's property and the Act is akin to a succession statute.[4] The *Texas v. New Jersey* rule, as the Supreine Court noted, is a variation of the common law concept of *mobilia sequunter personam,* according to which the law of the state of domicile of the intestate owner determines the right of succession to personal property. The state in which the owner last resided is a rough indicator of domicile, and that state is entitled to provide by legislation for succession. The state of last known address, succeeding to the right of the owner, is entitled to compel a holder to disclose the existence of property which belongs to the owner in the same manner that a conservator of an esstate of an incompetent or the administrator of the estate of a missing person or decedent can compel the holder of that

[3] Texas v. New Jersey did not decide whether the state which is entitled to the first priority claim can compel reporting by a foreign corporation. The issue was neither briefed nor argued in the case; however, footnote 8 of the decision implies that such a legislative power exists. The right given to creditor states would be meaningless without the remedy of compelling reports.

[4] The Court's decision in Connecticut Mutual Life Insurance Co. v. Moore, 333 U.S. 541, 546-47 (1947), described the state as a "conservator" when claiming property under a custodial unclaimed property law. The Court in Standard Oil Co. v. New Jersey, 347 U.S. 428, 437 (1951), characterized the Moore case as involving a "conservation statute".

person's propery to account for it.[5] That the state may not be able to assert its claim in its own courts, but would be required to use the courts of another jurisdiction, is not determinative of its power to act as a custodian.[6] Hence the suggestion that corporate holders not "doing business" in a state might escape their obligation to pay unclaimed property owing to persons with last known addresses in that state is incorrect.[7]

The Supreme Court's failure to expressly mandate a reporting requirement in *Texas v. New Jersey* does not appear significant. Holders rarely raise a defense of failure to "do business" in response to a request for reporting. In any event many major holders are subject to the regulatory jurisdiction of most states. Even in those instances in which a holder is not subject to the regulatory jurisdiction of a state, the claimant state can nevertheless require reporting under this succession analysis.

Other Changes in the Act

In recent years the National Association of Unclaimed Property Administrators has become an active group. There is growing cooperation among member states to exchange information. Several states have joined together to conduct joint investigations of holders. States also have agreed that they will collect property for each other from holders, and they regularly exchange property. This Act seeks to encourage further cooperation among the states by authorizing such joint agreements and by authorizing the adoption of uniform reporting forms. See Section 33. Neither the existing agreements among states nor the agreements envisioned under Section 33 require the consent of Congress under the Compact Clause of the Constitution, Art. I, § 10, cl. 3. The Supreme Court has held that the Compact Clause is limited to combinations or agreements that tend to increase the political power of the states to such an extent that it interferes with the supremacy of the United States. United States Steel v. Multi-State Comm., 434 U.S. 452 (1978).

---

[5] As the United States Supreme Court noted in upholding the constitutionality of the Massachusetts custodial unclaimed property laws: "[i]f the facts warrant it, a legal representative can be appointed at any time with all the rights incident to such appointment, including that of withdrawing the funds and holding them for the true owner when he shall establish his claim." Provident Institution for Savings v. Malone, 221 U.S. 660, 666 (1911).

[6] In this connection, see Commonwealth of Pennsylvania v. Kervick, 60 N.J. 289, 288 A.2d 289 (1972) (Pennsylvania held entitled to sue in New Jersey state courts for property owing to Pennsyivania residents.)

[7] "Doing business", for purposes of service of process is limited only by the Fourteenth Amendment of the United States Constitution. On the other hand, jurisdiction to regulate a foreign corporation in a substantive fashion must run the gauntlet of the Commerce Clause, the Equal Protection Clause, and the Impairment of Contracts Clause as well as the Due Process Clause. (See Miller Bros. Co. v. Maryland, 347 U.S. 340 (1954) (a Delaware business is not required to collect a sales tax from Maryland purchasers even though it makes some deliveries in Maryland)).

The 1966 Act provided a presumption of abandonment of unclaimed dividend or interest checks but arguably did not cover the underlying ownership interest represented by issued and outstanding securities certificates. In recent years several states have amended their statutes to authorize taking of this property and indications are that the trend is likely to continue. California, Florida, Indiana, Maine, Massachusetts, Montana, Rhode Island and Virginia have statutes with such provisions and other states are known to be considering similar proposals. The new Act specifically covers securities even though they are not in the possession of the issuer. See Section 10.

Two major concerns have been expressed with the concept of presuming abandonment of underlying shares of stock or principal amounts of debt securities where the dividends or interest payments have been unclaimed. First, under what circumstances is it proper to presume abandonment and, second, what are the rights of the various parties when the conditions precedent to abandonment have occurred? As to the first question, Section 10 of the Act requires that there must be the passage of at least 7 years after the failure of an entitled person to claim or inquire about a dividend, interest payment, or other distribution and also the payment of at least 7 dividends, interest sums, or other distributions during such period which remain unclaimed.

As to the rights of the parties under the Act, the Administrator is entitled to have duplicate certificates issued in the state's name. The issuer of the duplicate certificate is relieved of all liability respecting the property delivered (Section 19) and is protected against claims by virtue of the administrator's duty to defend on behalf of the issuer and to indemnify that party against any liability on account of such claims (Section 20).

Under the Act, the administrator may require any person who has not filed a report to file a verified statement that he has or has not any unclaimed and reportable property (Section 30). The administrator has a right to audit records not limited to cases where there is reason to believe a person is not complying with the Act (Section 30).

In keeping with the Act's focus on the last known address of an owner as vesting a state with a priority claim to property, the revision requires a holder who has a record of the last known address to retain it for 10 years after the property becomes reportable (Section 31).

The Act reflects a tendency among state legislatures in recent years to reduce dormancy periods. The current high inflation rate exacts a severe penalty from one who holds money or its equivalent for extended periods; an inference of loss or abandonment may be drawn more quickly than in 1966 when the value of money was more stable.

The general rule of presumed abandonment is 5 years (Section 2) as compared with 7 years in the 1966 Act. A one year dormancy period is provided for unclaimed wages (Section 15), utility deposits (Section 8), refunds due from utilities (Section 9), and property held by courts and government agencies (Section 13).

Another set of problems addressed in the revision has to do with service charges imposed on abandoned property. Experience has shown that service charges levied against outstanding items such as money orders and cashier's checks as well as inactive and dormant checking and saving accounts have completely wiped out otherwise reportable property. Sections 5(b) and 6(c) of this revision codify the case law which has limited these charges.

The 1966 Act did not address the small but active heir finder's industry; that is, those businesses which pursuant to contract attempt to locate owners of abandoned property. Some state statutes have placed limits on the role of heir finders from the time property becomes reportable until a specified time after it has been turned over to the state. Section 35 of the new Act prohibits heir finder activity during a two-year period after payment or delivery to the state.

Unclaimed Property (1981 Act)

§ 1. [Definitions and Use of Terms]

As used in this Act, unless the context otherwise requires:

(1) "Administrator" means [ ].

(2) "Apparent owner" means the person whose name appears on the records of the holder as the person entitled to property held, issued, or owing by the holder.

(3) "Attorney general" means the chief legal officer of this State.

(4) "Banking organization" means a bank, trust company, savings bank, [industrial bank, land bank, safe deposit company,] private banker, or any organization defined by other law as a bank or banking organization.

(5) "Business association" means a non-public corporation, joint stock company, investment company, business trust, partnership, or association for business purposes of 2 or more individuals, whether or

not for profit, including a banking organization, financial organization, insurance company, or utility.

(6) "Domicile" means the state of incorporation of a corporation and the state of the principal place of business of an unincorporated person.

(7) "Financial organization" means a savings and loan association, [cooperative bank,] building and loan association, or credit union.

(8) "Holder" means a person, wherever organized or domiciled, who is:

(i) in possession of property belonging to another,

(ii) a trustee, or

(iii) indebted to another on an obligation.

(9) "Insurance company" means an association, corporation, fraternal or mutual benefit organization, whether or not for profit, which is engaged in providing insurance coverage, including accident, burial, casualty, credit life, contract performance, dental, fidelity, fire, health, hospitalization, illness, life (including endowments and annuities), malpractice, marine, mortgage, surety, and wage protection insurance.

(10) "Intangible property" includes:

(i) monies, checks, drafts, deposits, interest, dividends, and income;

(ii) credit balances, customer overpayments, gift certificates, security deposits, refunds, credit memos, unpaid wages, unused airline tickets, and unidentified remittances;

(iii) stocks and other intangible ownership interests in business associations;

(iv) monies deposited to redeem stocks, bonds, coupons, and other securities, or to make distributions;

(v) amounts due and payable under the terms of insurance policies; and

(vi) amounts distributable from a trust or custodial fund established under a plan to provide health, welfare, pension, vacation, severance, retirement, death, stock purchase, profit sharing, employee savings, supplemental unemployment insurance, or similar benefits.

(11) "Last known address" means a description of the location of the apparent owner sufficient for the purpose of the delivery of mail.

(12) "Owner" means a depositor in the case of a deposit, a beneficiary in case of a trust other than a deposit in trust, a creditor, claimant,

or payee in the case of other intangible property, or a person having a legal or equitable interest in property subject to this Act or his legal representative.

(13) "Person" means an individual, business association, state or other government, governmental subdivision or agency, public corporation, public authority, estate, trust, 2 or more persons having a joint or common interest, or any other legal or commercial entity.

(14) "State" means any state, district, commonwealth, territory, insular possession, or any other area subject to the legislative authority of the United States.

(15) "Utility" means a person who owns or operates for public use any plant, equipment, property, franchise, or license for the transmission of communications or the production, storage, transmission, sale, delivery, or furnishing of electricity, water, steam, or gas.

Commissioners' Comment

The definitions have been revised to reflect, pursuant to *Texas v. New Jersey,* 379 U.S. 670 (1965), the fact that the Act applies to persons in other states who are holding property, eliminating any requirement that those persons be engaged in business in the enacting state.

Subsection (2) has been added to facilitate reference to the person who appears on the holder's records to be the person entitled to the property. The right of a state to claim abandoned property depends on the information in the holder's records concerning the apparent owner's identification. It is of no consequence that without notice to the holder, he may have transferred his interest to another person. In Nellins v. Tampax, Inc., 394 A.2d 333 (Del.Ch.Ct.1978), the court held that the address of the apparent, not the actual, owner controlled. The holder is not required to ascertain the name of the current owner or resolve a dispute between the owner of record and a successor contesting ownership. However, nothing in this Act prohibits the actual owner from recovering the property, pursuant to Sections 20 and 24, from the holder or the administrator. Similarly, the state of last known address of the actual owner can recover the property, pursuant to Section 25, from the state which initially receives custody.

The definition of "business association" in subsection (5) expressly includes non-profit corporations.

The Act provides exclusively for the disposition of unclaimed intangible property with one exception in Section 16 for tangible property contained in safe deposit boxes.

Subsection (10) is not intended as a substantive addition to the coverage of Section 9 of the prior Acts. Included as intangible property are a variety of items which are often overlooked by holders, all of which were included within the 1966 Act and are within the coverage of this Act.

Subsection (11) defines "last known address" as the location of the apparent owner for the purpose of mail delivery, consistent with most state laws which have defined an address.

§ 2. [Property Presumed Abandoned; General Rule]

(a) Except as otherwise provided by this Act, all intangible property, including any income or increment derived therefrom, less any lawful charges, that is held, issued, or owing in the ordinary course of a holder's business and has remained unclaimed by the owner for more than 5 years after it became payable or distributable is presumed abandoned.

(b) Property is payable or distributable for the purpose of this Act notwithstanding the owner's failure to make demand or to present any instrument or document required to receive payment.

Commissioners' Comment

Section 2 establishes as a general proposition that all intangible property held or owing in the ordinary course of the holder's business is within the coverage of this Act. See the comment to Section 1(10).

This section provides that unless a different time period is specified all intangible property which has remained unclaimed for more than 5 years is presumed abandoned. Sections 4-16 deal with specific types of property and prescribe the events which raise a presumption of abandonment.

The general dormancy period of the 1966 Uniform Act was 7 years. Some legislatures have recently shortened that time period. Likewise, a few recently enacted abandoned property laws have provided for a longer dormancy period. Given the greater mobility of the population in 1981 as compared with that of a quarter century ago when the 7-year dormancy period was first established, a reduction of the general dormancy period to 5 years is warranted. Additionally, the experiences of those states with shorter abandonment periods reveal that they are able to return to owners a substantially higher percentage of property reported as abandoned. There are exceptions in this Act to the 5-year dormancy period, however. For instance, statistical evidence indicates that a period of 15 years continues to be appropriate in the case of travelers checks. A majority of travelers checks will ultimately be presented for payment within the 15-year period. Also, in certain instances a shorter period is appropriate. For instance, the likelihood of finding the owner of a payroll check is materially decreased after one year. Hence, Section 15 has a one year dormancy period for unpaid wages.

Subsection (b) is intended to make clear that property is reportable notwithstanding that the owner, who has lost or otherwise forgotten his entitlement to property, fails to present to the holder evidence of his ownership or to make a demand for payment. See Connecticut Mutual Life Insurance Co. v. Moore, 333 U.S. 541 (1948), in which the Court stated: "When the state undertakes the protection of abandoned claims, it would be beyond a reasonable requirement to compel the state to comply with conditions that may be quite proper as between the contracting parties." See also Provident Institution for Savings v. Malone, 221 U.S. 660 (1911), involving savings accounts; Insurance Co. of North America v. Knight, 8 Ill.App.3d 871, 291 N.E.2d 40 (1972), involving negotiable instruments, and People v. Marshall Field & Co., 83 Ill.App.3d 811, 404 N.E.2d 368 (1980), involving gift certificates.

Section 2(b) obviates the result reached in Oregon Racing Comm. v. Multonamah Kennel Club, 242 Or. 572, 411 P.2d 63 (1963), involving unpresented winning parimutual tickets.

Since the holder is indemnified against any loss resulting from the delivery of the property to the administrator, no possible harm can result in requiring that holders turn over property, even though the owner has not presented proof of death or surrendered the insurance policy, savings account passbook, the gift certificate, winning racing ticket, or other memorandum of ownership.

A draft issued by a property or casualty insurance company as an offer of settlement of a claim for property damage or personal injury is not subject to the presumption of abandonment if the offer was not accepted by the payee. In this situation, the draft never became payable or distributable. The issue of whether a draft is accepted by a payee is a question of fact that is not addressed by the Act.

§ 3. [General Rules for Taking Custody of Intangible Unclaimed Property]

Unless otherwise provided in this Act or by other statute of this State, intangible property is subject to the custody of this State as unclaimed property if the conditions raising a presumption of abandonment under Sections 2 and 5 through 16 are satisfied and:

(1) the last known address, as shown on the records of the holder, of the apparent owner is in this State;

(2) the records of the holder do not reflect the identity of the person entitled to the property and it is established that the last known address of the person entitled to the property is in this State;

(3) the records of the holder do not reflect the last known address of the apparent owner, and it is established that:

> (i) the last known address of the person entitled to the property is in this State, or
>
> (ii) the holder is a domiciliary or a government or governmental subdivision or agency of this State and has not previously paid or delivered the property to the state of the last known address of the apparent owner or other person entitled to the property;

(4) the last known address, as shown on the records of the holder, of the apparent owner is in a state that does not provide by law for the escheat or custodial taking of the property or its escheat or unclaimed property law is not applicable to the property and the holder is a domiciliary or a government or governmental subdivision or agency of this State;

(5) the last known address, as shown on the records of the holder, of the apparent owner is in a foreign nation and the holder is a domiciliary or a government or governmental subdivision or agency of this State; or

(6) the transaction out of which the property arose occurred in this State, and

> (i)(A) the last known address of the apparent owner or other person entitled to the property is unknown, or
>
> (B) the last known address of the apparent owner or other person entitled to the property is in a state that does not

provide by law for the escheat or custodial taking of the property or its escheat or unclaimed property law is not applicable to the property, and

(ii) the holder is a domiciliary of a state that does not provide by law for the escheat or custodial taking of the property or its escheat or unclaimed property law is not applicable to the property.

Commissioners' Comment

Section 3 describes the general circumstances under which a state may claim abandoned intangible property. (There is a special provision for travelers checks and money orders in Section 4 infra). This section closely follows the language of *Texas v. New Jersey*,[8] in which the court reasoned that unclaimed property is an asset of the creditor and should generally be paid to the creditor state, i.e., the state of residence of the apparent owner. Consistent with that reasoning it held that unclaimed intangible property is subject to escheat or custody as unclaimed property first by the state of the owner's last known address. If that state cannot claim the property, the state of the holder's domicile is entitled to it. Consistent with the court's concern for a simple rule which would avoid the complexities of proving domicile and residence the court established the priority on the basis of information contained in the holder's records. Recognising that the holder's records might be incomplete, the court's ruling permits a claimant state to prove by other means that the last known address of the owner is within its boundaries. Where the holder's records do not show the owner's last address, the second priority claimant, the state of domicile of the holder, is entitled to claim the property. The state of the owner's last known address can later assume custody from the state of the holder's domicile by showing that the last known address of the owner is within its borders. Likewise, if the state of last known address does not have an unclaimed property law which applies to the property, the state of the holder's domicile can take the property, again subject to the right of the state of last known address to recover the property if and when it enacts an unclaimed property or escheat law.

Paragraph (1) restates the factual situation in *Texas v. New Jersey*. As the court there said ".. the address on the records of a debtor, which in most cases will be the only one available, should be the only relevant last known address." If the holder's records are erroneous and the actual last known address of the owner is in another state, that other state can reclaim the property pursuant to Section 25.

Paragraph (2) covers the situation in which the identity of the person entitled to the property is unknown, but it is established, either through the holder's records or by some other means, that the property was owned by or payable to a

[8] Section 3 is akin to a jurisdictional section, in that it empowers the state to assert custody. At the same time it limits that jurisdictional assertion and establishes a partial system of priorities. It would be possible, of course, to separate the two concepts of jurisdiction and priority. However, the court did not do so in Texas v. New Jersey, and to do so in this Act might have some unfortunate and unforseen consequences. The decision directs the state of corporate domicile to take only if the state of the owner cannot. If Section 3 established as an independent basis of jurisdiction that the state of the holder's domicile could take without regard to the prior claim of the creditor state, there might well be a race between holder and creditor states, with attendant confusion for both states and holders. A priority section ranking the order of asserting claims would diminish the race if it were uniformly enacted. However, there is a strong likelihood that the domiciliary states of major holders would not enact a priority section and thereby would frustrate the system established by Texas v. New Jersey. Section 3 combined with Section 25 establish a system of priorities consistent with Texas v. New Jersey.

person whose last known address was within the claiming state. This is a rational extension of *Texas v. New Jersey.* Reunification of the owner with his property in this circumstance is impossible, and insofar as that issue is concerned, it makes no difference whether the property is delivered to the state of the holder's domicile or the state of the owner's last known address. However, following the equitable concept of distributing unclaimed property among creditor states articulated by the Supreme Court in *Texas v. New Jersey,* the subsection directs that, where there is no record of a name but there is a record of last known address, the state of last known address can claim the property.

Paragraph (3) is the secondary rule of *Texas v. New Jersey.* The Supreme Court ruled that, when property is owed to persons for whom there are no addresses, the property will be subject to escheat by the state of the holder's domicile, provided that another state may later claim upon proof that the last known address of the person entitled to the property was within its borders. If the property is initially paid or turned over to the state of corporate domicile, the state of last known address is authorized to assert its claim pursuant to Section 25. However, unless the right to claim the property is initially conferred in this section, there would be no basis for a reclamation action under Section 25. Where a holder originally bad the address of the owner and it has been subsequently destroyed, a computer code may be one way of establishing an address within the state.

Paragraph (4) provides that, if the law of the state of the owner's last known address does not provide for escheat or taking custody of the unclaimed property or if that state's escheat or unclaimed property law is not applicable to the property in question, the property is subject to claim by the state in which the holder is domiciled. In that instance, the state of the owner's last known address may thereafter claim the property if it enacts an applicable unclaimed property law. The holder state will act as custodian and pay or deliver the property to the owner or the state which has priority under *Texas v. New Jersey* upon request; see also State v. Liquidating Trustees of Republic Petroleum Co., 510 S.W.2d 311 (Texas 1974). See Section 25.

Paragraph (5) provides that, when the last known address of the apparent owner is in a foreign nation the state in which the holder is domiciled may claim the property. This issue was not dealt with by the Supreme Court in *Texas v. New Jersey,* but is a rational extension of that ruling.

Paragraph (6) provides for a situation in which neither of the priority claims discussed in *Texas v. New Jersey* can be made, but the state has a genuine and important contact with the property. An example of the type of claim which might be made under paragraph (6) arose in O'Connor v. Sperry & Hutchinson Co., 412 A.2d 539 (Pa.1980). There Pennsylvania sought to escheat unredeemed trading stamps sold by a corporation domiciled in New Jersey to retailers located in Pennsylvania. Pennsylvania took the position that *Texas v. New Jersey* did not create a jurisdictional bar to escheat by other states when the states granted priority were unable to take. There was no first priority claim since there were no addresses of the trading stamp purchasers. The second priority claimant, the state of corporate domicile (New Jersey), was not permitted under its law to escheat trading stamps (see New Jersey v. Sperry & Hutchinson Co., 56 N.J.Super. 589, 153 A.2d 691 (1959), affirmed *per curiam,* 31 N.J. 385, 157 A.2d 505 (1960)) and hence Pennsylvania urged that in order to prohibit a corporate windfall it should be allowed to claim this property. The Pennsylvania Supreme Court affirmed a lower court decision which overruled Sperry & Hutchinson's motion to dismiss but did not reach the *Texas v. New Jersey* issue.

Gift certificates, unused airline tickets, and other property for which there is no last known address may be claimed by the state of purchase if the state of corporate domicile does not have an abandoned property law covering the property in question under paragraph (6).

Wholly foreign transactions are excluded from the coverage of the Act. See Section 36.

§ 4. [Travelers Checks and Money Orders]

(a) Subject to subsection (d), any sum payable on a travelers check that has been outstanding for more than 15 years after its issuance is presumed abandoned unless the owner, within 15 years, has communicated in writing with the issuer concerning it or otherwise indicated an interest as evidenced by a memorandum or other record on file prepared by an employee of the issuer.

(b) Subject to subsection (d), any sum payable on a money order or similar written instrument, other than a third-party bank check, that has been outstanding for more than 7 years after its issuance is presumed abandoned unless the owner, within 7 years, has communicated in writing with the issuer concerning it or otherwise indicated an interest as evidenced by a memorandum or other record on file prepared by an employee of the issuer.

(c) A holder may not deduct from the amount of a travelers check or money order any charge imposed by reason of the failure to present the instrument for payment unless there is a valid and enforceable written contract between the issuer and the owner of the instrument pursuant to which the issuer may impose a charge and the issuer regularly imposes such charges and does not regularly reverse or otherwise cancel them.

(d) No sum payable on a travelers check, money order, or similar written instrument, other than a third-party bank check, described in subsections (a) and (b) may be subjected to the custody of this State as unclaimed property unless:

(1) the records of the issuer show that the travelers check, money order, or similar written instrument was purchased in this State;

(2) the issuer has its principal place of business in this State and the records of the issuer do not show the state in which the travelers check, money order, or similar written instrument was purchased; or

(3) the issuer has its principal place of business in this State, the records of the issuer show the state in which the travelers check, money order, or similar written instrument was purchased and the laws of the state of purchase do not provide for the escheat or custodial taking of the property or

its escheat or unclaimed property law is not applicable to the property.

(e) Notwithstanding any other provision of this Act, subsection (d) applies to sums payable on travelers checks, money orders, and similar written instruments presumed abandoned on or after February 1, 1965, except to the extent that those sums have been paid over to a state prior to January 1, 1974.

Commissioners' Comment

Section 4 is concerned with travelers checks and money orders which are unclaimed. Subsections (a) and (b) deal with the substantive requirements for presuming this property abandoned and follow closely the provisions of Section 2 of the 1966 Act. Although the general dormancy period has been reduced for many kinds of property, the 15-year period for travelers checks and the 7-year period for money orders is retained. Statistical and economic evidence has shown that these periods continue to be appropriate.

Subsection (c) is consistent with those cases which have ruled on the issue of service charges by money order issuers under the 1966 Act.

Subsections (d) and (e) are new and adopt the rules, including the dates, provided by congressional legislation which determine the state entitled to claim sums payable on travelers checks, money orders, and similar instruments, see Pub.L. 93-495, §§603, 604 (Oct. 28, 1974), 88 Stat. 1525-26, 12 U.S.C. §§2501 et seq. The congressional action was in response to the Supreme Court decision in Pennsylvania v. New York, 407 U.S. 206 (1972), which held that the state of corporate domicile was entitled to escheat money orders when there was no last known address of the purchaser although the property had been purchased in other states. Subsection (d) substitutes as the test for asserting a claim to travelers checks and money orders the place of purchase rather than the state of incorporation of the issuer.

§ 5. [Checks, Drafts and Similar Instruments Issued or Certified by Banking and Financial Organizations]

(a) Any sum payable on a check, draft, or similar instrument, except those subject to Section 4, on which a banking or financial organization is directly liable, including a cashier's check and a certified check, which has been outstanding for more than 5 years after it was payable or after its issuance if payable on demand, is presumed abandoned, unless the owner, within 5 years, has communicated in writing with the banking or financial organization concerning it or otherwise indicated an interest as evidenced by a memorandum or other record on file prepared by an employee thereof.

(b) A holder may not deduct from the amount of any instrument subject to this section any charge imposed by reason of the failure to present the instrument for payment unless there is a valid and enforceable written contract between the holder and the owner of the instrument pursuant to which the holder may impose a charge, and the holder regularly imposes such charges and does not regularly reverse or otherwise cancel them.

Commissioners' Comment

Section 5 covers checks and similar instruments issued or certified by banking and financial organizations. Checks and other instruments issued by persons other than banking and financial organizations are covered generally by Section 2. Travelers checks and money orders are covered by Section 4.

§ 6. [Bank Deposits and Funds In Financial Organizations]

(a) Any demand, savings, or matured time deposit with a banking or financial organization, including a deposit that is automatically renewable, and any funds paid toward the purchase of a share, a mutual investment certificate, or any other interest in a banking or financial organization is presumed abandoned unless the owner, within 5 years has:

(1) in the case of a deposit, increased or decreased its amount or presented the passbook or other similar evidence of the deposit for the crediting of interest;

(2) communicated in writing with the banking or financial organization concerning the property;

(3) otherwise indicated an interest in the property as evidenced by a memorandum or other record on file prepared by an employee of the banking or financial organization;

(4) owned other property to which paragraph (1), (2), or (3) applies and if the banking or financial organization communicates in writing with the owner with regard to the property that would otherwise be presumed abandoned under this subsection at the address to which communications regarding the other property regularly are sent; or

(5) had another relationship with the banking or financial organization concerning which the owner has

(i) communicated in writing with the banking or financial organization; or

(ii) otherwise indicated an interest as evidenced by a memorandum or other record on file prepared by an employee of the banking or financial organization and if the banking or financial organization communicates in writing with the owner with regard to the property that would otherwise be abandoned under this subsection at the address to which communications regarding the other relationship regularly are sent.

(b) For purposes of subsection (a) property includes interest and dividends.

(c) A holder may not impose with respect to property described in subsection (a) any charge due to dormancy or inactivity or cease payment of interest unless:

> (1) there is an enforceable written contract between the holder and the owner of the property pursuant to which the holder may impose a charge or cease payment of interest;
>
> (2) for property in excess of $2.00, the holder, no more than 3 months before the initial imposition of those charges or cessation of interest, has given written notice to the owner of the amount of those charges at the last known address of the owner stating that those charges will be imposed or that interest will cease, but the notice provided in this section need not be given with respect to charges imposed or interest ceased before the effective date of this Act; and
>
> (3) the holder regularly imposes such charges or ceases payment of interest and does not regularly reverse or otherwise cancel them or retroactively credit interest with respect to the property.

(d) Any property described in subsection (a) that is automatically renewable is matured for purposes of subsection (a) upon the expiration of its initial time period, but in the case of any renewal to which the owner consents at or about the time of renewal by communicating in writing with the banking or financial organization or otherwise indicating consent as evidenced by a memorandum or other record on file prepared by an employee of the organization, the property is matured upon the expiration of the last time period for which consent was given. If, at the time provided for delivery in Section 19, a penalty or forfeiture in the payment of interest would result from the delivery of the property, the time for delivery is extended until the time when no penalty or forfeiture would result.

Commissioners' Comment

Section 6 covers bank accounts and follows closely Section 2(a) of the 1966 Act. In addition to the depositor or owner contacts contained in the 1966 Act which will prevent a presumption of abandonment, paragraphs (4) and (5) of subsection (a) add two additional tests rebutting the presumption of abandonment. Activity by an owner with another account in the bank or another active relationship between the owner and the holder such as a loan will prevent abandonment provided the holder gives notice to the owner of the inactive account. These changes will conform the Act to the practices of financial organizations which issue unified bank statements or which are otherwise able to cross reference owners of inactive accounts with owners of active accounts.

Subsection (c) is consistent with those cases which have construed the 1966 Act to require the reporting of savings accounts (together with interest thereon) and checking accounts where the holder for purposes of reporting seeks to impose service charges and cease the payment of interest but regularly reverses or cancels such charges and cessation of interest for customers that reactivate their accounts. If the holder does not have a contract with the owner providing for charges he must, in any event, report and deliver the property.

Subsection (c) may change banking statutes or regulations in certain states.

Paragraph (2) of subsection (c) imposes the additional requirement that notice of the imposition of such charges must be provided to the owner at his last known address. Since the cost of mailing such a notice might approximate the amount of a $2.00 balance, notices are required only when the balance exceeds $2.00.

Subsection (d) prevents a certificate of deposit with automatic renewal provisions from being treated as perpetually exempt from a presumption of abandonment. The subsection also insures that no interest penalty will result from the delivery of such property during the interest term then in effect. Although delivery of such property is deferred, reporting is not.

§ 7. [Funds Owing Under Life Insurance Policies]

(a) Funds held or owing under any life or endowment insurance policy or annuity contract that has matured or terminated are presumed abandoned if unclaimed for more than 5 years after the funds became due and payable as established from the records of the insurance company holding or owing the funds, but property described in subsection (c)(2) is presumed abandoned if unclaimed for more than 2 years.

(b) If a person other than the insured or annuitant is entitled to the funds and an address of the person is not known to the company or it is not definite and certain from the records of the company who is entitled to the funds, it is presumed that the last known address of the person entitled to the funds is the same as the last known address of the insured or annuitant according to the records of the company.

(c) For purposes of this Act, a life or endowment insurance policy or annuity contract not matured by actual proof of the death of the insured or annuitant according to the records of the company is matured and the proceeds due and payable if:

(1) the company knows that the insured or annuitant has died; or

(2)(i) the insured has attained, or would have attained if he were living, the limiting age under the mortality table on which the reserve is based;

(ii) the policy was in force at the time the insured attained, or would have attained, the limiting age specified in subparagraph (i); and

(iii) neither the insured nor any other person appearing to have an interest in the policy within the preceding 2 years, according to the records of the company, has assigned, readjusted, or paid premiums on the policy, subjected the policy to a loan, corresponded in writing with the company concerning the policy, or otherwise indicated an interest as evidenced by a memorandum or other record on file prepared by an employee of the company.

(d) For purposes of this Act, the application of an automatic premium loan provision or other nonforfeiture provision contained in an insurance policy does not prevent a policy from being matured or terminated under subsection (a) if the insured has died or the insured or the beneficiary of the policy otherwise has become entitled to the proceeds thereof before the depletion of the cash surrender value of a policy by the application of those provisions.

(e) If the laws of this State or the terms of the life insurance policy require the company to give notice to the insured or owner that an automatic premium loan provision or other nonforfeiture provision has been exercised and the notice, given to an insured or owner whose last known address according to the records of the company is in this State, is undeliverable, the company shall make a reasonable search to ascertain the policyholder's correct address to which the notice must be mailed.

(f) Notwithstanding any other provision of law, if the company learns of the death of the insured or annuitant and the beneficiary has not communicated with the insurer within 4 months after the death, the company shall take reasonable steps to pay the proceeds to the beneficiary.

(g) Commencing 2 years after the effective date of this Act, every change of beneficiary form issued by an insurance company under any life or endowment insurance policy or annuity contract to an insured or owner who is a resident of this State must request the following information:

(1) the name of each beneficiary, or if a class of beneficiaries is named, the name of each current beneficiary in the class;

(2) the address of each beneficiary; and

(3) the relationship of each beneficiary to the insured.

Commissioners' Comment

Subsections (a) and (b) restate the substance of Section 3(a) of the 1966 Act. Paragraph (1) of subsection (c) provides that proceeds of a life insurance policy are presumed abandoned if the insurer is aware that the insured has died even though actual proof of death has not been furnished to the insurer. Under the 1966 Act these proceeds generally would not have been reportable until the 103rd anniversary of the decedent's birth. Paragraph (2) of subsection (c) provides that the policy proceeds are payable if the limiting age under the mortality table on which the reserve is based is reached and there has been no activity with respect to the policy for 2 years. This is a restatement of a similar provision in subsection (b) of Section 3 of the 1966 Act; however, the abandonment period has been reduced from 7 to 2 years.

Subsection (d) provides that the application of an automatic premium loan provision will not be used to consume the proceeds of a policy and prevent the policy from being matured under subsection (a) if the insured has died or if the beneficiaries have otherwise become entitled to the proceeds of the policy.

Subsection (e) in certain instances imposes an affirmative duty upon the insurer to ascertain a correct address of an insured who fails to receive notice of the exercise of the nonforfeiture option. In these cases it is expected that as a result of the search the insurer will become aware that the insured is deceased. Subsection (f) then requires the insurer to attempt to locate the beneficiaries and pay the policy proceeds, a duty apparently not heretofore imposed on insurance companies. See *Insurer's Duty to Disclose the Existence of a Policy,* 76 Colum.L.Rev. 825 (1976).

Subsection (f) provides for the insurer to request the addresses of beneficiaries if the insured changes a beneficiary designation. Most insurance companies do not request address information for beneficiaries. Since in many instances the initial beneficiary resides in the same household as the insured and the administrative burden of accumulating address information is thought to be considerable, the obligation to obtain the address is deferred until such time as a change of beneficiary occurs. This subsection will assist in locating this limited class of beneficiaries. By making the commencement date of this subsection 2 years after enactment, insurers will be provided sufficient time within which to undertake the necessary administrative steps to implement this provision.

Civil penalties are provided by Section 34(b) for failure to perform the duties imposed by subsections (f) and (g).

§ 8. [Deposits Held by Utilities]

A deposit, including any interest thereon, made by a subscriber with a utility to secure payment or any sum paid in advance for utility services to be furnished, less any lawful deductions, that remains unclaimed by the owner for more than one year after termination of the services for which the deposit or advance payment was made is presumed abandoned.

Commissioners' Comment

The requirement that the services be furnished in the state before a presumption of abandonment arises is eliminated. This is consistent with Texas v. New Jersey, 379 U.S. 670 (1965). The dormancy period for the property is one year. The fact that a deposit in the hands of the utility can be of no benefit to the former subscriber raises a strong inference that it has been forgotten by the owner.

See Section 1(10) for the definition of "utility."

Intangible property held by utilities other than deposits are subject to the 5-year period set forth in Section 2(a).

§ 9. [Refunds Held by Business Associations]

Except to the extent otherwise ordered by the court or administrative agency, any sum that a business association has been ordered to refund by a court or administrative agency which has remained unclaimed by the owner for more than one year after it became payable in accordance with the final determination or order providing for the refund, whether or not the final determination or order requires any person entitled to a refund to make a claim for it, is presumed abandoned.

Commissioners' Comment

Section 9 provides that court or administrative agency ordered refunds which remain unclaimed for more than one year are presumed abandoned. The short dormancy period of one year is justified since no possible advantage can occur to the owner by leaving his property with the holder, and failure to claim a refund is strong evidence that the property has been abandoned.

§ 10. [Stock and Other Intangible Interests in Business Associations]

(a) Except as provided in subsections (b) and (e), stock or other intangible ownership interest in a business association, the existence of which is evidenced by records available to the association, is presumed abandoned and, with respect to the interest, the association is the holder, if a dividend, distribution, or other sum payable as a result of the interest has remained unclaimed by the owner for 7 years and the owner within 7 years has not:

(1) communicated in writing with the association regarding the interest or a dividend, distribution, or other sum payable as a result of the interest; or

(2) otherwise communicated with the association regarding the interest or a dividend, distribution, or other sum payable as a result of the interest, as evidenced by a memorandum or other record on file with the association prepared by an employee of the association.

(b) At the expiration of a 7-year period following the failure of the owner to claim a dividend, distribution, or other sum payable to the owner as a result of the interest, the interest is not presumed abandoned unless there have been at least 7 dividends, distributions, or other sums paid during the period, none of which has been claimed by the owner. If 7 dividends, distributions, or other sums are paid during the 7-year period, the period leading to a presumption of abandonment commences on the date payment of the first such unclaimed dividend, distribution, or other sum became due and payable. If 7 dividends, distributions, or other sums are not paid during the presumptive period, the period continues to run until there have been 7 dividends, distributions, or other sums that have not been claimed by the owner.

(c) The running of the 7-year period of abandonment ceases immediately upon the occurrence of a communication referred to in subsection (a). If any future dividend, distribution, or other sum payable to the owner as a result of the interest is subsequently not claimed by the owner, a new period of abandonment commences and relates back to the time a subsequent dividend, distribution, or other sum became due and payable.

(d) At the time an interest is presumed abandoned under this section, any dividend, distribution, or other sum then held for or owing to the owner as a result of the interest, and not previously presumed abandoned, is presumed abandoned.

(e) This Act does not apply to any stock or other intangible ownership interest enrolled in a plan that provides for the automatic reinvestment of dividends, distributions, or other sums payable as a result of the interest unless the records available to the administrator of the plan show, with respect to any intangible ownership interest not enrolled in the reinvestment plan, that the owner has not within 7 years communicated in any manner described in subsection (a).

Commissioners' Comment

Section 10 covers underlying shares of stock and principal amounts of debt securities, i.e., stock certificates in the possession of the record owner.[9] Dividends and other distributions which were included in Section 5 of the 1966 Act are to be reported pursuant to Section 2 of this Act.

Several states have enacted specific provisions for the presumption of abandonment of underlying share certificates. Typical is the provision of California (Cal.Civ.Pro.Code § 1516) which provides that the underlying intangible interest is presumed abandoned if the owner has not contacted the company within the abandonment period and he cannot be found

[9] It has generally been assumed that Section 5 of the 1966 Act did not cover underlying shares unless those shares were in the actual possession of the issuer (i.e., as undeliverable stock). However, the Supreme Court's analysis of the New Jersey escheat statute in Standard Oil Co. v. New Jersey, 341 U.S. 428 (1951), suggests that Sections 5 and 9 of the 1966 Act apply to underlying shares even though they are not in the possession of the issuer but have been delivered to an owner who is lost and has made no claim on the stock. It has generally been assumed that actual certificates for the abandoned shares in Standard Oil were in the possession of the company or its transfer agent. However, the record clearly reflects that neither the company nor its transfer agent had custody of the shares. (See Stipulation Of Facts Entered Between the state of New Jersey and the Standard Oil Company, Exhibit 3, Clerks Transcript, pp. 198a and 199a, see also, p. 77a, p. 233a.) The Supreme Court affirmed New Jersey's claim to escheat the shares notwithstanding that its laws did not expressly refer to underlying shares.

Even if underlying shares not in the possession of the issuer were not within the coverage of Section 5 of the 1966 Act, the comment to Section 9 of that Act, the omnibus provision, indicate that this type of property was within the coverage of Section 9. However, the fact remains that no states with the Uniform Act have sought to recover this property in a systematic way.

whether or not dividends on that interest are paid. Connecticut, Florida, Indiana, Massachusetts, Montana, New York, Rhode Island, Wisconsin and Virginia also have specific provisions for the presumption of abandonment of underlying shares. States with escheat laws similar to New Jersey's would be entitled to claim underlying shares based on the *Standard Oil* precedent.

Two major concerns have been expressed with the concept of presuming abandonment of underlying stock interests. The first deals with the evidential showing necessary to raise a presumption of abandonment, and the second concerns the rights of the various parties when underlying stock interests are presumed abandoned.

Under what set of circumstances is it appropriate to presume that stock has been abandoned when the shares have been delivered to an owner and are no longer in the possession of the issuer? Section 10 establishes a longer dormancy period, (7 years) for this property than for other property covered by this Act. Further, Section 10 requires that there must be at least 7 consecutive dividend checks issued during this period of dormancy which remain uncashed. Additionally, the presumption of abandonment will not arise in the event the missing owner has communicated with the association. In this regard, the communication would normally be with an agent of the association such as a transfer agent or a dividend disbursing agent. Of course, such communication would satisfy the provision of this section. The existing underlying shares statutes make no formal distinction between dividend and nondividend paying stock and provide that the mere passage of time with no contact is sufficient to raise the presumption of abandonment. Section 10 combines both a period of inactivity, 7 years, with the requirement that distributions paid on the underlying intangible interest remain unclaimed, thus avoiding concerns that abandonment should not be presumed where a shareholder has not contacted a non-dividend paying company.

If the conditions leading to a presumption of abandonment have occurred, the holder (issuer of the security) must report to the state pursuant to Section 17, and if the holder has in its records an address of the owner, it must send written notice to the owner in an effort to reunite the owner with his property. Thereafter the administrator must give notice by advertising the existence of the property and send mailed notice to owners of property valued at $50 or more. See Section 18.

Many owners will be located through the publication and mail notice requirements of the Act. In the event abandonment is presumed and the owner subsequently appears, there are at least 3 formal opportunities to reunite that owner with the issuer before a duplicate certificate is turned over to the administrator.

If the owner is not located, however, a duplicate certificate is issued to the administrator pursuant to Section 19(d) and the original certificate will be cancelled. Thereafter, if the owner appears, the duplicate certificate may be claimed from the administrator. The Act is designed to encourage the administrator to hold the certificate for at least 3 years. (See Section 22(d).) If the administrator does sell the stock before the expiration of this 3-year period, the original owner may recover the net proceeds of sale or the market value of the property at the time he makes a claim, whichever is higher. If the owner appears after the 3-year holding period and after his interest has been sold, he recovers the net proceeds of sale.

The issuer who delivers a duplicate certificate under the Act is protected, because upon delivery it is relieved of all liability to the extent of the value of the property delivered under Section 20. If any person thereafter makes a claim against the holder, the administrator is required to indemnify the holder against any liability on the claim. The required indemnity is complete, and it is not restricted to the value of the property turned over.

If a purchaser from the owner turns up and presents the original share for registration after the property has been presumed abandoned, his claim is initially under the UCC. However, because of the indemnity provision in Section 20, the state will be required to assume all liability. UCC § 8-405 provides that the issuer must register the transfer unless to do so would result in overissue. In this event, the purchaser's rights are determined by UCC § 8-104 and, if a similar security is not reasonably available for purchase, he recovers the price he paid the original owner. Presumably the issuer would call on the administrator to fulfill his requirement of indemnity. If the administrator still has the duplicate certificate, he would turn it over to the purchaser.

Subsection (e) would not require the reporting of interests enrolled in dividend reinvestment plans unless the owner has other stock which is not in dividend reinvestment and which would be presumed abandoned under Section 10.

§ 11. [Property of Business Associations Held in Course of Dissolution]

Intangible property distributable in the course of a dissolution of a business association which remains unclaimed by the owner for more than one year after the date specified for final distribution is presumed abandoned.

Commissioners' Comment

This section closely follows Section 6 of the 1966 Act except that the dormancy period has been reduced to one year from 2 years. This section covers both voluntary and involuntary dissolutions.

§ 12. [Property Held By Agents and Fiduciaries]

(a) Intangible property and any income or increment derived therefrom held in a fiduciary capacity for the benefit of another person is presumed abandoned unless the owner, within 5 years after it has become payable or distributable, has increased or decreased the principal, accepted payment of principal or income, communicated concerning the property, or otherwise indicated an interest as evidenced by a memorandum or other record on file prepared by the fiduciary.

(b) Funds in an individual retirement account or a retirement plan for self-employed individuals or similar account or plan established pursuant to the Internal Revenue laws of the United States are not payable or distributable within the meaning of subsection (a) unless, under the terms of the account or plan, distribution of all or part of the funds would then be mandatory.

(c) For the purpose of this section, a person who holds property as an agent for a business association is deemed to hold the property in a fiduciary capacity for that business association alone, unless the agreement between him and the business association provides otherwise.

(d) For the purposes of this Act, a person who is deemed to hold property in a fiduciary capacity for a business association alone is the holder of the property only insofar as the interest of the business association in the property is concerned, and the business association is the holder of the property insofar as the interest of any other person in the property is concerned.

Commissioners' Comment

Intangible property is not "payable or distributable" under subsection (a) if the fiduciary possesses merely the discretion to pay or distribute property and has not exercised the discretion.

Subsection (d) is designed to clarify the status of transfer agents. That is, they are agents for the business association and the administrator must look to the principal, the business association, as the holder, unless they have contractually undertaken the obligation to report the property. A later section provides that the administrator is authorized to examine the records of the holder or records relating to the holder which are in the possession of the transfer agent. See Section 30.

§ 13. [Property Held by Courts and Public Agencies]

Intangible property held for the owner by a court, state or other government, governmental subdivision or agency, public corporation, or public authority which remains unclaimed by the owner for more than one year after becoming payable or distributable is presumed abandoned.

§ 14. [Gift Certificates and Credit Memos]

(a) A gift certificate or a credit memo issued in the ordinary course of an issuer's business which remains unclaimed by the owner for more than 5 years after becoming payable or distributable is presumed abandoned.

(b) In the case of a gift certificate, the amount presumed abandoned is the price paid by the purchaser for the gift certificate. In the case of a credit memo, the amount presumed abandoned is the amount credited to the recipient of the memo.

Commissioners' Comment

Section 14 should be read in conjunction with Section 2. The comment to Section 2 is particularly pertinent to this section. Holders did not routinely report gift certificates and credit memos under the 1966 Act, but it has been held that both kinds of property are within the coverage of Section 9 of that Act. See, for instance, People v. Marshall Field & Co., 83 Ill.App.3d 811, 404 N.E.2d 368 (1980).

Subsection (b) is intended to clarify the amount reportable which is represented by gift certificates and credit memos. In the case of a gift certificate, it is the price paid by the purchaser. In the case of a credit memo, it is the amount credited to the recipient's account.

§ 15. [Wages]

Unpaid wages, including wages represented by unpresented payroll checks, owing in the ordinary course of the holder's business which remain unclaimed by the owner for more than one year after becoming payable are presumed abandoned.

Commissioners' Comment

Since the chance of locating the missing owner of a wage check materially decreases with the passage of time, this property is presumed abandoned at an earlier period than that for most other property.

§ 16. [Contents of Safe Deposit Box or Other Safekeeping Repository]

All tangible and intangible property held in a safe deposit box or any other safekeeping repository in this State in the ordinary course of the holder's business and proceeds resulting from the sale of the property permitted by other law, which remain unclaimed by the owner for more than 5 years after the lease or rental period on the box or other repository has expired, are presumed abandoned.

Commissioners' Comment

Section 16 parallels Section 2(d) of the 1966 Act. This Section is not intended to cover property left in places other than safekeeping repositories, for example, airport lockers or field warehouses. Its coverage is limited to safe deposit boxes in banks and other financial institutions. Most states have statutory provisions apart from the unclaimed property law for the disposition of property abandoned in such places as airport lockers.

§ 17. [Report of Abandoned Property]

(a) A person holding property tangible or intangible, presumed abandoned and subject to custody as unclaimed property under this Act shall report to the administrator concerning the property as provided in this section.

(b) The report must be verified and must include:

(1) except with respect to travelers checks and money orders, the name, if known, and last known address, if any, of each person appearing from the records of the holder to be the owner of property of the value of $25 or more presumed abandoned under this Act;

(2) in the case of unclaimed funds of $25 or more held or owing under any life or endowment insurance policy or annuity contract, the full name and last known address of the insured or annuitant and of the beneficiary according to the records of the insurance company holding or owing the funds;

(3) in the case of the contents of a safe deposit box or other safekeeping repository or of other tangible property, a description of the property and the place where it is held and

may be inspected by the administrator and any amounts owing to the holder;

(4) the nature and identifying number, if any, or description of the property and the amount appearing from the records to be due, but items of value under $25 each may be reported in the aggregate;

(5) the date the property became payable, demandable, or returnable, and the date of the last transaction with the apparent owner with respect to the property; and

(6) other information the administrator prescribes by rule as necessary for the administration of this Act.

(c) If the person holding property presumed abandoned and subject to custody as unclaimed property is a successor to other persons who previously held the property for the apparent owner or the holder has changed his name while holding the property, he shall file with his report all known names and addresses of each previous holder of the property.

(d) The report must be filed before November 1 of each year as of June 30, next preceding, but the report of any life insurance company must be filed before May 1 of each year as of December 31 next preceding. On written request by any person required to file a report, the administrator may postpone the reporting date.

(e) Not more than 120 days before filing the report required by this section, the holder in possession of property presumed abandoned and subject to custody as unclaimed property under this Act shall send written notice to the apparent owner at his last known address informing him that the holder is in possession of property subject to this Act if:

(i) the holder has in its records an address for the apparent owner which the holder's records do not disclose to be inaccurate,

(ii) the claim of the apparent owner is not barred by the statute of limitations, and

(iii) the property has a value of $50 or more.

Commissioners' Comment

The $25 minimum provided in subsection (b)(1)(2) and (4) represents an increase from $3.00 in the 1966 Act in order to minimize reporting expenses. Almost every state which enacted the prior Uniform Act now provides for a $25 minimum.

Before filing its report, the holder must send written notice to the apparent owner, if the owner's claim is not barred by the statute of limitations, the property has a value of $50 of more, and the holder's records do not disclose the address to be inaccurate. Other efforts to locate the owner are no longer required. Since most notifications under the 1966 Act were returned as undeliverable, and the administrator must also mail a notice under Section 18 to owners of property having a value of $50 or more, the holder should not be compelled to incur the expense of preparing and mailing notices under all circumstances.

The subsection now requires that the notice be sent not more than 120 days before the filing of the report. The previous subsection did not specify when the notice was to be given, and some holders felt that notices given years earlier were sufficient.

§ 18. [Notice and Publication of Lists of Abandoned Property]

(a) The administrator shall cause a notice to be published not later than March 1, or in the case of property reported by life insurance companies, September 1, of the year immediately following the report required by Section 17 at least once a week for 2 consecutive weeks in a newspaper of general circulation in the [county] of this State in which is located the last known address of any person to be named in the notice. If no address is listed or the address is outside this State, the notice must be published in the [county] in which the holder of the property has its principal place of business within this State.

(b) The published notice must be entitled "Notice of Names of Persons Appearing to be Owners of Abandoned Property" and contain:

(1) the names in alphabetical order and last known address, if any, of persons listed in the report and entitled to notice within the [county] as specified in subsection (a);

(2) a statement that information concerning the property and the name and last known address of the holder may be obtained by any person possessing an interest in the property by addressing an inquiry to the administrator; and

(3) a statement that if proof of claim is not presented by the owner to the holder and the owner's right to receive the property is not established to the holder's satisfaction before April 20, or, in the case of property reported by life insurance companies, before October 20, the property will be placed not later than May 1, or in the case of property reported by life insurance companies, not later than November 1, in the custody of the administrator and all further claims must thereafter be directed to the administrator.

(c) The administrator is not required to publish in the notice any items of less than $[50] unless the administrator considers their publication to be in the public interest.

(d) Not later than March 1, or in the case of property reported by life insurance companies, not later than September 1, of the year immediately following the report required by Section 17, the administrator shall mail a notice to each person whose last known address is listed in the report and who appears to be entitled to property of the value of $[50] or more presumed abandoned under this Act and any beneficiary of a life or endowment insurance policy or annuity contract for whom the administrator has a last known address.

(e) The mailed notice must contain:

(1) a statement that, according to a report filed with the administrator, property is being held to which the addressee appears entitled;

(2) the name and last known address of the person holding the property and any necessary information regarding the changes of name and last known address of the holder; and

(3) a statement that, if satisfactory proof of claim is not presented by the owner to the holder by the date specified in the published notice, the property will be placed in the custody of the administrator and all further claims must be directed to the administrator.

(f) This section is not applicable to sums payable on travelers checks, money orders, and other written instruments presumed abandoned under Section 4.

Commissioners' Comment

Subsections (a) and (b)(3) set forth the dates by which the administrator must publish the names of missing owners and mail notification to the last known address of each owner. This section eliminates the requirement of the 1966 Act that a separate notification be given by the administrator to the holder to establish when the final report and remittance is required.

Subsections (c) and (d) have increased from $25 to $50 the minimum value required for advertising and notification. The amounts were increased because the costs of publishing newspaper advertisements now range from $12 to $22 per name. Because most mailed notifications are returned to administrators as undeliverable, the mailing minimum was also increased.

§ 19. [Payment or Delivery of Abandoned Property]

(a) Except as otherwise provided in subsections (b) and (c), a person who is required to file a report under Section 17, within 6 months after the final date for filing the report as required by Section 17, shall pay or deliver to the administrator all abandoned property required to be reported.

(b) If the owner establishes the right to receive the abandoned property to the satisfaction of the holder before the property has been delivered or it appears that for some other reason the presumption of abandonment is erroneous, the holder need not pay or deliver the property to the administrator, and the property will no longer be presumed abandoned. In that case, the holder shall file with the administrator a verified written explanation of the proof of claim or of the error in the presumption of abandonment.

(c) Property reported under Section 17 for which the holder is not required to report the name of the apparent owner must be delivered to the administrator at the time of filing the report.

(d) The holder of an interest under Section 10 shall deliver a duplicate certificate or other evidence of ownership if the holder does not issue certificates of ownership to the administrator. Upon delivery of a duplicate certificate to the administrator, the holder and any transfer agent, registrar, or other person acting for or on behalf of a holder in executing or delivering the duplicate certificate is relieved of all liability of every kind in accordance with the provision of Section 20 to every person, including any person acquiring the original certificate or the duplicate of the certificate issued to the administrator, for any losses or damages resulting to any person by the issuance and delivery to the administrator of the duplicate certificate.

Commissioners' Comment

Subsections (a) through (c) restate the substance of Section 13 of the 1966 Act. The holder is required to pay over the property within 6 months after reporting its existence. However, if the holder does not know the owner's name or the value of the property is less than $25, then the property must be turned over to the administrator at the time of filing the report. The notification provisions of Sections 17 and 18 often stimulate owners to reclaim their property and the retention period of 6 months permits the holder to honor these claims.

Subsection (d) provides that the holder of an underlying stock interest presumed abandoned under Section 10 shall deliver a duplicate certificate to the administrator. Upon delivery the holder, in accordance with the provisions of Section 20, is relieved of all liability to any person occasioned by the reappearance of the original certificate or the issuance of the duplicate certificate. In this connection, see the comment to Section 10.

§ 20. [Custody by State; Holder Relieved from Liability; Reimbursement of Holder Paying Claim; Reclaiming for Owner; Defense of Holder; Payment of Safe Deposit Box or Repository Charges]

(a) Upon the payment or delivery of property to the administrator, the state assumes custody and responsibility for the safekeeping of the property. A person who pays or delivers property to the administrator in good faith is relieved of all liability to the extent of the value of the property paid or delivered for any claim then existing or which thereafter may arise or be made in respect to the property.

(b) A holder who has paid money to the administrator pursuant to this Act may make payment to any person appearing to the holder to be entitled to payment and, upon filing proof of payment and proof that the payee was entitled thereto, the administrator shall promptly reimburse the holder for the payment without imposing any fee or other charge. If reimbursement is sought for a payment made on a negotiable instrument, including a travelers check or money order, the holder must be reimbursed under this subsection upon filing proof that the instrument was duly presented and that payment was made to a person who appeared to the holder to be entitled to payment. The holder must be reimbursed for payment made under this subsection even if the payment was made to a person whose claim was barred under Section 29(a).

(c) A holder who has delivered property (including a certificate of any interest in a business association) other than money to the administrator pursuant to this Act may reclaim the property if still in the possession of the administrator, without paying any fee or other charge, upon filing proof that the owner has claimed the property from the holder.

(d) The administrator may accept the holder's affidavit as sufficient proof of the facts that entitle the holder to recover money and property under this section.

(e) If the holder pays or delivers property to the administrator in good faith and thereafter another person claims the property from the holder or another state claims the money or property under its laws relating to escheat or abandoned or unclaimed property, the administrator, upon written notice of the claim, shall defend the holder against the claim and indemnify the holder against any liability on the claim.

(f) For the purposes of this section, "good faith" means that

(1) payment or delivery was made in a reasonable attempt to comply with this Act;

(2) the person delivering the property was not a fiduciary then in breach of trust in respect to the property and had a reasonable basis for believing, based on the facts then known to him, that the property was abandoned for the purposes of this Act; and

(3) there is no showing that the records pursuant to which the delivery was made did not meet reasonable commercial standards of practice in the industry.

(g) Property removed from a safe deposit box or other safekeeping repository is received by the administrator subject to the holder's right under this subsection to be reimbursed for the actual cost of the opening and to any valid lien or contract providing for the holder to be reimbursed for unpaid rent or storage charges. The administrator shall reimburse or pay the holder out of the proceeds remaining after deducting the administrator's selling cost.

Commissioners' Comment

When property is turned over to the state, the holder is relieved of all liability for any turnover made in good faith. Subsection (f) sets forth a definition of good faith which *inter alia* allows the holder to rely on its records if they meet reasonable commercial standards of practice in the industry.

The section also permits the holder to obtain reimbursement for claims it elected to pay to owners who appeared after the property was turned over. If a state in enacting Section 24(c) provides for the payment of interest on property delivered to the administrator, then the holder will add such interest when paying the claim. See Section 24(d).

If after turnover, any person or another state makes a claim on the holder, the state, upon request, is required to defend the holder and indemnify him against any liability. This provision is particularly important in light of the underlying share provisions of Section 10. The comment to that section is pertinent here as well.

§ 21. [Crediting of Dividends, Interest, or Increments to Owner's Account]

Whenever property other than money is paid or delivered to the administrator under this Act, the owner is entitled to receive from the administrator any dividends, interest, or other increments realized or accruing on the property at or before liquidation or conversion thereof into money.

Commissioners' Comment

This section changes Section 15 of the 1966 Act which provided that the owner was not entitled to receive any income or other increment accruing after the delivery of unclaimed property to the administrator. This Act provides for some substantial retention periods by the administrator. For instance, securities obtained pursuant to Section 10 will generally be held for a 3-year period prior to sale. The owner will be entitled to dividends, interest or other increment realized or accruing on the property during this 3-year period.

§ 22. [Public Sale of Abandoned Property]

(a) Except as provided in subsections (b) and (c), the administrator, within 3 years after the receipt of abandoned property, shall sell it to the highest bidder at public sale in whatever city in the state affords in the judgment of the administrator the most favorable market for the property involved. The administrator may decline the highest bid and reoffer the property for sale if in the judgment of the administrator the bid is insufficient. If in the judgment of the administrator the probable cost of sale exceeds the value of the property, it need not be offered for sale. Any sale held under this section must be preceded by a single publication of notice, at least [3] weeks in advance of sale, in a newspaper of general circulation in the [county] in which the property is to be sold.

(b) Securities listed on an established stock exchange must be sold at prices prevailing at the time of sale on the exchange. Other securities may be sold over the counter at prices prevailing at the time of sale or by any other method the administrator considers advisable.

(c) Unless the administrator considers it to be in the best interest of the state to do otherwise, all securities, other than those presumed abandoned under Section 10, delivered to the administrator must be held for at least one year before he may sell them.

(d) Unless the administrator considers it to be in the best interest of the state to do otherwise, all securities presumed abandoned under Section 10 and delivered to the administrator must be held for at least 3 years before he may sell them. If the administrator sells any securities delivered pursuant to Section 10 before the expiration of the 3-year period, any person making a claim pursuant to this Act before the end of the 3-year period is entitled to either the proceeds of the sale of the securities or the market value of the securities at the time the claim is made, whichever amount is greater, less any deduction for fees pursuant to Section 23(b). A person making a claim under this Act after the expiration of this period is entitled to receive either the securities delivered to the administrator by the holder, if they still remain in the hands of the administrator, or the proceeds received from sale, less any amounts deducted pursuant to Section 23(b), but no person has any claim under this Act against the state, the holder, any transfer agent, registrar, or other person acting for or on behalf of a holder for any appreciation in the value of the property occurring after delivery by the holder to the administrator.

(e) The purchaser of property at any sale conducted by the administrator pursuant to this Act takes the property free of all claims of the owner or previous holder thereof and of all persons claiming through or under them. The administrator shall execute all documents necessary to complete the transfer of ownership.

Commissioners' Comment

In order to give additional protection to the missing owner of a security which has been presumed abandoned and is not subject to Section 10, this section directs the administrator to hold that security for at least one year.

If the security is one which has been presumed abandoned pursuant to Section 10 the administrator is expected to hold the security for 3 years. He is permitted to sell the security within this 3-year period, but if the missing owner appears and makes claim for the security within this 3-year period after the administrator has sold it, the missing owner is entitled to receive the proceeds of the sale or the market value of the securities at the time the claim is made. Thus there is a genuine incentive for an administrator to hold this property for the requisite 3-year period.

Subsection (b) permits an administrator to sell securities at prevailing prices directly to the issuing companies.

§ 23. [Deposit of Funds]

[(a)] Except as otherwise provided by this section, the administrator shall promptly deposit in the [general fund] of this State all funds received under this Act, including the proceeds from the sale of abandoned property under Section 22. The administrator shall retain in a separate trust fund an amount not less than $[100,000] from which prompt payment of claims duly allowed must be made by him. Before making the deposit, the administrator shall record the name and last known address of each person appearing from the holders' reports to be entitled to the property and the name and last known address of each insured person or annuitant and beneficiary and with respect to each policy or contract listed in the report of an insurance company its number, the name of the company, and the amount due. The record must be available for public inspection at all reasonable business hours.

[(b) Before making any deposit to the credit of the [general fund], the administrator may deduct:

(1) any costs in connection with the sale of abandoned property;

(2) costs of mailing and publication in connection with any abandoned property;

(3) reasonable service charges; and

(4) costs incurred in examining records of holders of property and in collecting the property from those holders.]

Commissioners' Comment

This section increases from $25,000 to $100,000 the sum which is recommended to be retained in a trust account for payment of claims. Each state based on its own experience will establish a minimum amount to be kept on hand in order that claims will be quickly paid. If a state receives substantial amounts represented by underlying stock certificates pursuant to Section 10, it is contemplated that the amount of the trust fund which it selects will reflect its experience in paying owners' claims. The practice in most states is for the legislature in its appropriation bill to provide for a continuing appropriation of general funds to pay abandoned property claims.

§ 24. [Filing of Claim with Administrator]

(a) A person, excluding another state, claiming an interest in any property paid or delivered to the administrator may file with him a claim on a form prescribed by him and verified by the claimant.

(b) The administrator shall consider each claim within 90 days after it is filed and give written notice to the claimant if the claim is denied in whole or in part. The notice may be given by mailing it to the last address, if any, stated in the claim as the address to which notices are to be sent. If no address for notices is stated in the claim, the notice may be mailed to the last address, if any, of the claimant as stated in the claim. No notice of denial need be given if the claim fails to state either the last address to which notices are to be sent or the address of the claimant.

(c) If a claim is allowed, the administrator shall pay over or deliver to the claimant the property or the amount the administrator actually received or the net proceeds if it has been sold by the administrator, together with any additional amount required by Section 21. If the claim is for property presumed abandoned under Section 10 which was sold by the administrator within 3 years after the date of delivery, the amount payable for that claim is the value of the property at the time the claim was made or the net proceeds of sale, whichever is greater. If the property claimed was interest-bearing to the owner on the date of surrender by the holder, the administrator also shall pay interest at a rate of [ ] percent a year or any lesser rate the property earned while in the possession of the holder. Interest begins to accrue when the property is delivered to the administrator and ceases on the earlier of the expiration of 10 years after delivery or the date on which payment is made to the owner. No interest on interest-bearing property is payable for any period before the effective date of this Act.

(d) Any holder who pays the owner for property that has been delivered to the state and which, if claimed from the administrator, would be subject to subsection (c) shall add interest as provided in subsection (c). The added interest must be repaid to the holder by the administrator in the same manner as the principal.

Commissioners' Comment

If a valid claim to property turned over to the administrator is made, the administrator is to return the property or, if it has been sold, to pay the net proceeds of sale. If the claim is for an underlying share interest presumed abandoned under Section 10 and the administrator has sold the property within 3 years, the claimant is entitled to the net proceeds of sale or the market value of the property at the time claim was made for it, whichever is higher, together with any additional amount payable under Section 21.

Several states have added to the 1966 Act a provision for paying interest on property which was interest-bearing to the owner. Subsections (c) and (d) set forth provisions which a state may wish to enact providing for the payment of interest.

Subsection (c) provides for the administrator to pay interest on property which was interest bearing to the owner. The rate of interest will be fixed by each state enacting the Act and should fairly reflect prevailing rates.

§ 25. [Claim of Another State to Recover Property; Procedure]

(a) At any time after property has been paid or delivered to the administrator under this Act another state may recover the property if:

(1) the property was subjected to custody by this State because the records of the holder did not reflect the last known address of the apparent owner when the property was presumed abandoned under this Act, and the other state establishes that the last known address of the apparent owner or other person entitled to the property was in that state and under the laws of that state the property escheated to or was subject to a claim of abandonment by that state;

(2) the last known address of the apparent owner or other person entitled to the property, as reflected by the records of the holder, is in the other state and under the laws of that state the property has escheated to or become subject to a claim of abandonment by that state;

(3) the records of the holder were erroneous in that they did not accurately reflect the actual owner of the property and the last known address of the actual owner is in the other state and under the laws of that state the property escheated to or was subject to a claim of abandonment by that state;

(4) the property was subjected to custody by this State under Section 3(6) and under the laws of the state of domicile of the holder the property has escheated to or become subject to a claim of abandonment by that state; or

(5) the property is the sum payable on a travelers check, money order, or other similar instrument that was subjected to custody by this State under Section 4, and the instrument was purchased in the other state, and under the laws of that state the property escheated to or became subject to a claim of abandonment by that state.

(b) The claim of another state to recover escheated or abandoned property must be presented in a form prescribed by the administrator, who shall decide the claim within 90 days after it is presented. The administrator shall allow the claim if he determines that the other state is entitled to the abandoned property under subsection (a).

(c) The administrator shall require a state, before recovering property under this section, to agree to indemnify this State and its officers and employees against any liability on a claim for the property.

Commissioners' Comment

Section 25 should be read together with Sections 3 and 4. Sections 3 and 25 are designed to carry out the priority scheme enunciated in Texas v. New Jersey, 379 U.S. 670 (1965). In general the state of last known address is entitled to claim abandoned property. Where there is insufficient information to permit this assertion of custody, the state of the holder's domicile takes the property subject to a later claim by the state of the last known address.

Paragraph 1 provides that, if property was paid to the state of the holder's domicile because the last known address of the owner was unknown and it is later established that the last known address of the person entitled to the property was in another state, the state of domicile should pay over to the state of last known address.

Paragraph 2 parallels subsection (3)(d), which permits the state of corporate domicile to take if the state of the last known address does not provide for the escheat or custodial taking of the property. If the state of the last known address subsequently enacts an unclaimed property law which covers the property, the taking state must turn it over.

Paragraph 3 addresses the problem of Nellius v. Tampax, Inc., 394 A.2d 333 (Del.Ch.Ct.1978) in which the holder's records did not reflect the fact that the record owner had sold the property to another. The court concluded, under *Texas v. New Jersey,* that the holder's records were controlling and that the apparent and not actual owner state could initially claim the property. Paragraph 3 provides that the state of the actual owner can reclaim this property from the taking state.

Paragraph 4, parallelling subsection (3)(f), provides that property initially claimed under a "contacts" test because there was no last known address and the state of domicile had no applicable unclaimed property law may be reclaimed by the state of corporate domicile if it enacts an applicable unclaimed property law.

Subsection (c) provides that the state that initially receives the property and which is requested to remit it to another state should be indemnified by the claiming state.

§ 26. [Action to Establish Claim]

A person aggrieved by a decision of the administrator or whose claim has not been acted upon within 90 days after its filing may bring an action to establish the claim in the [ ] court, naming the administrator as a defendant. The action must be brought within [90] days after the decision of the administrator or within [180] days after the filing of the claim if he has failed to act on it. [If the aggrieved person establishes the claim in an action against the administrator, the court shall award him costs and reasonable attorney's fees.]

Commissioners' Comment

After property is presumed abandoned and reported to the administrator (Section 17) the administrator must attempt to locate the missing owner (Section 18). Thereafter, if the property has been delivered to the administrator (Section 19) and the owner or his representative appears, the administrator must pay the claim (Section 24). The owner's rights are never cut off. If one claiming to be the owner cannot satisfy the administrator of his right to claim the property in an administrative proceeding pursuant to Section 24, he retains a right to assert his claim in a court of appropriate jurisdiction under this section.

§ 27. [Election to Take Payment or Delivery]

(a) The administrator may decline to receive any property reported under this Act which he considers to have a value less than the expense of giving notice and of sale. If the administrator elects not to receive custody of the property, the holder shall be notified within [120] days after filing the report required under Section 17.

(b) A holder, with the written consent of the administrator and upon conditions and terms prescribed by him, may report and deliver property before the property is presumed abandoned. Property delivered under this subsection must be held by the administrator and is not presumed abandoned until such time as it otherwise would be presumed abandoned under this Act.

Commissioners' Comment

Subsection (b) is new. It authorizes the administrator to assume custody of property prior to the time for presuming abandonment. Administrators have expressed a need for this authority to enable them to take possession of property, such as the contents of a safe deposit box repository, when the holder is terminating business but the property is not yet reportable. Additionally, other holders which have conducted business in the state and are ceasing operations might use the provisions of this section. The property must be held by the administrator until the abandonment period runs and then the property will be subject to the other provisions of the Act.

§ 28. [Destruction or Disposition of Property Having Insubstantial Commercial Value; Immunity from Liability]

If the administrator determines after investigation that any property delivered under this Act has insubstantial commercial value, the administrator may destroy or otherwise dispose of the property at any time. No action or proceeding may be maintained against the state or any officer or against the holder for or on account of any action taken by the administrator pursuant to this section.

Commissioners' Comment

This section provides for the disposition of property which has no commercial value. As an example, the contents of safety deposit boxes often include such items as rent receipts, personal correspondence and lapsed insurance policies. In such cases, these contents might have some personal significance to the owner, which the administrator would take into consideration in determining for what period of time he will hold the property awaiting a claim by the owner. However, in the usual situation there will be no interest to be preserved by maintaining this property under state custody.

Under this section the administrator would be free to retain property having no commercial value. Further, the administrator could transfer it to other agencies or institutions which might have an interest in the property because of its historical value or other independent significance.

This section provides that the administrator in exercising his discretion in disposing of such property is not subject to a claim by the missing owner.

§ 29. [Periods of Limitation]

(a) The expiration, before or after the effective date of this Act, of any period of time specified by contract, statute, or court order, during which a claim for money or property can be made or during which an action or proceeding may be commenced or enforced to obtain payment of a claim for money or to recover property, does not prevent the money or property from being presumed abandoned or affect any duty to file a report or to pay or deliver abandoned property to the administrator as required by this Act.

(b) No action or proceeding may be commenced by the administrator with respect to any duty of a holder under this Act more than 10 years after the duty arose.

Commissioners' Comment

Section 29 has an added provision that the expiration of time periods set forth in contracts will not prevent the property from becoming reportable. See People v. Marshall Field & Co., 83 Ill.App.3d 811, 404 N.E.2d 368 (1980); Screen Actors Guild, Inc. v. Cory, 91 Cal.App.3d 111, 154 Cal.Rptr. 77 (1979); State v. Jefferson Lake Sulphur Co., 36 N.J. 577, 178 A.2d 329 (1962). Section 2 abrogates another contractual condition often asserted as a defense to reporting property otherwise presumed abandoned, the failure to present the evidence of indebtedness.

Subsection (a) is written to insure that although the owner's claim against the holder may be barred by the statute of limitations prior to the effective date of the Act, the holder is not relieved of his obligation to pay abandoned property to the administrator. The comment to Section 16 of the 1966 Act noted that local law must be consulted in order to ascertain whether legislation constitutionally may be enacted reviving a cause of action barred by the statute of limitations. This issue has been litigated in several states, e.g., Country Mutual Insurance Co. v. Knight, 40 Ill.2d 523, 240 N.E.2d 612 (1968); Douglas Aircraft Co. v. Cranston, 24 Cal.Rptr. 851, 374 P.2d 819 (1962); cf. Standard Oil v. New Jersey, 5 N.J. 281, 74 A.2d 565 (1950). Even though the statute of limitations has run before the effective date of the Act, the holder must report and deliver the property to the state if the holder does not regularly enforce the statute. See South Carolina Tax Commission v. Metropolitan Life Insurance Co., 266 S.C. 34, 221 S.E.2d 522 (1975).

Subsection (b) provides that an administrator must commence an action against a holder within 10 years after the time the property was first reportable. Under existing law it is not clear that statutes of limitations apply to the state in compelling a holder to report or deliver unclaimed property. A holder may under the 1966 Act be subject to suit for an indeterminate period. Certain states have argued that Section 16 of the 1966 Act applies to states and thus there is no statute of limitations. The 10-year limitation period will provide a holder with a cutoff date on which it can rely.

§ 30. [Requests for Reports and Examination of Records]

(a) The administrator may require any person who has not filed a report to file a verified report stating whether or not the person is holding any unclaimed property reportable or deliverable under this Act.

(b) The administrator, at reasonable times and upon reasonable notice, may examine the records of any person to determine whether the person has complied with the provisions of this Act. The administrator may conduct the examination even if the person believes it is not in possession of any property reportable or deliverable under this Act.

(c) If a person is treated under Section 12 as the holder of the property only insofar as the interest of the business association in the property is concerned, the administrator, pursuant to subsection (b), may examine the records of the person if the administrator has given the notice required by subsection (b) to both the person and the business association at least 90 days before the examination.

(d) If an examination of the records of a person results in the disclosure of property reportable and deliverable under this Act, the administrator may assess the cost of the examination against the holder at the rate of $[ ] a day for each examiner, but in no case may the charges exceed the value of the property found to be reportable and deliverable. The cost of examination made pursuant to subsection (c) may be imposed only against the business association.

(e) If a holder fails after the effective date of this Act to maintain the records required by Section 31 and the records of the holder available for the periods subject to this Act are insufficient to permit the preparation of a report, the administrator may require the holder to report and pay such amounts as may reasonably be estimated from any available records.

Commissioners' Comment

This section is designed to facilitate compliance with the Act. Subsection (a) provides for the filing of a negative report if the administrator requires such a report and will minimize disruption which would otherwise be caused to the holder if an examination of records instead were conducted by the administrator. Subsection (b) is based on Section 23 of the 1966 Act. The 1966 Act authorizes examination if the administrator has reason to believe the holder has failed to report property. To require as prerequisite for an examination that a state has reason to believe information has been withheld *encourages litigation* and imposes an unnecessary burden on the state.

Subsection (c) is intended to provide a useful method whereby the administrator can conduct a single examination of a dividend disbursing agent or transfer agent serving in such capacity for numerous business associations. Under the 1966 Act, dividend disbursing agents and transfer agents have refused to permit any examination of records unless the affirmative consent of the business association was first obtained. This procedure has proved unwieldy and very expensive to the enforcing states. By requiring prior notice to the dividend disbursing agent and the business association, the agent will have an opportunity to make the necessary arrangements with its principal, the business association, to provide the necessary information in the event that the business association elects not to report the property in question voluntarily. This section, together with Section 33, will enable several states to conduct joint examinations of numerous holders at one time, saving substantial expense and thus permitting examinations which might otherwise be economically unfeasible.

Subsection (e) permits the use of estimates in instances where the holder has failed to report and deliver property that is abandoned and no longer has records with which to prepare such a report. Additionally, if the holder fails to maintain records of the last known address, states can assert claims based on any other records which might exist. Resort may be had to computer codes. This subsection does not resolve the issue of whether the domiciliary state of the holder can also claim the property from the holder. See comment to Section 1(11). While the holding in *Texas v. New Jersey* is intended to prevent multiple liability of holders, this subsection, viewed as a penalty for failure to maintain records of names and last known address, is not inconsistent with that decision. Subsection (e) is prospective only.

§ 31. [Retention of Records]

(a) Every holder required to file a report under Section 17, as to any property for which it has obtained the last known address of the owner, shall maintain a record of the name and last known address of the owner for 10 years after the property becomes reportable, except to the extent that a shorter time is provided in subsection (b) or by rule of the administrator.

(b) Any business association that sells in this State its travelers checks, money orders, or other similar written instruments, other than third-party bank checks on which the business association is directly liable, or that provides such instruments to others for sale in this State, shall maintain a record of those instruments while they remain outstanding, indicating the state and date of issue for 3 years after the date the property is reportable.

Commissioners' Comment

Many holders are not retaining records of addresses of owners. While Section 11(e) of the 1966 Act may be interpreted to require that those records be kept, this section makes express such a requirement if the holder initially had an address. The experience of several states has confirmed that substantial amounts of unclaimed property, for which at one time the holder had records of address, are now subject to claim only by the domiciliary state of the holder since the recorded address has not been retained.

This section does not require that the holder in the first instance obtain the address of the owner, a matter which each state may wish to consider as to specific types of property. For example, a record of the address of the purchaser or recipient of a gift certificate customarily is not obtained.

Initially, the period for which records of address must be obtained is established at 10 years from the date the property was first reportable as abandoned property. However, this section permits a state to shorten this period by rule. Because the reporting practices of holders vary, an administrator will want to consider such factors as the burden imposed on the holder in maintaining such records, the opportunity of returning the property, and the type of business of the holder. For example, in the case of property that would be reportable in the aggregate without the name and address of the apparent owner under Section 17, a state might adopt a rule providing for a relatively short record retention period on condition that the holder maintain a record sufficient to satisfy the requirements of *Texas v. New Jersey* that there be a last known address or that the state can prove that the last known address of the creditor was within its borders.

Subsection (b) is designed to insure that the information required for asserting a claim to travelers checks and money orders specified in subsection 4(c) is retained by the issuers of travelers checks and money orders.

§ 32. [Enforcement]

The administrator may bring an action in a court of competent jurisdiction to enforce this Act.

Commissioners' Comment

Section 32 authorises suit by the administrator in any court of competent jurisdiction. Although generally an administrator would be expected to sue in his own state, he can use the courts of another forum to enforce the Act. See Section 33. See also, Commonwealth of Pennsylvania v. Kervick, 60 N.J. 289, 288 A.2d 289 (1972).

§ 33. [Interstate Agreements and Cooperation; Joint and Reciprocal Actions With Other States]

(a) The administrator may enter into agreements with other states to exchange information needed to enable this or another state to audit or otherwise determine unclaimed property that it or another state may be entitled to subject to a claim of custody. The administrator by rule may require the reporting of information needed to enable compliance with agreements made pursuant to this section and prescribe the form.

(b) To avoid conflicts between the administrator's procedures and the procedures of administrators in other jurisdictions that enact the Uniform Unclaimed Property Act, the administrator, so far as is consistent with the purposes, policies, and provisions of this Act, before adopting, amending or repealing rules, shall advise and consult with administrators in other jurisdictions that enact substantially the Uniform Unclaimed Property Act and take into consideration the rules of administrators in other jurisdictions that enact the Uniform Unclaimed Property Act.

(c) The administrator may join with other states to seek enforcement of this Act against any person who is or may be holding property reportable under this Act.

(d) At the request of another state, the attorney general of this State may bring an action in the name of the administrator of the other state in any court of competent jurisdiction to enforce the unclaimed property laws of the other state against a holder in this State of property subject to escheat or a claim of abandonment by the other state, if the other state has agreed to pay expenses incurred by the attorney general in bringing the action.

(e) The administrator may request that the attorney general of another state or any other person bring an action in the name of the administrator in the other state. This State shall pay all expenses including attorney's fees in any action under this subsection. [The administrator may agree to pay the person bringing the action attorney's fees based in whole or in part on a percentage of the value of any property recovered in the action.] Any expenses paid pursuant to this subsection may not be deducted from the amount that is subject to the claim by the owner under this Act.

Commissioners' Comment

Cooperation among states is essential if abandoned property programs are to be efficiently administered. In recent years several states have joined together to audit major holders. Additionally, several states have entered into agreements to act as collection agents for each other. Interstate cooperation and the development of uniform reporting forms and uniform regulations will be of assistance to holders as well as program administrators. Section 33 encourages joint agreements and cooperation among the states.

In many instances holders apparently fail to report based on the correct assumption that individual and distant states will not go to the expense of auditing records. This section will permit spreading the very real expense of conducting audits among several collecting states and the pooling of information which should make enforcement of the Act less burdensome to the state and potentially less burdensome to major corporate holders. An agreement among the states might expressly relieve holders from reporting piecemeal to separate states. Instead, they might be able to file a single report of all abandoned property, wherever located, and regardless of the address of the owner.

Reciprocal agreements envisioned under subsection (c) do not require the consent of Congress under the Compact Clause of the Constitution, Art. I, § 10, cl. 3. The Supreme Court has held that the restriction of the Compact Clause is limited to combinations or agreements that tend to increase the political power of the states to such an extent that it interferes with the supremacy of the United States. United States Steel v. Multi-State Tax Commission, 434 U.S. 452 (1978). In *Multi-State Tax Commission* the Court upheld a tax compact, that had not been approved by Congress creating a permanent administrative body to perform audits of multi-state taxpayer operations, and at the request of a member state, to sue to enforce the audits in the courts of the member states.

This section simply authorises an economical approach to enforcing a state's claim under *Texas v. New Jersey*. Each state retains discretion to bring suit or to decide against such action, remaining free to adopt its own abandoned property policies. The position of the states will not be politically improved at the expense of the federal government although the process for claiming abandoned property will be more efficient.

Action by one state for another is expressly permitted by this section. In some cases the administrator of a state may deem it wise to seek counsel in a foreign jurisdiction. There may be small claims which would not justify individual action by the claimant state in a foreign forum, but if several states join forces and retain counsel in the holder state to sue for all of them, it might be administratively justified. This section expressly permits such joint action.

§ 34. [Interest and Penalties]

(a) A person who fails to pay or deliver property within the time prescribed by this Act [shall] [may be required to] pay to the administrator interest at the annual rate of [18 percent] [10 percent above the annual rate of discount, in effect on the date the property should have been paid or delivered, for the most recent issue of 52-week United States Treasury bills] on the property or value thereof from the date the property should have been paid or delivered.

(b) A person who willfully fails to render any report or perform other duties required under this Act shall pay a civil penalty of $[100] for each day the report is withheld or the duty is not performed, but not more than $[5000].

(c) A person who willfully fails to pay or deliver property to the administrator as required under this Act shall pay a civil penalty equal to 25 percent of the value of the property that should have been paid or delivered.

(d) A person who willfully refuses after written demand by the administrator to pay or deliver property to the administrator as required under this Act is guilty of a [ ] and upon conviction may be punished by a fine of not less than $[ ] nor more than $[ ], or imprisonment for not more than [ ] months, or both.

Commissioners' Comment

A major weakness of the 1966 Act was its ineffective penalty provision. Primary reliance on the criminal law as a compliance mechanism is misplaced. Often the reason for withholding property is economic, and economic sanctions in those cases are generally more effective in assuring compliance.

The experience of several states is that many holders find the economic incentive for noncompliance so great that violations of the law are frequent and extensive. The holder who neglects to report or pay has the use of property which is extremely valuable to it. The provision for civil penalties in subsection (a) is designed to give a holder sufficient incentive to report and pay over abandoned property. It is also designed to ensure that the true owners or their representatives, the states, receive the income from the property while it is wrongfully withheld. Similar provisions have been enacted by several states, for example, California (Cal.Civ.Pro.Code § 1577 (Supp.1981)) and Minnesota (Minn. Stat. § 345.55 subd. 3).

Criminal penalties are provided in subsection (d) for willful refusal, after written demand by an administrator, to pay or deliver property.

§ 35. [Agreement To Locate Reported Property]

All agreements to pay compensation to recover or assist in the recovery of property reported under Section 17, made within 24 months after the date payment or delivery is made under Section 19, are unenforceable.

Commissioners' Comment

This section is in part based on Cal.Civ.Pro.Code § 1582 (Supp.1981).

§ 36. [Foreign Transactions]

This Act does not apply to any property held, due and owing in a foreign country and arising out of a foreign transaction.

Commissioners' Comment

This provision is designed to exclude from the coverage of the Act wholly foreign transactions.

§ 37. [Effect of New Provisions; Clarification of Application]

(a) This Act does not relieve a holder of a duty that arose before the effective date of this Act to report, pay, or deliver property. A holder who did not comply with the law in effect before the effective date of this Act is subject to the applicable enforcement and penalty provisions that then existed and they are continued in effect for the purpose of this subsection, subject to Section 29(b).

(b) The initial report filed under this Act for property that was not required to be reported before the effective date of this Act but which is subject to this Act must include all items of property that would have been presumed abandoned during the 10-year period preceding the effective date of this Act as if this Act had been in effect during that period.

Commissioners' Comment

This Act adds, amends, clarifies and repeals sections of the 1966 Act. The new Act may provide for the presumption of abandonment of one type of property that arguably was not subject to a presumption of abandonment under the 1966 Act. For example, the 1966 Act did not expressly cover underlying share certificates unless they were held or owing by business associations. Underlying share certificates are now expressly covered in this Act pursuant to Section 10. Additionally, the state of last known address under the 1966 Act perhaps could not reach property otherwise presumed abandoned where the holder was not doing business in the state of last known address.

Subsection (a) provides that if a state had an unclaimed property law prior to the adoption of this Act, a holder is not relieved of his duty to report and pay over the property abandoned under the Act then existing.

Subsection (b) deals with the problem of how far back a holder must property not subject to the prior Act must be paid to the state under this Act. The period chosen is 10 years. A holder is required to pay to the state any property which 10 years before the date of enactment would have been payable in the enacting state if this Act had been in effect. For example, if a state enacts the new Act effective January 1, 1983 for property not previously presumed abandoned, the holder must report it if, as of January 1, 1973, it had been unclaimed for the abandonment period. A similar provision is found in Section 11(g) of the 1966 Act.

However, some property subject to this Act but which was not covered by the then existing Act may have been paid to another state. If a holder has already paid this property to another state under its then existing unclaimed or abandoned property laws, it is not required to pay again to this State. Nothing in this section, however, prohibits this State from making a claim on the state to which the property was originally paid.

§ 38. [Rules]

The administrator may adopt necessary rules to carry out the provisions of this Act.

§ 39. [Severability]

If any provision of this Act or the application thereof to any person or circumstance is held invalid, the invalidity shall not affect other provisions or applications of this Act which can be given effect without the invalid provision or application, and to this end the provisions of this Act are severable.

§ 40. [Uniformity of Application and Construction]

This Act shall be applied and construed as to effectuate its general purpose to make uniform the law with respect to the subject of this Act among states enacting it.

§ 41. [Short Title]

This Act may be cited as the Uniform Unclaimed Property Act (1981).

§ 42. [Repeal]

The following acts and parts of acts are hereby repealed:

(a)

(b)

(c)

§ 43. [Time of Taking Effect]

This Act shall take effect ________

Unclaimed Property (1981 Act)

Table of Comparative Sections

Showing Sections of the Uniform Unclaimed Property Act (1981) and the 1966 Uniform Disposition of Unclaimed Property Act.

Uniform Unclaimed Property Act	*1966 Uniform Act*
Section 1 [Definitions and Use of Terms.]	Section 1
Section 2 [Property Presumed Abandoned; General Rule.]	Section 9
Section 3 [General Rules for Taking Custody of Intangible Unclaimed Property.]	No comparable section
Section 4 [Travelers Checks and Money Orders.]	Section 2
Section 5 [Checks, Drafts and Similar Instruments Issued or Certified by Banking and Financial Organizations.]	Section 2
Section 6 [Bank Deposits and Funds in Financial Organizations.]	Section 2
Section 7 [Funds Owing Under Life Insurance Policies.]	Section 3
Section 8 [Deposits Held by Utilities.]	Section 4
Section 9 [Refunds Held by Business Associations.]	Section 4
Section 10 [Stock and Other Intangible Interests in Business Associations.]	Section 5
Section 11 [Property of Business Associations Held in Course of Dissolution.]	Section 6
Section 12 [Property Held by Agents and Fiduciaries.]	Section 7
Section 13 [Property Held by Courts and Public Agencies.]	Section 8
Section 14 [Gift Certificates and Credit Memos.]	Section 9
Section 15 [Wages.]	Section 9
Section 16 [Contents of Safe Deposit Box or Other Safekeeping Repository.]	Section 2(d)
Section 17 [Report of Abandoned Property.]	Section 11
Section 18 [Notice and Publication of Lists of Abandoned Property.]	Section 12
Section 19 [Payment or Delivery of Abandoned Property.]	Section 13
Section 20 [Custody by State; Holder Relieved From Liability; Reimbursement of Holder Paying Claim; Reclaiming for Owner; Defense of Holder; Payment of Safe Deposit Box or Repository Charges.]	Section 14
Section 21 [Crediting of Dividends, Interest or Increments to Owner's Account.]	No comparable section

Uniform Unclaimed Property Act	*1966 Uniform Act*
Section 22 [Public Sale of Abandoned Property.]	Section 17
Section 23 [Deposit of Funds.]	Section 18
Section 24 [Filing of Claim With Administrator.]	Sections 19 and 20
Section 25 [Claim of Another State to Recover Property; Procedure.]	No comparable section
Section 26 [Action to Establish Claim.]	Section 21
Section 27 [Election to Take Payment or Delivery.]	Section 22
Section 28 [Destruction or Disposition of Property Having Insubstantial Commercial Value; Immunity from Liability.]	No comparable section
Section 29 [Periods of Limitation.]	Section 16
Section 30 [Requests for Reports and Examination of Records.]	Section 23
Section 31 [Retention of Records.]	No comparable section
Section 32 [Enforcement.]	Section 24
Section 33 [Interstate Agreements and Cooperation; Joint and Reciprocal Actions with Other States.]	No comparable section
Section 34 [Interest and Penalties.]	Section 25
Section 35 [Agreement to Locate Reported Property.]	No comparable section
Section 36 [Foreign Transactions.]	No comparable section
Section 37 [Effect of New Provisions; Clarification of Application.]	No comparable section
Section 38 [Rules.]	Section 26
Section 39 [Severability.]	Section 28
Section 40 [Uniformity of Application and Construction.]	Section 29
Section 41 [Short Title.]	Section 30
Section 42 [Repeal.]	Section 31
Section 43 [Time of Taking Effect.]	Section 32

¶ 12,005 Uniform Unclaimed Property Act (1995)

Drafted by the National Conference of Commissioners on Uniform State Laws and by it approved and recommended for enactment in all the states at its annual conference meeting in its one-hundred-and-fourth year in Kansas City, Missouri, July 28–August 4, 1995. With Prefatory Note and comments. Copyright 1995 by National Conference of Commissioners on Uniform State Laws. Approved by the American Bar Association, Orlando, Florida, August 6, 1996.

Copies of this Act may be obtained from:

National Conference of Commissioners on Uniform State Laws
211 East Ontario Street, Suite 1300
Chicago, Illinois 60611
312-915-0195

Uniform Unclaimed Property Act (1995)

The Committee that acted for the National Conference of Commissioners on Uniform State Laws in preparing the Uniform Unclaimed Property Act (1995) was as follows:

Willis E. Sullivan, III, P.O. Box 359, 1423 Tyrell Lane, Boise, ID 83701, *Chair*

Owen L. Anderson, University of Oklahoma, College of Law, 300 Timberdell Road, Norman, OK 73019

David D. Biklen, Law Revision Commission, Room 509A, State Capitol, Hartford, CT 06106

Fred C. Cornish, Suite 917, 321 South Boston, Tulsa, OK 74103

Edward I. Cutler, P.O. Box 3239, Tampa, FL 33601

Stanley M. Fisher, 1100 Huntington Building, Cleveland, OH 44115

Patrick C. Guillot, Suite 900, 8080 North Central Expressway, Dallas, TX 75206

John F. Hayes, Suite 260, 335 North Washington, Hutchinson, KS 67504

Raymond P. Pepe, 13th Floor, 240 North Third Street, Harrisburg, PA 17101

Robert E. Sullivan, 112 Hillcrest Loop, Missoula, MT 59803

Robert Williams, Suite 800, 770 L Street, Sacramento, CA 95814

Curtis D. Forslund, 5555 Via Entrada, Tucson, AZ 85718, *Reporter*

EX OFFICIO

Richard C. Hite, 200 West Douglas Avenue, Suite 600, Wichita, KS 67202, *President*

W. Jackson Willoughby, Placer County Municipal Court, 300 Taylor Street, Roseville, CA 95678, *Chair, Division B*

EXECUTIVE DIRECTOR

Fred H. Miller, University of Oklahoma, College of Law, 300 Timberdell Road, Norman, OK 73019, *Executive Director*

William J. Pierce, 1505 Roxbury Road, Ann Arbor, MI 48104, *Executive Director Emeritus*

ADVISORS

E. Suzanne Darling, *National Association of Unclaimed Property Administrators*

Sonya M. Davis, *American Bar Association*

David J. Epstein, *Boston, MA*

ADDITIONAL PARTICIPANTS

Thomas E. Haider, *Travelers Express Company, Inc.*

Todd D. Lebsack, *National Retail Federation*

Stephen P. Norman, *American Society of Corporate Secretaries, Inc.*

Carol B. Rosen, *Keane Tracers Inc.*

Paula Young Smith, *National Association of Division Order Analysts*

Todd R. Stimmel, *The National Abandoned Property Processing Corporation*

Mathew H. Street, *American Bankers Association*

Robert A. Wittie, *Investment Company Institute*

Contents

Prefatory Note

Statement of the History of the Act

This Act is preceded by the 1954 Uniform Disposition of Unclaimed Property Act (1954), which was revised in 1966, and the Uniform Unclaimed Property Act (1981). The 1954 Act was drafted during a period of conflicting legislation among the various States and several Supreme Court decisions in the late 1940's and early 1950's. In 1965, these conflicts were resolved by the decision in *Texas v. New Jersey*, 379 U.S. 674 (1965), which established a set of priorities for claimant States. These rules of priority were then adopted in the 1981 Act. They were re-examined and reaffirmed in *Delaware v. New York*, — U.S. —, 113 S.Ct. 1550, 123 L.Ed.2d 211 (1993). Although the *Delaware* Court made no change in the rules of priority, it clarified the issue of how to determine the identity of the "debtor"—the "holder" under this Act—when payments by intermediaries are at stake. The "debtor" will be defined by reference to the state law that creates the property interest; an intermediary which holds property in its own name will generally be the debtor, and not the original obligor which has satisfied its obligation by transmitting payment to the intermediary. *Delaware v. New York* also makes it clear that no State may supersede the Court's priority rules by seeking to establish different priorities under state law. See Comments to Section 1 and Section 4 for further discussion of these rules.

This Act retains the custodial features of the 1954 Act and the 1981 Act. Thus, the State does not take title to unclaimed property, but takes custody only, and holds the property in perpetuity for the owner.

A State may enforce its claim of custody in the courts of other jurisdictions, see *Commonwealth of Pennsylvania v. Kervick*, 60 N.J. 289, 288 A.2d 289 (1972), or in its own courts. Even if a holder does not do business in the State, that State should be able to require the holder to report and deliver unclaimed property in the State, under the *Texas v. New Jersey* rationale, based on the common law rule of *mobilia sequunter personam*: the right of succession to personal property is governed by the law of the owner's domicile. See also *Connecticut Mutual Life Insurance Co. v. Moore*, 333 U.S. 541, 546-47 (1947), where the Supreme Court described the State as a "conservator" when claiming property under a custodial unclaimed property law. The Court in *Standard Oil Co. v. New Jersey*, 347 U.S. 428, 437 (1951), characterized the Moore case as involving a "conservation statute." See generally Epstein, McThenia and Forslund, "Unclaimed Property Law and Reporting Forms," sections 2.01, 3.02, 4.01 (Matt. Bend. 1984).

Uniform Unclaimed Property Act (1995)

SECTION 1. DEFINITIONS. In this [Act]:

(1) "Administrator" means [insert name of appropriate officer].

(2) "Apparent owner" means a person whose name appears on the records of a holder as the person entitled to property held, issued, or owing by the holder.

(3) "Business association" means a corporation, joint stock company, investment company, partnership, unincorporated association, joint venture, limited liability company, business trust, trust company, [land bank], safe deposit company, [safekeeping depository], financial organization, insurance company, mutual fund, utility, or other business entity consisting of one or more persons, whether or not for profit.

(4) "Domicile" means the State of incorporation of a corporation and the State of the principal place of business of a holder other than a corporation.

(5) "Financial organization" means a savings and loan association, [building and loan association, savings bank, industrial bank,] bank, banking organization, or credit union.

(6) "Holder" means a person obligated to hold for the account of, or deliver or pay to, the owner property that is subject to this [Act].

(7) "Insurance company" means an association, corporation, or fraternal or mutual benefit organization, whether or not for profit, engaged in the business of providing life endowments, annuities, or insurance, including accident, burial, casualty, credit life, contract performance, dental, disability, fidelity, fire, health, hospitalization, illness, life, malpractice, marine, mortgage, surety, wage protection, and workers' compensation insurance.

(8) "Mineral" means gas; oil; coal; other gaseous, liquid, and solid hydrocarbons; oil shale; cement material; sand and gravel; road material; building stone; chemical raw material; gemstone; fissionable and nonfissionable ores; colloidal and other clay; steam and other geothermal resource; or any other substance defined as a mineral by the law of this State.

(9) "Mineral proceeds" means amounts payable for the extraction, production, or sale of minerals, or, upon the abandonment of those payments, all payments that become payable thereafter. The term includes amounts payable:

(i) for the acquisition and retention of a mineral lease, including bonuses, royalties, compensatory royalties, shut-in royalties, minimum royalties, and delay rentals;

(ii) for the extraction, production, or sale of minerals, including net revenue interests, royalties, overriding royalties, extraction payments, and production payments; and

(iii) under an agreement or option, including a joint operating agreement, unit agreement, pooling agreement, and farm-out agreement.

(10) "Money order" includes an express money order and a personal money order, on which the remitter is the purchaser. The term does not include a bank money order or any other instrument sold by a financial organization if the seller has obtained the name and address of the payee.

(11) "Owner" means a person who has a legal or equitable interest in property subject to this [Act] or the person's legal representative. The term includes a depositor in the case of a deposit, a beneficiary in the case of a trust other than a deposit in trust, and a creditor, claimant, or payee in the case of other property.

(12) "Person" means an individual, business association, financial organization, estate, trust, government, governmental subdivision, agency, or instrumentality, or any other legal or commercial entity.

(13) "Property" means tangible property described in Section 3 or a fixed and certain interest in intangible property that is held, issued, or owed in the course of a holder's business, or by a government, governmental subdivision, agency, or instrumentality, and all income or increments therefrom. The term includes property that is referred to as or evidenced by:

(i) money, a check, draft, deposit, interest, or dividend;

(ii) credit balance, customer's overpayment, gift certificate, security deposit, refund, credit memorandum, unpaid wage, unused ticket, mineral proceeds, or unidentified remittance;

(iii) stock or other evidence of ownership of an interest in a business association or financial organization;

(iv) a bond, debenture, note, or other evidence of indebtedness;

(v) money deposited to redeem stocks, bonds, coupons, or other securities or to make distributions;

(vi) an amount due and payable under the terms of an annuity or insurance policy, including policies providing life insurance, property and casualty insurance, workers' compensation insurance, or health and disability insurance; and

(vii) an amount distributable from a trust or custodial fund established under a plan to provide health, welfare, pension, vacation, severance, retirement, death, stock purchase, profit sharing, employee savings, supplemental unemployment insurance, or similar benefits.

(14) "Record" means information that is inscribed on a tangible medium or that is stored in an electronic or other medium and is retrievable in perceivable form.

(15) "State" means a State of the United States, the District of Columbia, the Commonwealth of Puerto Rico, or any territory or insular possession subject to the jurisdiction of the United States.

(16) "Utility" means [a person who owns or operates for public use any plant, equipment, real property, franchise, or license for the transmission of communications or the production, storage, transmission, sale, delivery, or furnishing of electricity, water, steam, or gas] [insert cross reference to statute defining public utility].

Comment

The definitions reflect, pursuant to *Texas v. New Jersey*, 379 U.S. 674, 85 S.Ct. 626, 13 L.Ed. 2d 596 (1965), the fact that the Act applies to persons in other States who are holding property, eliminating any requirement that those persons be engaged in business in the enacting State. The obligation of a holder to report to all States in which a creditor had an address, or in which a transaction took place, or which is the holder's domicile, is now well established in the abandoned property statutes of the States and in the decisions of the Supreme Court. The holder's obligation to report is not confined to situations where the holder is authorized to do business or actually transacts business in a State. These jurisdictional rules are spelled out in detail in Section 4.

Paragraph (2) defines "apparent owner" in terms of reference to the person who appears on the holder's records to be the person entitled to the property. The right of a State to claim abandoned property depends on the information in the holder's records concerning the apparent owner's identification. It is of no consequence that without notice to the holder, the owner may have transferred the property to another person. In *Nellius v. Tampax, Inc.*, 394 A.2d 333 (Del. Ch. Ct. 1978), the court held that the address of the apparent, not the actual, owner controlled. The holder is not required to ascertain the name of the current owner or resolve a dispute between the owner of record and a successor contesting ownership. However, nothing in this Act prohibits the actual owner from recovering the property, pursuant to Sections 10 and 15, from the holder or the administrator. Similarly, the State of last known address of the actual owner can recover the property, pursuant to Section 14, from the State which initially receives custody.

The definition of "business association" in paragraph (3) expressly includes mutual funds, which previously were covered in general terms.

The definition of "holder" in paragraph 5 is a clarification. There had been some confusion in the past over the identity of the holder of an obligation that had been transferred by the original obligor, as in the payment of dividends on corporate stock. As held by the Supreme Court in *Delaware v. New York*, the holder is the person indebted under the applicable state law. Thus, if the original debtor, the dividend-paying corporation, has satisfied its debt under its share contract and under state law by transmitting payment to an intermediary, which has undertaken to make the payment, the intermediary becomes the debtor. The holder thus is "a person obligated," *i.e.*, a person who could be sued successfully by the owner for refusing to make payment.

Although the 1981 Act defined "last known address" as "a description of the location of the apparent owner sufficient for the purpose of the delivery of mail," that Act indicated some uncertainty over whether this was an accurate interpretation of *Texas v. New Jersey*, since this definition was accompanied by a Commissioners' Comment that appeared to be at odds with the definition itself. Thus, the Comment stated that "Where a holder originally had the address of the owner and it has been subsequently destroyed, a computer code may be one way of establishing an address within the state." "Last known address" is no longer defined in the Act; instead, the sections dealing with the jurisdictional rules (Sections 4 and 14) are rewritten so that they define, individually, the rules of the States' priorities of taking.

The touchstone of those rules of priority is *Texas v. New Jersey*, 379 U.S. 674, 85 S.Ct. 626, 13 L.Ed. 2d 596 (1965), in which the Court established as a primary rule that unclaimed property goes to "the State of the last known address of the creditor, as shown by the debtor's books and records." *Id.* at 681-82, 85 S.Ct. at 631, 13 L.Ed. 2d at 601. Where the debtor has "no record of any address at all," the state of corporate domicile could take, *id.* at 682, 85 S.Ct. at 631, 13 L.Ed. 2d at 601, subject to proof by another State "that the last known address of the creditor was within its borders." *Id.*, 13 L.Ed. 2d at 602. See also *Pennsylvania v. New York*, 407 U.S. 206, 32 L.Ed. 2d 693, 92 S.Ct. 2075 (1972).

In *Delaware v. New York*, the Court reaffirmed the rules of *Texas v. New Jersey*: Delaware, as the State of corporate domicile, would take the property initially where the holder's records did not contain a last known address. That delivery of the property to Delaware, however, would not cut off the rights of another State to later claim the property from Delaware. For instance:

On remand, if New York can establish by reference to debtors' records that the creditors who were owed particular securities distributions had last known addresses in New York, New York's right to escheat under the primary rule will supersede Delaware's right under the secondary rule. As we noted in *Texas*, "the State of corporate domicile should be allowed to ... retai[n] the property for itself only until some other State comes forward with proof that it has a superior right to escheat." 379 U.S., at 682. Accord, *Pennsylvania*, 407 U.S., at 210-211. If New York or any other claimant State fails to offer such proof on a transaction-by-transaction basis or to provide some other proper mechanism for ascertaining creditors' last known addresses, the creditor's State will not prevail under the primary rule, and the secondary rule will control.

Id. at ___, 113 S.Ct. at 1561-62, 123 L.Ed. 2d at 227-28. (Deletions in original.)

In sum, *Delaware v. New York* requires that some "proper mechanism" show that the owner had an address within the State that asserts a primary claim. A computer code would appear to be such a means of proof. On the other hand, showing that the transaction took place in the State would not be sufficient proof of an owner's address. *Pennsylvania v. New York*, 407 U.S. 206, 92 S.Ct. 2075, 32 L.Ed. 2d 693 (1972).

For purposes other than these jurisdictional rules—i.e., the holder's duties of reporting and maintenance of records and the States' duties of publication—the "last known address" will depend on the nature and extent of the holder's records. Thus, the holder will include in its report the best address it has, which may or may not include a street address, or, for example, an "E mail" address.

The definition of "money order" in paragraph (10) is designed to distinguish between personal money orders issued by business entities which are not financial organizations, which have a seven year holding period, and those issued by financial organizations, which have a five year holding period.

The Act provides exclusively for the disposition of unclaimed intangible property and does not apply to tangible property, with one exception: Section 3 applies to tangible property contained in safe deposit boxes. Paragraph (12), defining property, is not intended as a substantive addition to the coverage of the 1981 Act. It is, however, intended to be all-inclusive; the descriptions of property interests that are set forth as examples are not limiting, but are stated to help holders identify kinds of property interests which otherwise may be overlooked. Thus, "property" is not the check, note, certificate or other document that evidences the property interest, but the underlying right or obligation. See *Blue Cross of Northern California v. Cory*, 120 Cal. App. 3d 723, 174 Cal. Rptr. 901 (1981) ("right to be paid" is the "'intangible personal property' (or 'chose in action') ... which is recognized in the UPL"). The requirement that the right be "fixed and certain" excludes unliquidated claims from the coverage of the Act, such as disputed tort claims.

Many States already have laws that define utilities. Paragraph (15) gives a State the option to adopt the Act's definition of a utility, or another definition contained in existing law. The term is intended to be broadly applied.

SECTION 2. PRESUMPTIONS OF ABANDONMENT.

(a) Property is presumed abandoned if it is unclaimed by the apparent owner during the time set forth below for the particular property:

(1) traveler's check, 15 years after issuance;

(2) money order, seven years after issuance;

(3) stock or other equity interest in a business association or financial organization, including a security entitlement under [Article 8 of the Uniform Commercial Code], five years after the earlier of (i) the date of the most recent dividend, stock split, or other distribution unclaimed by the apparent owner, or (ii) the date of the second mailing of a statement of account or other notification or communication that was returned as undeliverable or after the holder discontinued mailings, notifications, or communications to the apparent owner;

(4) debt of a business association or financial organization, other than a bearer bond or an original issue discount bond, five years after the date of the most recent interest payment unclaimed by the apparent owner;

(5) a demand, savings, or time deposit, including a deposit that is automatically renewable, five years after the earlier of maturity or the date of the last indication by the owner of interest in the property; but a deposit that is automatically renewable is deemed matured for purposes of this section upon its initial date of maturity, unless the owner has consented to a renewal at or about the time of the renewal and the consent is in writing or is evidenced by a memorandum or other record on file with the holder;

(6) money or credits owed to a customer as a result of a retail business transaction, three years after the obligation accrued;

(7) gift certificate, three years after December 31 of the year in which the certificate was sold, but if redeemable in merchandise only, the amount abandoned is deemed to be [60] percent of the certificate's face value;

(8) amount owed by an insurer on a life or endowment insurance policy or an annuity that has matured or terminated, three years after the obligation to pay arose or, in the case of a policy or annuity payable upon proof of death, three years after the insured has attained, or would have attained if living, the limiting age under the mortality table on which the reserve is based;

(9) property distributable by a business association or financial organization in a course of dissolution, one year after the property becomes distributable;

(10) property received by a court as proceeds of a class action, and not distributed pursuant to the judgment, one year after the distribution date;

(11) property held by a court, government, governmental subdivision, agency, or instrumentality, one year after the property becomes distributable;

(12) wages or other compensation for personal services, one year after the compensation becomes payable;

(13) deposit or refund owed to a subscriber by a utility, one year after the deposit or refund becomes payable;

(14) property in an individual retirement account, defined benefit plan, or other account or plan that is qualified for tax deferral under the income tax laws of the United States, three years after the earliest of the date of the distribution or attempted distribution of the property, the date of the required distribution as stated in the plan or trust agreement governing the plan, or the date, if determinable by the holder, specified in the income tax laws of the United States by which distribution of the property must begin in order to avoid a tax penalty; and

(15) all other property, five years after the owner's right to demand the property or after the obligation to pay or distribute the property arises, whichever first occurs.

(b) At the time that an interest is presumed abandoned under subsection (a), any other property right accrued or accruing to the owner as a result of the interest, and not previously presumed abandoned, is also presumed abandoned.

(c) Property is unclaimed if, for the applicable period set forth in subsection (a), the apparent owner has not communicated in writing or by other means reflected in a contemporaneous record prepared by or on behalf of the holder, with the holder concerning the property or the account in which the property is held, and has not otherwise indicated an interest in the property. A communication with an owner by a person other than the holder or its representative who has not in writing identified the property to the owner is not an indication of interest in the property by the owner.

(d) An indication of an owner's interest in property includes:

(i) the presentment of a check or other instrument of payment of a dividend or other distribution made with respect to an account or underlying stock or other interest in a business association or financial organization or, in the case of a distribution made by electronic or similar means, evidence that the distribution has been received;

(ii) owner-directed activity in the account in which the property is held, including a direction by the owner to increase, decrease, or change the amount or type of property held in the account;

(iii) the making of a deposit to or withdrawal from a bank account; and

(iv) the payment of a premium with respect to a property interest in an insurance policy; but the application of an automatic premium loan provision or other nonforfeiture provision contained in an insurance policy does not prevent a policy from maturing or terminating if the insured has died or the insured or the beneficiary of the policy has otherwise become entitled to the proceeds before the depletion of the cash surrender value of a policy by the application of those provisions.

(e) Property is payable or distributable for purposes of this [Act] notwithstanding the owner's failure to make demand or present an instrument or document otherwise required to obtain payment.

Comment

Section 2 continues the general proposition that all intangible property is within the coverage of this Act. It provides in a single section for all the various periods of abandonment that were separately stated in several sections of the 1981 Act. With limited exceptions this reorganization does not alter the bases for presuming abandonment of the property from that established in the 1981 Act, but merely restates those standards in a unified section, more easily applied, with less repetition. One exception is that whereas the 1981 Act exempted from the presumption of abandonment certain property held by a bank if the bank held other property of the depositor not presumptively abandoned, the present Act does not. It was the conclusion of the Commissioners that an owner's knowledge of some property does not necessarily imply knowledge of all his or her property held by the bank, and that the owner is entitled to the protection of this Act as to all the owner's property.

This section treats underlying bond obligations the same as underlying stock, except as to bearer bonds and original issue discount bonds. Thus, registered interest paying bonds will be presumed abandoned five years after the date of an unpresented instrument issued to pay interest. In the case of bearer bonds, however, although interest held on deposit for more than five years that has not been paid out as a result of failure to present a coupon for payment will be considered abandoned, the underlying principal represented by the bearer certificate, provided such certificate is not held by an agent due to a mail return or other similar circumstance, will not be considered abandoned even if the coupons that were attached to that certificate at the time of original issuance have not been presented for payment. Where interest is accrued but not paid until the return of principal at the time the obligation matures or is called, and there is no making of periodic interest payments, there is not the same motivation for bond holders to communicate with the trustee or paying agent as in the case of interest paying bonds, and a lack of communication should not give rise to a presumption of abandonment. Therefore, bearer bonds and original issue discount bonds are excluded from paragraph (4) of this section, and will fall instead under paragraph (15). Those bonds will be presumed abandoned five years after the issuer's obligation to pay arises, i.e., five years after call or maturity.

The 1981 Act shortened the general dormancy period from 7 years to 5 years. Certain exceptions continue to be appropriate. For instance, statistical evidence indicates that a period of 15 years continues to be appropriate in the case of travelers checks, and seven years in the case of personal money orders and money orders issued by express companies. Also, in certain instances shorter periods are appropriate. For instance, the likelihood of finding the owner of a payroll check is materially decreased after one year. Hence, there is a one year dormancy period for unclaimed wages. Coverage of consumer credits is specifically provided, which is a clarification of the 1981 Act. The term covers credits owed on consumer transactions such as returns of merchandise, cancellation of layaways, and various kinds of deposits. The existence and amounts of such credits will of course be dependent on the terms of the contract between the holder and the consumer.

The dormancy period for unpaid distributions from retirement accounts and plans has been modified to shorten the period of presumed abandonment from five to three years, since an earlier date of presumed abandonment should be of assistance in assuring that the assets of the plan are ultimately claimed by their owner.

Because the unclaimed property laws are matters of traditional state powers, are laws of general application, and have only a tenuous, remote and peripheral impact on ERISA plans, it has been held that they are not pre-empted by federal law. *Aetna Life Ins. Co. v. Borges*, 869 F.2d 142 (2nd Cir. 1989); *Attorney General v. Blue Cross and Blue Shield of Michigan*, 168 Mich. App. 372, 424 N.W.2d 54 (Ct. App. 1988), *appeal denied*, No. 83788 (March 31, 1989). These cases declined to follow two advisory opinions to the contrary, issued by the Department of Labor (Opinions 78-32A, December 22, 1978, and 79-30A, May 14, 1979). Thereafter, notwithstanding the Second Circuit and Michigan decisions, the Department continued to adhere to its position that unclaimed property laws "relate to" ERISA, and are thus pre-empted, in a letter opinion issued March 3, 1995. 22 BNA Pension & Benefits Reporter 743 (1995). That opinion relied on *Ingersoll-Rand Co. v. McClendon*, 498 U.S. 133 (1990), as holding that pre-emption extended to state laws that had only an indirect economic affect on ERISA plans. Subsequently, the Supreme Court in *New York State Conference of Blue Cross & Blue Shield Plans v. Travelers Ins. Co.*, ___ U.S. ___ (63 Law Week 4372, April 26, 1995), expounded a much narrower meaning of *Ingersoll-Rand*. The case held that ERISA does not pre-empt the imposition of statutorily-man-dated surcharges on bills of hospital patients whose commercial insurance coverage is purchased by an ERISA plan, or on HMOs insofar as their membership fees are paid by an ERISA plan. The Court emphasized that even though such state statutes would affect choices made by plan administrators, the ERISA pre-emption was not so broad as to nullify those state laws. The Court emphasized the basic presumption that "Congress does not intend to supplant state law" (63 LW at 4374). The Court said that *Ingersoll-Rand* does not hold that "merely economic influence" on administrative decisions will trigger pre-emption. (63 LW at 4376.) *Ingersoll-Rand* was explained to hold only that pre-emption would be found where state law produced "such acute, albeit indirect, economic effects" as to force a certain substantive scheme of coverage or effectively restrict insurance choices. (*Id.* at 4375.) Thus, "the basic thrust of the

[ERISA] pre-emption clause, then, was to avoid a multiplicity of regulation in order to permit the nationally uniform administration of employee benefit plans." (*Id.* at 4375.) *See also Mackey v. Lanier Collection Agency & Service, Inc.*, 486 U.S. 825 (1988), holding that ERISA does not preempt a state garnishment statute under which a creditor may reach plan participants' benefits. A state claim under its unclaimed property law would appear to be no more intrusive to the federal regulatory scheme than its garnishment laws. Accordingly, with one exception, the final distribution of assets of a terminated plan, which is governed by 29 U.S.C. sec. 1350, this Act presumes that it is not preempted by ERISA.

Intangible property held by a utility other than subscribers' deposits and refunds are subject to the five year rule of subsection (a)(15).

Subsection (e) is intended to make clear that property is reportable notwithstanding that the owner, who has lost or otherwise forgotten his or her entitlement to property, fails to present to the holder evidence of ownership or to make a demand for payment. See *Connecticut Mutual Life Insurance Co. v. Moore*, 333 U.S. 541 (1948), in which the Court stated: "When the state undertakes the protection of abandoned claims, it would be beyond a reasonable requirement to compel the state to comply with conditions that may be quite proper as between the contracting parties." See also *Provident Institution for Savings v. Malone*, 221 U.S.. 660 (1911), involving savings account; *Insurance Co. of North America v. Knight*, 8 Ill. App. 3d 871, 291 N.E.2d 40 (1972), involving negotiable instruments, and *People v. Marshall Field & Co.*, 83 Ill. App. 3d 811, 404 N.E.2d 368 (1980), involving gift certificates. With respect to gift certificates, see also Section 19(a), which invalidates private periods of limitation. Thus, gift certificates will be reportable notwithstanding language on the certificate purporting to avoid escheat by creating an expiration date prior to the time of presumed abandonment. Section (c) also obviates the result reached in *Oregon Racing Comm. v. Multonamah Kennel Club*, 242 Or. 572, 411 P.2d 63 (1963), involving unpresented winning parimutuel tickets.

Since the holder is indemnified against any loss resulting from the delivery of the property to the administrator, no possible harm can result in requiring that holders turn over the property, even though the owner has not presented proof of death or surrendered the insurance policy, savings account passbook, the gift certificate, winning racing ticket, or other memorandum of ownership.

SECTION 3. CONTENTS OF SAFE DEPOSIT BOX OR OTHER SAFEKEEPING DEPOSITORY. Tangible property held in a safe deposit box or other safekeeping depository in this State in the ordinary course of the holder's business and proceeds resulting from the sale of the property permitted by other law, are presumed abandoned if the property remains unclaimed by the owner for more than five years after expiration of the lease or rental period on the box or other depository.

Comment

Section 3 parallels Section 2(d) of the 1966 Act and Section 16 of the 1981 Act. This section is not intended to cover property left in places other than safekeeping depositories, for example, airport lockers or field warehouses. Its coverage is limited to tangible property held in safe deposit boxes in banks and financial institutions. Intangible property, evidence of which is found in a safe deposit box, is covered by Section 2.

SECTION 4. RULES FOR TAKING CUSTODY. Except as otherwise provided in this [Act] or by other statute of this State, property that is presumed abandoned, whether located in this or another State, is subject to the custody of this State if:

(1) the last known address of the apparent owner, as shown on the records of the holder, is in this State;

(2) the records of the holder do not reflect the identity of the person entitled to the property and it is established that the last known address of the person entitled to the property is in this State;

(3) the records of the holder do not reflect the last known address of the apparent owner and it is established that:

> (i) the last known address of the person entitled to the property is in this State; or
>
> (ii) the holder is domiciled in this State or is a government or governmental subdivision, agency, or instrumentality of this State and has not previously paid or delivered the property to the State of the last known address of the apparent owner or other person entitled to the property;

(4) the last known address of the apparent owner, as shown on the records of the holder, is in a State that does not provide for the escheat or custodial taking of the property and the holder is domiciled in this State or is a government or governmental subdivision, agency, or instrumentality of this State;

(5) the last known address of the apparent owner, as shown on the records of the holder, is in a foreign country and the holder is domiciled in this State or is a government or governmental subdivision, agency, or instrumentality of this State;

(6) the transaction out of which the property arose occurred in this State, the holder is domiciled in a State that does not provide for the escheat or custodial taking of the property, and the last known address of the apparent owner or other person entitled to the property is unknown or is in a State that does not provide for the escheat or custodial taking of the property; or

(7) the property is a traveler's check or money order purchased in this State, or the issuer of the traveler's check or money order has its principal place of business in this State and the issuer's records show that the instrument was purchased in a State that does not provide for the escheat or custodial taking of the property, or do not show the State in which the instrument was purchased.

Comment

Section 4 describes the general circumstances under which a State may claim abandoned intangible property. This section closely follows the language of *Texas v. New Jersey*, in which the court reasoned that unclaimed property is an asset of the creditor and should generally be paid to the creditor State, i.e., the State of residence of the apparent owner. Consistent with that reasoning it held that unclaimed intangible property is subject to escheat or custody as unclaimed property first by the State of the owner's last known address. (See Section 1(7) and the Comment with regard to "last known address.") If that State cannot claim the property, the State of the holder's domicile is entitled to custody. Consistent with the court's concern for a simple rule which would avoid the complexities of proving domicile and residence the court established the priority on the basis of information contained in the holder's records. Where the holder's records do not show that the owner had an address within the State, the second priority claimant, the State of domicile of the holder, is entitled to claim the property. Another State can later assume custody from the State of the holder's domicile by showing that the last known address of the owner was within its borders. Likewise, if the State of last known address does not have an unclaimed property law which applies to the property, the State of the holder's domicile can take the property, again subject to the right of the State of last known address to recover the property if and when it enacts an unclaimed property or escheat law.

Paragraph (1) restates the factual situation in *Texas v. New Jersey*. As the court there said "... the address on the records of a debtor, which in most cases will be the only one available, should be the only relevant last known address."

Paragraph (2) covers the situation in which, on the basis of the holder's records, the identity of the person entitled to the property is unknown, and the holder therefore reports to the State of its domicile, but it is later established by another State that the property was owned by or payable to a person whose last known address was within the claiming State. This is a rational extension of *Texas v. New Jersey*. Reunification of the owner with his or her property in this circumstance is impossible, and insofar as that issue is concerned, it makes no difference whether the property is delivered to the State of the holder's domicile or the State of the owner's last known address. However, following the equitable concept of distributing unclaimed property among creditor States articulated by the Supreme Court in *Texas v. New Jersey*, and reaffirmed in *Delaware v. New York*, the subsection directs that where there is no record of a name but there is a record that the last known address was within the State, that State where the owner had an address can claim the property.

Paragraph (3) is the secondary rule of *Texas v. New Jersey*. The Supreme Court ruled that when property is owed to persons for whom there are no addresses, the property will be subject to escheat by the State of the holder's domicile, provided that another State may later claim upon proof that the last known address of the person entitled to the property was within its borders.

Paragraph (4) provides that if the law of the State of the owner's last known address does not provide for escheat or taking custody of the unclaimed property or if that State's escheat or unclaimed property law is not applicable to the property in question, the property is subject to claim by the State in which the holder is domiciled. In that instance, the State of the owner's last known address may thereafter claim the property if it enacts an applicable unclaimed property law. The holder State will act as custodian and pay or deliver the property to the owner or the State which has priority under *Texas v. New Jersey* upon request. As held in *State v. Liquidating Trustees of Republic Petroleum Co.*, 510 S.W.2d 311 (Texas 1974), *Texas v. New Jersey* dealt only with conflicting claims of two or more States, and provides no basis for a holder to object to the claim of its State of domicile by asserting that another State has a superior claim, if the holder has not already reported the property to that other State. Therefore a State which claims custody on the ground that it is the holder's domicile is not required to prove that the laws of some or all of the other 49 States do not "provide" for the taking of the property; if the holder has not reported and paid the property to another State, as between the domiciliary State and the holder, it will be presumed that such other State's laws do not apply. If another State does claim the property, it may of course proceed under Section 14.

Paragraph (5) provides that when the last known address of the apparent owner is in a foreign nation the State in which the holder is domiciled may claim the property. This issue was not dealt with by the Supreme Court in *Texas v. New Jersey,* but is a rational extension of that ruling.

Paragraph (6) provides for a situation in which neither of the priority claims discussed in *Texas v. New Jersey* can be made, but the State has a genuine and important contact with the property. An example of the type of claim which might be made under paragraph (6) arose in *O'Connor v. Sperry & Hutchinson Co.,* 412 A.2d 539 (Pa.1980). There Pennsylvania sought to escheat unredeemed trading stamps sold by a corporation domiciled in New Jersey to retailers located in Pennsylvania. Pennsylvania took the position that *Texas v. New Jersey* did not create a jurisdictional bar to escheat by other States when the States granted priority were unable to take. There was no first priority claim since there were no addresses of the trading stamp purchasers. The second priority claimant, the State of corporate domicile (New Jersey), was not permitted under its law to escheat trading stamps (see *New Jersey v. Sperry & Hutchinson Co.,* 56 N.J.Super. 589, 153 A.2d 691 (1959), *affirmed per curiam,* 31 N.J. 385, 157 A.2d 505 (1960)) and hence Pennsylvania urged that in order to prohibit a corporate windfall it should be allowed to claim this property. The Pennsylvania Supreme Court affirmed a lower court decision which overruled Sperry & Hutchinson's motion to dismiss but did not reach the *Texas v. New Jersey* issue.

Gift certificates, unused airline tickets, and other property for which there is no last known address may be claimed by the State where the purchase was made if the State of corporate domicile does not have an abandoned property law covering the property in question under paragraph (6).

Travelers checks and money orders are covered under paragraph (7), which states the rule adopted by Congress in 12 U.S.C. sections 2501 *et seq.* The congressional action was in response to the Supreme Court decision in *Pennsylvania v. New York,* 407 U.S. 206 (1972), which held that the State of corporate domicile was entitled to escheat money orders when there was no last known address of the purchaser although the property had been purchased in other States. Paragraph (7), pursuant to the congressional mandate, substitutes as the test for asserting a claim to travelers checks and money orders the place of purchase rather than the State of incorporation of the issuer.

Wholly foreign transactions are excluded from the coverage of the Act. See Section 26.

SECTION 5. DORMANCY CHARGE. A holder may deduct from property presumed abandoned a charge imposed by reason of the owner's failure to claim the property within a specified time only if there is a valid and enforceable written contract between the holder and the owner under which the holder may impose the charge and the holder regularly imposes the charge, which is not regularly reversed or otherwise canceled. The amount of the deduction is limited to an amount that is not unconscionable.

Comment

This section is consistent with those cases which have ruled on the issue of service charges under the 1966 Act and the 1981 Act. Section 5 is a limitation on the deduction of charges based solely on dormancy and is applicable to all intangible property presumed abandoned. This section, which applies to all unclaimed property, replaces similar limitations that were specifically focused on various types of property in the 1981 Act. The limitation of a service charge to an amount that is not unconscionable is new and is drawn from Article 2, Section 302, of the Uniform Commercial Code.

SECTION 6. BURDEN OF PROOF AS TO PROPERTY EVIDENCED BY RECORD OF CHECK OR DRAFT. A record of the issuance of a check, draft, or similar instrument is prima facie evidence of an obligation. In claiming property from a holder who is also the issuer, the administrator's burden of proof as to the existence and amount of the property and its abandonment is satisfied by showing issuance of the instrument and passage of the requisite period of abandonment. Defenses of payment, satisfaction, discharge, and want of consideration are affirmative defenses that must be established by the holder.

Comment

This provision clarifies the burden of proof in situations where the obligation evidenced by a negotiable instrument is disputed by the holder, and is consistent with cases which have ruled on the matter. See *Insurance Co. of North America v. Knight,* 8 Ill.App.3d 871, 291 N.E.2d 40 (1972), *app. dismissed* 414 U.S. 804, 38 L.Ed.2d 40, 94 S.Ct. 165 (1973), *Blue Cross of Northern Cal. v. Cory,* 120 Cal. App.3d 723, 174 Cal. Rptr. 901 (1981), and *Revenue Cabinet v. Blue Cross & Blue Shield,* 702 S.W.2d 433, 435 (Ky. 1986). See also *Riggs Nat'l Bank v. District of Columbia,* 581 A.2d 1229 (D.C.App. 1990). It is also consistent with the cases holding that when claiming abandoned property the State steps into the shoes of the owner (see Epstein, McThenia and Forslund, "Unclaimed Property and Reporting Forms," sec. 3.02 (Matt. Bend. 1984), and Article 3-308 of the Uniform Commercial Code. Under U.C.C. Section 3-308(2), "When signatures are admitted or established, production of the instrument entitles a holder to recover on it unless the defendant establishes a defense." The reason for requiring a plaintiff to produce the instrument is "to show that the plaintiff is in fact the holder, and in order to protect the defendant from double liability." 6 Anderson, Uniform Commercial Code, sec. 3-307:4, p. 158 (3rd ed., 1993). The administrator, by proving issuance of the instrument, succeeds to all rights of the payee. Because the issuer is relieved of all liability on the instrument by paying the obligation to the State as unclaimed property, and is indemnified by the State, there is no chance that the issuer would be held liable twice, and therefore the administrator is not required to produce the instrument in order to possess the same rights as a holder in due course.

SECTION 7. REPORT OF ABANDONED PROPERTY.

(a) A holder of property presumed abandoned shall make a report to the administrator concerning the property.

(b) The report must be verified and must contain:

(1) a description of the property;

(2) except with respect to a traveler's check or money order, the name, if known, and last known address, if any, and the social security number or taxpayer identification number, if readily ascertainable, of the apparent owner of property of the value of $50 or more;

(3) an aggregated amount of items valued under $50 each;

(4) in the case of an amount of $50 or more held or owing under an annuity or a life or endowment insurance policy, the full name and last known address of the annuitant or insured and of the beneficiary;

(5) in the case of property held in a safe deposit box or other safekeeping depository, an indication of the place where it is held and where it may be inspected by the administrator, and any amounts owing to the holder;

(6) the date, if any, on which the property became payable, demandable, or returnable, and the date of the last transaction with the apparent owner with respect to the property; and

(7) other information that the administrator by rule prescribes as necessary for the administration of this [Act].

(c) If a holder of property presumed abandoned is a successor to another person who previously held the property for the apparent owner or the holder has changed its name while holding the property, the holder shall file with the report its former names, if any, and the known names and addresses of all previous holders of the property.

(d) The report must be filed before November 1 of each year and cover the 12 months next preceding July 1 of that year, but a report with respect to a life insurance company must be filed before May 1 of each year for the calendar year next preceding.

(e) The holder of property presumed abandoned shall send written notice to the apparent owner, not more than 120 days or less than 60 days before filing the report, stating that the holder is in possession of property subject to this [Act], if:

(1) the holder has in its records an address for the apparent owner which the holder's records do not disclose to be inaccurate;

(2) the claim of the apparent owner is not barred by a statute of limitations; and

(3) the value of the property is $50 or more.

(f) Before the date for filing the report, the holder of property presumed abandoned may request the administrator to extend the time for filing the report. The administrator may grant the extension for good cause. The holder, upon receipt of the extension, may make an interim payment on the amount the holder estimates will ultimately be due, which terminates the accrual of additional interest on the amount paid.

(g) The holder of property presumed abandoned shall file with the report an affidavit stating that the holder has complied with subsection (e).

Comment

The $50 minimum provided in subsection (b)(1), (2), and (3) represents an increase from $3.00 in the 1966 Act and $25 in the 1981 Act in order to minimize reporting expenses. Almost every State which enacted the prior Uniform Act now provides for a $25 minimum.

Before filing its report, the holder must send written notice to the apparent owner, if the owner's claim is not barred by the statute of limitations, the property has a value of $50 or more, and the holder's records do not disclose the address to be inaccurate. Other efforts to locate the owner are no longer required.

Subsection (f) provides new flexibility to the holder and to the administrator in cases where the holder's timely compliance is not feasible. In the past, some administrators have felt themselves to be without authority to extend the filing deadlines, or to accept less than a final report. It is now made clear that an extension can be had for good cause, and the holder can limit its exposure to interest by making a partial payment.

SECTION 8. PAYMENT OR DELIVERY OF ABANDONED PROPERTY.

(a) Except for property held in a safe deposit box or other safekeeping depository, upon filing the report required by Section 7, the holder of property presumed abandoned shall pay, deliver, or cause to be paid or delivered to the administrator the property described in the report as unclaimed, but if the property is an automatically renewable deposit, and a penalty or forfeiture in the payment of interest would result, the time for compliance is extended until a penalty or forfeiture would no longer result. Tangible property held in a safe deposit box or other safekeeping depository may not be delivered to the administrator until [120] days after filing the report required by Section 7.

(b) If the property reported to the administrator is a security or security entitlement under [Article 8 of the Uniform Commercial Code], the administrator is an appropriate person to make an indorsement, instruction, or entitlement order on behalf of the apparent owner to invoke the duty of the issuer or its transfer agent or the securities intermediary to transfer or dispose of the security or the security entitlement in accordance with [Article 8 of the Uniform Commercial Code].

(c) If the holder of property reported to the administrator is the issuer of a certificated security, the administrator has the right to obtain a replacement certificate pursuant to [Section 8-408 of the Uniform Commercial Code], but an indemnity bond is not required.

(d) An issuer, the holder, and any transfer agent or other person acting pursuant to the instructions of and on behalf of the issuer or holder in accordance with this section is not liable to the apparent owner and must be indemnified against claims of any person in accordance with Section 10.

Comment

Subsections (b) and (c) particularize the general duty stated in subsection (a) with respect to investment securities, including securities positions held directly and securities positions held through accounts with brokers or other intermediaries (referred to as security entitlements" under revised Article 8 of the Uniform Commercial Code). UCC Article 8 provides that the issuer of a security, or intermediary with respect to a security entitlement, has a duty to act at the direction of the "appropriate person." Subsection (b) provides that with respect to securities and security entitlements that have been reported as abandoned property pursuant to Section 7, the administrator is an "appropriate person." Accordingly, the administrator has the same rights under UCC Article 8 as other persons who succeed by operation of law to securities or security entitlements, such as the executor or administrator of a decedent. Subsection (c) deals with situations where the holder reporting abandoned property is itself the issuer of a certificated security, and hence does not have the original certificate to turn over to the administrator. Accordingly, subsection (b) provides that the administrator can invoke the provisions of UCC Article 8 governing replacement certificates, without an indemnity bond.

Subsection (d) indemnifies a person causing a replacement certificate to be issued to the administrator from any claims that the person acted wrongfully in so doing. This indemnification is desireable in that it eliminates any duty of the transferring authority to make an independent investigation into whether the listed owner of the security is in fact missing, or into other factors which might affect the administrator's right to obtain custody of the property.

SECTION 9. NOTICE AND PUBLICATION OF LISTS OF ABANDONED PROPERTY.

(a) The administrator shall publish a notice not later than November 30 of the year next following the year in which abandoned property has been paid or delivered to the administrator. The notice must be published in a newspaper of general circulation in the [county] of this State in which is located the last known address of any person named in the notice. If a holder does not report an address for the apparent owner, or the address is outside this State, the notice must be published in the [county] in which the holder has its principal place of business within this State or another [county] that the administrator reasonably selects. The advertisement must be in a form that, in the judgment of the administrator, is likely to attract the attention of the apparent owner of the unclaimed property. The form must contain:

(1) the name of each person appearing to be the owner of the property, as set forth in the report filed by the holder;

(2) the last known address or location of each person appearing to be the owner of the property, if an address or location is set forth in the report filed by the holder;

(3) a statement explaining that property of the owner is presumed to be abandoned and has been taken into the protective custody of the administrator; and

(4) a statement that information about the property and its return to the owner is available to a person having a legal or beneficial interest in the property, upon request to the administrator.

(b) The administrator is not required to advertise the name and address or location of an owner of property having a total value less than $50, or information concerning a traveler's check, money order, or similar instrument.

Comment

This section sets forth the minimum requirements for advertisement. The administrator may publish more frequently or extensively. The Act does not establish a specific time for the publication so that the administrator can choose a time that will provide the best exposure and flexibility in scheduling the workload and personnel available.

The advertisement must contain a minimum of two items of information, one of which explains that the abandoned property has been paid into the protective custody of the administrator. Since abandoned property is delivered with the report under the revisions of this Act, this statement is necessary to explain the location of the property and to insure that inquiries are directed to the administrator.

Subsection (b) limits the duty to advertise in recognition of the fact in the specified circumstances the value of the property is so slight as to negate the benefits of the advertising, or the names and addresses of the owners of the instruments are not maintained by the holder, or in the case of travelers checks, after 15 years the advertisement is unlikely to be productive.

SECTION 10. CUSTODY BY STATE; RECOVERY BY HOLDER; DEFENSE OF HOLDER.

(a) In this section, payment or delivery is made in "good faith" if:

(1) payment or delivery was made in a reasonable attempt to comply with this [Act];

(2) the holder was not then in breach of a fiduciary obligation with respect to the property and had a reasonable basis for believing, based on the facts then known, that the property was presumed abandoned; and

(3) there is no showing that the records under which the payment or delivery was made did not meet reasonable commercial standards of practice.

(b) Upon payment or delivery of property to the administrator, the State assumes custody and responsibility for the safekeeping of the property. A holder who pays or delivers property to the administrator in good faith is relieved of all liability arising thereafter with respect to the property.

(c) A holder who has paid money to the administrator pursuant to this [Act] may subsequently make payment to a person reasonably appearing to the holder to be entitled to payment. Upon a filing by the holder of proof of payment and proof that the payee was entitled to the payment, the administrator shall promptly reimburse the holder for the payment without imposing a fee or other charge. If reimbursement is sought for a payment made on a negotiable instrument, including a traveler's check or money order, the holder must be reimbursed upon filing proof that the instrument was duly presented and that payment was made to a person who reasonably appeared to be entitled to payment. The holder must be reimbursed for payment made even if the payment was made to a person whose claim was barred under Section 19(a).

(d) A holder who has delivered property other than money to the administrator pursuant to this [Act] may reclaim the property if it is still in the possession of the administrator, without paying any fee or other charge, upon filing proof that the apparent owner has claimed the property from the holder.

(e) The administrator may accept a holder's affidavit as sufficient proof of the holder's right to recover money and property under this section.

(f) If a holder pays or delivers property to the administrator in good faith and thereafter another person claims the property from the holder or another State claims the money or property under its laws relating to escheat or abandoned or unclaimed property, the administrator, upon written notice of the claim, shall defend the holder against the claim and indemnify the holder against any liability on the claim resulting from payment or delivery of the property to the administrator.

(g) Property removed from a safe deposit box or other safekeeping depository is received by the administrator subject to the holder's right to be reimbursed for the cost of the opening and to any valid lien or contract providing for the holder to be reimbursed for unpaid rent or storage charges. The administrator shall reimburse the holder out of the proceeds remaining after deducting the expense incurred by the administrator in selling the property.

Comment

When property is turned over to the State, the holder is relieved of all liability for any turnover made in good faith. Subsection (a) sets forth a definition of good faith which *inter alia* allows the holder to rely on its records if they meet reasonable commercial standards of practice in the industry.

The section also permits the holder to obtain reimbursement for claims it elected to pay to owners who appeared after the property was turned over. If a State in enacting Section 12(b) provides for the payment of interest on property delivered to the administrator, then the holder will add such interest when paying the claim.

If after turnover, any person or another State makes a claim on the holder, the State, upon request, is required to defend the holder and provide indemnification against any liability.

SECTION 11. CREDITING OF DIVIDENDS, INTEREST, AND INCREMENTS TO OWNER'S ACCOUNT. If property other than money is delivered to the administrator under this [Act], the owner is entitled to receive from the administrator any income or gain realized or accruing on the property at or before liquidation or conversion of the property into money. If the property was an interest bearing demand, savings, or time deposit, including a deposit that is automatically renewable, the administrator shall pay interest at a rate of [insert legal rate] percent a year or any lesser rate the property earned while in the possession of the holder. Interest begins to accrue when the property is delivered to the administrator and ceases on the earlier of the expiration of 10 years after delivery or the date on which payment is made to the owner. Interest on interest bearing property is not payable for any period before the effective date of this [Act], unless authorized by law superseded by this [Act].

Comment

Under this section the owner of interest earning bonds or bank deposits, or dividend paying stock, will generally receive interest or income which the property earned while in the State's custody.

SECTION 12. PUBLIC SALE OF ABANDONED PROPERTY.

(a) Except as otherwise provided in this section, the administrator, within three years after the receipt of abandoned property, shall sell it to the highest bidder at public sale at a location in the State which in the judgment of the administrator affords the most favorable market for the property. The administrator may decline the highest bid and reoffer the property for sale if the administrator considers the bid to be insufficient. The administrator need not offer the property for sale if the administrator considers that the probable cost of sale will exceed the proceeds of the sale. A sale held under this section must be preceded by a single publication of notice, at least three weeks before sale, in a newspaper of general circulation in the [county] in which the property is to be sold.

(b) Securities listed on an established stock exchange must be sold at prices prevailing on the exchange at the time of sale. Other securities may be sold over the counter at prices prevailing at the time of sale or by any reasonable method selected by the administrator. If securities are sold by the administrator before the expiration of three years after their delivery to the administrator, a person making a claim under this [Act] before the end of the three-year period is entitled to the proceeds of the sale of the securities or the market value of the securities at the time the claim is made, whichever is greater, plus dividends, interest, and other increments thereon up to the time the claim is made, less any deduction for expenses of sale. A person making a claim under this [Act] after the expiration of the three-year period is entitled to receive the securities delivered to the administrator by the holder, if they still remain in the custody of the administrator, or the net proceeds received from sale, and is not entitled to receive any appreciation in the value of the property occurring after delivery to the administrator, except in a case of intentional misconduct or malfeasance by the administrator.

(c) A purchaser of property at a sale conducted by the administrator pursuant to this [Act] takes the property free of all claims of the owner or previous holder and of all persons claiming through or under them. The administrator shall execute all documents necessary to complete the transfer of ownership.

Comment

If the security is stock or other intangible interest in a business association, the administrator is permitted to sell the security, but if the missing owner appears and makes claim for the security within three years after the administrator has sold it, the missing owner is entitled to receive the proceeds of the sale or the market value of the securities at the time the claim is made. Thus there is a genuine incentive for an administrator to hold this property for the requisite three-year period.

Subsection (b) permits an administrator to sell securities at prevailing prices directly to the issuing companies.

This section is not intended as a direction to the administrator to sell "money," although money is included in the definition of property, unless it is a collector's specie having value greater than the face value of the money as cash.

SECTION 13. DEPOSIT OF FUNDS.

[(a) Except as otherwise provided by this section, the] [The] administrator shall promptly deposit in the [general fund] of this State all funds received under this [Act], including the proceeds from the sale of abandoned property under Section 12. [The administrator shall retain in a separate trust fund at least [$100,000] from which the administrator shall pay claims duly allowed.] The administrator shall record the name and last known address of each person appearing from the holders' reports to be entitled to the property and the name and last known address of each insured person or annuitant and beneficiary and with respect to each policy or annuity listed in the report of an insurance company, its number, the name of the company, and the amount due.

[(b) Before making a deposit to the credit of the [general fund], the administrator may deduct:

(1) expenses of sale of abandoned property;

(2) costs of mailing and publication in connection with abandoned property;

(3) reasonable service charges; and

(4) expenses incurred in examining records of holders of property and in collecting the property from those holders.]

Comment

This section increases from $25,000 to $100,000 the sum which is recommended to be retained in a trust account for payment of claims. It is contemplated that the amount of the trust fund which is ultimately established will reflect a State's experience in paying owners' claims.

SECTION 14. CLAIM OF ANOTHER STATE TO RECOVER PROPERTY.

(a) After property has been paid or delivered to the administrator under this [Act], another State may recover the property if:

(1) the property was paid or delivered to the custody of this State because the records of the holder did not reflect a last known location of the apparent owner within the borders of the other State and the other State establishes that the apparent owner or other person entitled to the property was last known to be located within the borders of that State and under the laws of that State the property has escheated or become subject to a claim of abandonment by that State;

(2) the property was paid or delivered to the custody of this State because the laws of the other State did not provide for the escheat or custodial taking of the property, and under the laws of that State subsequently enacted the property has escheated or become subject to a claim of abandonment by that State;

(3) the records of the holder were erroneous in that they did not accurately identify the owner of the property and the last known location of the owner within the borders of another State and under the laws of that State the property has escheated or become subject to a claim of abandonment by that State;

(4) the property was subjected to custody by this State under Section 4(6) and under the laws of the State of domicile of the holder the property has escheated or become subject to a claim of abandonment by that State; or

(5) the property is a sum payable on a traveler's check, money order, or similar instrument that was purchased in the other State and delivered into the custody of this State under Section 4(7), and under the laws of the other State the property has escheated or become subject to a claim of abandonment by that State.

(b) A claim of another State to recover escheated or abandoned property must be presented in a form prescribed by the administrator, who shall decide the claim within 90 days after it is presented. The administrator shall allow the claim upon determining that the other State is entitled to the abandoned property under subsection (a).

(c) The administrator shall require another State, before recovering property under this section, to agree to indemnify this State and its officers and employees against any liability on a claim to the property.

Comment

Section 14 should be read together with Section 4. Sections 4 and 14 are designed to carry out the priority scheme enunciated in *Texas v. New Jersey*, 379 U.S. 674 (1965). In general the State in which the owner had his or her last known address is entitled to claim abandoned property. Where there is insufficient information to permit this assertion of custody, the State of the holder's domicile takes the property subject to a later claim by the State of the last known address.

Paragraph (1) of subsection (a) provides that if property was paid to the State of the holder's domicile because the last known address of the owner was unknown and it is later established by another State that the last known address of the person entitled to the property was in the other State, the State of domicile should pay the property over to the other State.

Paragraph (2) parallels Section 4, paragraph (4), which permits the State of corporate domicile to take if the State of the last known address does not provide for the escheat or custodial taking of the property. If the State of the last known address subsequently enacts an unclaimed property law which covers the property, the taking State must turn it over.

Paragraph (3) addresses the problem of *Nellius v. Tampax, Inc.*, 394 A.2d 333 (Del. Ch. Ct. 1978) in which the holder's records did not reflect the fact that the record owner had sold the property to another. The court concluded, under *Texas v. New Jersey*, that the holder's records were controlling and that it could properly report and deliver the property to the State in which its records showed the owner to be resident. However, as provided in *Texas v. New Jersey* and in paragraph 4, the State of the owner's actual residence could then claim the property from the State to which it was initially reported.

Paragraph (4), paralleling Section 4(6), provides that property initially claimed under a "contacts" test because there was no last known address and the State of domicile had no applicable unclaimed property law may be reclaimed by the State of corporate domicile if it enacts an applicable unclaimed property law.

Subsection (c) provides that the State that initially receives property later claimed by another State may require an indemnification agreement from the claiming State.

SECTION 15. FILING CLAIM WITH ADMINISTRATOR; HANDLING OF CLAIMS BY ADMINISTRATOR.

(a) A person, excluding another State, claiming property paid or delivered to the administrator may file a claim on a form prescribed by the administrator and verified by the claimant.

(b) Within 90 days after a claim is filed, the administrator shall allow or deny the claim and give written notice of the decision to the claimant. If the claim is denied, the administrator shall inform the claimant of the reasons for the denial and specify what additional evidence is required before the claim will be allowed. The claimant may then file a new claim with the administrator or maintain an action under Section 16.

(c) Within 30 days after a claim is allowed, the property or the net proceeds of a sale of the property must be delivered or paid by the administrator to the claimant, together with any dividend, interest, or other increment to which the claimant is entitled under Sections 11 and 12.

(d) A holder who pays the owner for property that has been delivered to the State and which, if claimed from the administrator by the owner would be subject to an increment under Sections 11 and 12, may recover from the administrator the amount of the increment.

Comment

A person claiming property from the administrator is not limited to the number of times the claim may be filed or refiled prior to commencing an action under Section 16. The administrator's decision on a claim does not operate as collateral estoppel or *res judicata*. A person who has commenced an action under Section 16 may also reassert a claim before the administrator if the action has been dismissed without prejudice. A claim which has become the subject of a final judgment may not thereafter by refiled with the administrator.

SECTION 16. ACTION TO ESTABLISH CLAIM. A person aggrieved by a decision of the administrator or whose claim has not been acted upon within 90 days after its filing may maintain an original action to establish the claim in the [appropriate] court, naming the [administrator] as a defendant. [If the aggrieved person establishes the claim in an action against the administrator, the court may award the claimant reasonable attorney's fees.]

Comment

After property is presumed abandoned and reported to the administrator the administrator must attempt to locate the missing owner. Thereafter, if the property has been delivered to the administrator and the owner or his representative appears, the administrator must pay the claim. The owner's rights are never cut off; under this Act, the owner's rights exist in perpetuity. Although some state administrators have urged legislation that would terminate an owner's right to the property merely by the passage of time, such enactments may be unconstitutional. In *Hamilton v. Brown*, 161 U.S. 256, 275, 16 S. Ct. 585, 592, 40 L. Ed. 691, 699, (1896), the Supreme Court held that any procedure by which the State seeks to cut off the owner's title through escheat must include "actual notice by service of summons to all known claimants, and constructive notice by publication to all possible claimants who are unknown...." Any lesser procedure appears to fall short of due process. The history of escheat, as compared with modern unclaimed property legislation, is discussed in "Unclaimed Property and Reporting Forms," Epstein, McThenia & Forslund, ch. 1 (Matt. Bend. 1984).

In any judicial action commenced to recover the property from the administrator, the claimant may proceed *de novo*, and the court will not be limited to a mere review of the administrator's decision.

SECTION 17. ELECTION TO TAKE PAYMENT OR DELIVERY.

(a) The administrator may decline to receive property reported under this [Act] which the administrator considers to have a value less than the expenses of notice and sale.

(b) A holder, with the written consent of the administrator and upon conditions and terms prescribed by the administrator, may report and deliver property before the property is presumed abandoned. Property so delivered must be held by the administrator and is not presumed abandoned until it otherwise would be presumed abandoned under this [Act].

Comment

Subsection 17(b) authorizes the administrator to assume custody of property prior to the time for presuming abandonment. Administrators have expressed a need for this authority to enable them to take possession of property, such as the contents of a safe deposit box repository, when the holder is terminating business but the property is not yet reportable. Additionally, other holders which have conducted business in the State and are ceasing operations might use the provisions of this section. The property must be held by the administrator until the abandonment period runs and then the property will be subject to the other provisions of the Act.

SECTION 18. DESTRUCTION OR DISPOSITION OF PROPERTY HAVING NO SUBSTANTIAL COMMERCIAL VALUE; IMMUNITY FROM LIABILITY. If the administrator determines after investigation that property delivered under this [Act] has no substantial commercial value, the administrator may destroy or otherwise dispose of the property at any time. An action or proceeding may not be maintained against the State or any officer or against the holder for or on account of an act of the administrator under this section, except for intentional misconduct or malfeasance.

Comment

This section provides for the disposition of property which has no commercial value. As an example, the contents of safety deposit boxes often include such items as rent receipts, personal correspondence and lapsed insurance policies. In such cases, these contents might have some personal significance to the owner, which the administrator would take into consideration in determining for what period of time he will hold the property awaiting a claim by the owner. However, in the usual situation there will be no interest to be preserved by maintaining this property under state custody.

Under this section the administrator would be free to retain property having no commercial value. Further, the administrator could transfer it to other agencies or institutions which might have an interest in the property because of its historical value or other independent significance.

SECTION 19. PERIODS OF LIMITATION.

(a) The expiration, before or after the effective date of this [Act], of a period of limitation on the owner's right to receive or recover property, whether specified by contract, statute, or court order, does not preclude the property from being presumed abandoned or affect a duty to file a report or to pay or deliver or transfer property to the administrator as required by this [Act].

(b) An action or proceeding may not be maintained by the administrator to enforce this [Act] in regard to the reporting, delivery, or payment of property more than 10 years after the holder specifically identified the property in a report filed with the administrator or gave express notice to the administrator of a dispute regarding the property. In the absence of such a report or other express notice, the period of limitation is tolled. The period of limitation is also tolled by the filing of a report that is fraudulent.

Comment

Subsection (a) is consistent with cases such as *People v. Marshall Field & Co.,* 83 Ill. App. 3d 811, 404 N.E.2d 368 (1980), *Screen Actors Guild, Inc. v. Cory,* 91 Cal.App.3d 111, 154 Cal.Rptr. 77 (1979), and *State v. Jefferson Lake Sulphur Co.,* 36 N.J. 577, 178 A.2d 329 (1962). It also abrogates another contractual condition often asserted as a defense to reporting property otherwise presumed abandoned, the failure to present the evidence of indebtedness.

Subsection (a) is written to insure also that although the owner's claim against the holder may be barred by the statute of limitations prior to the effective date of the Act, the holder is not relieved of his obligation to pay abandoned property to the administrator. The Comment to Section 16 of the 1966 Act noted that local law must be consulted in order to ascertain whether legislation constitutionally may be enacted reviving a cause of action barred by the statute of limitations. This issue has been litigated in several States, *e.g., Country Mutual Insurance Co. v. Knight,* 40 Ill.2d 523, 240 N.E.2d 612 (1968); *Douglas Aircraft Co. v. Cranston,* 24 Cal.Rptr. 851, 374 P.2d 819 (1962); *cf. Standard Oil v. New Jersey,* 5 N.J. 281, 74 A.2d 565 (1950). Even though the statute of limitations has run before the effective date of the Act, the holder may be required to report and deliver the property to the State if the holder does not regularly enforce the statute. *See South Carolina Tax Commission v. Metropolitan Life Insurance Co.,* 266 S.C. 34, 221 S.E.2d 522 (1975). *But see State of Washington v. Puget Sound Power & Light Co.,* 103 Wash.2d 501, 694 P.2d 7, 10 (1985).

Subsection (b) provides that an administrator must commence an action against a holder within 10 years after the time the property was first reported or specifically placed in issue. The 1995 amendment clarifies existing law and codifies the holdings of abandoned property cases that have ruled on issues of limitations. See *Blue Cross of Northern California v. Cory,* 174 Cal. Rptr. 901, 913, 120 Cal. App.3d 743 (App., 1981) (no statute of limitations will commence to run against the State until after the holder duly reports in compliance with the unclaimed property act); *Travelers Express Co., Inc. v. Cony,* 664 F.2d 763 (9th Cir. 1981) (statute of limitations commences to run only after filing of report which contains written explanation of why property is not subject to the act); *Employers Insurance of Wausau v. Smith,* 453 N.W.2d 856 (Wis. 1990) (filing of report essential to running of statute of limitations, since unclaimed property act depends on self-reporting); *Sennet v. Insurance Co. of North America,* 432 Pa. 5215, 247 A.2d 774, 777-78 (1968) (same; "INA simply has to take its stand: if it reports the holding [of funds in issue] (as a precautionary measure), the statute will run; if it does not, the Commonwealth is not precluded...."); *State of New Jersey v. U.S. Steel Corporation,* 22 N.J. 341, 126 A.2d 168 (1956) (same); *Treasurer and Rec. Gen. v. John Hancock Mut. Life Ins. Co.,* 388 Mass. 410, 446 N.E.2d 1376 (1983) (same). The provision also parallels the Internal Revenue Code, 26 U.S.C. sec. 6501(c). Since the Unclaimed Property Act is based on a theory of truthful self-reporting, a holder which conceals property, wilfully or otherwise, cannot expect the protection of the stated limitations period.

SECTION 20. REQUESTS FOR REPORTS AND EXAMINATION OF RECORDS.

(a) The administrator may require a person who has not filed a report, or a person who the administrator believes has filed an inaccurate, incomplete, or false report, to file a verified report in a form specified by the administrator. The report must state whether the person is holding property reportable under this [Act], describe property not previously reported or as to which the administrator has made inquiry, and specifically identify and state the amounts of property that may be in issue.

(b) The administrator, at reasonable times and upon reasonable notice, may examine the records of any person to determine whether the person has complied with this [Act]. The administrator may conduct the examination even if the person believes it is not in possession of any property that must be reported, paid, or delivered under this [Act]. The administrator may contract with any other person to conduct the examination on behalf of the administrator.

(c) The administrator at reasonable times may examine the records of an agent, including a dividend disbursing agent or transfer agent, of a business association or financial association that is the holder of property presumed abandoned if the administrator has given the notice required by subsection (b) to both the association or organization and the agent at least 90 days before the examination.

(d) Documents and working papers obtained or compiled by the administrator, or the administrator's agents, employees, or designated representatives, in the course of conducting an examination are confidential and are not public records, but the documents and papers may be:

(1) used by the administrator in the course of an action to collect unclaimed property or otherwise enforce this [Act];

(2) used in joint examinations conducted with or pursuant to an agreement with another State, the federal government, or any other governmental subdivision, agency, or instrumentality;

(3) produced pursuant to subpoena or court order; or

(4) disclosed to the abandoned property office of another State for that State's use in circumstances equivalent to those described in this subdivision, if the other State is bound to keep the documents and papers confidential.

(e) If an examination of the records of a person results in the disclosure of property reportable under this [Act], the administrator may assess the cost of the examination against the holder at the rate of [$200] a day for each examiner, or a greater amount that is reasonable and was incurred, but the assessment may not exceed the value of the property found to be reportable. The cost of an examination made pursuant to subsection (c) may be assessed only against the business association or financial organization.

(f) If, after the effective date of this [Act], a holder does not maintain the records required by Section 21 and the records of the holder available for the periods subject to this [Act] are insufficient to permit the preparation of a report, the administrator may require the holder to report and pay to the administrator the amount the administrator reasonably estimates, on the basis of any available records of the holder or by any other reasonable method of estimation, should have been but was not reported.

Comment

This section is designed to facilitate compliance with the Act. Subsection (a) provides for the filing of a negative report if the administrator requires such a report and will minimize disruption which would otherwise be caused to the holder if an examination of records instead were conducted by the administrator. Subsection (b) is based on Section 30 of the 1981 Act. Aside from the requirement that the administrator conduct the examination at reasonable times and upon reasonable notice, the only limitations on the administrator's right to examine are constitutional limitations. Even though the Fourth Amendment does not extend as broadly to corporations as to individuals, *Oklahoma Press Pub. Co. v. Walling,* 327 U.S. 186, 90 L.Ed. 614, 66 S.Ct. 494 (1946), inspections of commercial property may be unreasonable if they are not authorized by law or are unnecessary for the furtherance of a governmental interest. *Donovan v. Dewey,* 452 U.S. 594, 55 L.Ed.2d 486, 98 S.Ct. 1942 (1980). This Act is deemed to meet that standard. Also, since one of the dual purposes of this Act is the collection of revenue, reference may be made to the cases holding that it is not an unreasonable search to require taxpayers to produce their books and records. See Annot., "Constitutionality of statutory provisions for examination of records, books, or documents for taxation purposes," 103 ALR 522.

Subsection (c) is intended to provide a useful method whereby the administrator can conduct a single examination of a dividend disbursing agent or transfer agent serving in such capacity for numerous business associations.

Subsection (f) permits the use of estimates in instances where the holder has failed to report and deliver property that is abandoned and no longer has reasonably accessible records sufficient to prepare a specific report. Additionally, if the holder fails to maintain records of the last known address, States can assert claims based on any other records which might exist. Resort may be had to computer codes. While the holding in *Texas v. New Jersey* is intended to prevent multiple liability of holders, this subsection, viewed as a penalty for failure to maintain records of names and last known address, is not inconsistent with that decision. That part of subsection (f) which permits the State to make estimates was prospective only from the date of adoption of the 1981 Act. This Act expressly states the bases on which estimates may be made. Thus, the State may use estimating techniques—where a holder has not maintained records as required by statute—based on industry averages, and may rely on inferences that may be based on statistics drawn from a broader basis than that of the holder in question who has failed to keep records. This section, together with Section 23, also clarifies the administrator's authority to enter into agreements to enforce the State's custodial powers in all States.

SECTION 21. RETENTION OF RECORDS.

(a) Except as otherwise provided in subsection (b), a holder required to file a report under Section 7 shall maintain the records containing the information required to be included in the report for 10 years after the holder files the report, unless a shorter period is provided by rule of the administrator.

(b) A business association or financial organization that sells, issues, or provides to others for sale or issue in this State, traveler's checks, money orders, or similar instruments other than third-party bank checks, on which the business association or financial organization is directly liable, shall maintain a record of the instruments while they remain outstanding, indicating the State and date of issue, for three years after the holder files the report.

Comment

This section does not require that the holder in the first instance obtain the address of the owner. For example, a record of the address of the purchaser or recipient of a gift certificate customarily is not obtained.

Initially, the period for which records of address must be obtained is established at 10 years from the date the property was first reportable as abandoned property. However, this section permits a State to shorten this period by rule. Because the reporting practices of holders vary, an administrator will want to consider such factors as the burden imposed on the holder in maintaining such records, the opportunity of returning the property, and the type of business of the holder. For example, in the case of property that would be reportable in the aggregate without the name and address of the apparent owner under Section 7, a State might adopt a rule providing for a relatively short record retention period on condition that the holder maintain a record sufficient to satisfy the requirements of *Texas v. New Jersey* that there be a last known address or that the State can prove that the last known address of the creditor was within its borders.

Subsection (b) is designed to assure that the information required for asserting a claim to travelers checks and money orders is retained by the issuers of travelers checks and money orders.

SECTION 22. ENFORCEMENT. The administrator may maintain an action in this or another State to enforce this [Act]. The court may award reasonable attorney's fees to the prevailing party.

Comment

Although generally an action would be brought in an administrator's own State, action to enforce the Act may also be brought in the courts of another State. See Section 23. See also, *Commonwealth of Pennsylvania v. Kervick*, 60 N.J. 289, 288 A.2d 289 (1972).

SECTION 23. INTERSTATE AGREEMENTS AND COOPERATION; JOINT AND RECIPROCAL ACTIONS WITH OTHER STATES.

(a) The administrator may enter into an agreement with another State to exchange information relating to abandoned property or its possible existence. The agreement may permit the other State, or another person acting on behalf of a State, to examine records as authorized in Section 20. The administrator by rule may require the reporting of information needed to enable compliance with an agreement made under this section and prescribe the form.

(b) The administrator may join with another State to seek enforcement of this [Act] against any person who is or may be holding property reportable under this [Act].

(c) At the request of another State, the attorney general of this State may maintain an action on behalf of the other State to enforce, in this State, the unclaimed property laws of the other State against a holder of property subject to escheat or a claim of abandonment by the other State, if the other State has agreed to pay expenses incurred by the attorney general in maintaining the action.

(d) The administrator may request that the attorney general of another State or another attorney commence an action in the other State on behalf of the administrator. With the approval of the attorney general of this State, the administrator may retain any other attorney to commence an action in this State on behalf of the administrator. This State shall pay all expenses, including attorney's fees, in maintaining an action under this subsection. With the administrator's approval, the expenses and attorney's fees may be paid from money received under this [Act]. [The administrator may agree to pay expenses and attorney's fees based in whole or in part on a percentage of the value of any property recovered in the action.] Any expenses or attorney's fees paid under this subsection may not be deducted from the amount that is subject to the claim by the owner under this [Act].

Comment

To avoid conflicts between the administrator's procedures and the procedures of administrators in other jurisdictions that enact the Uniform Unclaimed Property Act, the administrator, before adopting, amending or repealing rules, should advise and consult with administrators in other jurisdictions that adopt this Act substantially and take into consideration the rules of administrators in other jurisdictions that enact the Uniform Unclaimed Property Act.

Cooperation among States is essential if abandoned property programs are to be efficiently administered. In recent years several States have joined together to audit major holders. Additionally, several States have entered into agreements to act as collection agents for each other. Interstate cooperation and the development of uniform reporting forms and uniform regulations will be of assistance to holders as well as program administrators. This section encourages joint agreements and cooperation among the States. An agreement among the States might expressly relieve holders from reporting piecemeal to separate States. Instead, they might be able to file a single report of all abandoned property, wherever located, and regardless of the address of the owner.

Reciprocal agreements envisioned under subsection (c) do not require the consent of Congress under the Compact Clause of the Constitution, Art. I, § 10, cl. 3. The Supreme Court has held that the restriction of the Compact Clause is limited to combinations or agreements that tend to increase the political power of the States to such an extent that it interferes with the supremacy of the United States. *United States Steel v. Multi-State Tax Commission*, 434 U.S. 452 (1978). In *Multi-State Tax Commission* the Court upheld a tax compact, that had not been approved by Congress creating a permanent administrative body to perform audits of multi-state taxpayer operations, and at the request of a member State, to sue to enforce the audits in the courts of the member States.

This section simply authorizes an economical approach to enforcing a State's claim under *Texas v. New Jersey*. Each State retains discretion to bring suit or to decide against such action, remaining free to adopt its own abandoned property policies. The position of the States will not be politically improved at the expense of the federal government although the process for claiming abandoned property will be more efficient.

Action by one State for another is expressly permitted by this section. In some cases the administrator of a State may deem it wise to seek counsel in a foreign jurisdiction. There may be small claims which would not justify individual action by the claimant State in a foreign forum, but if several States join forces and retain counsel in the holder State to sue for all of them, it might be administratively justified. This section expressly permits such joint action.

SECTION 24. INTEREST AND PENALTIES.

(a) A holder who fails to report, pay, or deliver property within the time prescribed by this [Act] shall pay to the administrator interest at the annual rate of [12 percent] [two percentage points above the annual rate of discount in effect on the date the property should have been paid or delivered for the most recent issue of 52-week United States Treasury bills] on the property or value thereof from the date the property should have been reported, paid or delivered.

(b) Except as otherwise provided in subsection (c), a holder who fails to report, pay, or deliver property within the time prescribed by this [Act], or fails to perform other duties imposed by this [Act], shall pay to the administrator, in addition to interest as provided in subsection (a), a civil penalty of [$200] for each day the report, payment, or delivery is withheld, or the duty is not performed, up to a maximum of [$5,000].

(c) A holder who willfully fails to report, pay, or deliver property within the time prescribed by this [Act], or willfully fails to perform other duties imposed by this [Act], shall pay to the administrator, in addition to interest as provided in subsection (a), a civil penalty of [$1,000] for each day the report, payment, or delivery is withheld, or the duty is not performed, up to a maximum of [$25,000], plus 25 percent of the value of any property that should have been but was not reported.

(d) A holder who makes a fraudulent report shall pay to the administrator, in addition to interest as provided in subsection (a), a civil penalty of [$1,000] for each day from the date a report under this [Act] was due, up to a maximum of [$25,000], plus 25 percent of the value of any property that should have been but was not reported.

(e) The administrator for good cause may waive, in whole or in part, interest under subsection (a) and penalties under subsections (b) and (c), and shall waive penalties if the holder acted in good faith and without negligence.

Comment

A major weakness of the 1966 Act was its ineffective penalty provision. Although the 1981 Act increased penalties for non-compliance, voluntary compliance with the Act continued to be a problem. In this Act, compliance failures not accompanied by willfulness are dealt with by moderate increases in the applicable penalties, and the administrator simultaneously is given authority to waive both interest and penalties where the holder has attempted in good faith to comply, or where the failure has been due to excusable neglect. Where the holder's failure is willful or fraudulent, and not in good faith, penalties are increased more substantially.

Criminal penalties, which were the sole enforcement mechanism of the 1954 Act and which were retained in the 1981 Act have been eliminated, as they were not effective and rarely, if ever, pursued.

The provision for the discretionary waiver of interest upon a showing of good cause is intended to apply to situations in which the holder has attempted to comply with the Act. Establishment of "good cause" is likely to be difficult where the holder has failed to file a report.

SECTION 25. AGREEMENT TO LOCATE PROPERTY.

(a) An agreement by an owner, the primary purpose of which is to locate, deliver, recover, or assist in the recovery of property that is presumed abandoned is void and unenforceable if it was entered into during the period commencing on the date the property was presumed abandoned and extending to a time that is 24 months after the date the property is paid or delivered to the administrator. This subsection does not apply to an owner's agreement with an attorney to file a claim as to identified property or contest the administrator's denial of a claim.

(b) An agreement by an owner, the primary purpose of which is to locate, deliver, recover, or assist in the recovery of property is enforceable only if the agreement is in writing, clearly sets forth the nature of the property and the services to be rendered, is signed by the apparent owner, and states the value of the property before and after the fee or other compensation has been deducted.

(c) If an agreement covered by this section applies to mineral proceeds and the agreement contains a provision to pay compensation that includes a portion of the underlying minerals or any mineral proceeds not then presumed abandoned, the provision is void and unenforceable.

(d) An agreement covered by this section which provides for compensation that is unconscionable is unenforceable except by the owner. An owner who has agreed to pay compensation that is unconscionable, or the administrator on behalf of the owner, may maintain an action to reduce the compensation to a conscionable amount. The court may award reasonable attorney's fees to an owner who prevails in the action.

(e) This section does not preclude an owner from asserting that an agreement covered by this section is invalid on grounds other than unconscionable compensation.

Comment

This section is intended to enhance the likelihood that the owner of the abandoned property will be located by the efforts of the State, and will receive a return of the property without payment of a "finder's fee." In the past, it appears to have been the practice in many States for unclaimed property locators or heir finders to utilize the State's lists of names and addresses of missing owners to contact them and propose to find their property for them for a fee, before the State has had an opportunity to locate the missing owners. Some States have enacted legislation that prohibits examination of these lists by anyone except an apparent owner or other person having a legal interest in the property, but in many States that kind of provision may be in conflict with the State's public records laws.

Subsections (b) and (d) apply to agreements entered into at any time. These subsections apply to all finders' and locators' contracts, regardless of when the contract is made, including agreements with an owner as a result of a holder providing to private parties, the holder's information regarding an inactive account.

This section is not intended to apply to situations such as the probating of an estate, which may incidentally include a necessity of locating unclaimed property. Agreements in such cases do not have as their principal purpose, the rendition of services to locate, deliver or recover unclaimed property. This section also does not apply to agreements for legal representation of an owner who is claiming property the identity of which is already known to the owner.

SECTION 26. FOREIGN TRANSACTIONS. This [Act] does not apply to property held, due, and owing in a foreign country and arising out of a foreign transaction.

SECTION 27. TRANSITIONAL PROVISIONS.

(a) An initial report filed under this [Act] for property that was not required to be reported before the effective date of this [Act] but which is subject to this [Act] must include all items of property that would have been presumed abandoned during the 10-year period next preceding the effective date of this [Act] as if this [Act] had been in effect during that period.

(b) This [Act] does not relieve a holder of a duty that arose before the effective date of this [Act] to report, pay, or deliver property.

Except as otherwise provided in Section 19(b), a holder who did not comply with the law in effect before the effective date of this [Act] is subject to the applicable provisions for enforcement and penalties which then existed, which are continued in effect for the purpose of this section.

Comment

Paragraph (a) is retained from the 1981 Act and deals with the problem of how far back a holder must check its records to determine what property not subject to the prior Act must be paid to the State under this Act. Thus, property which was not covered by any unclaimed property law prior to adoption of the 1981 Act, but was covered by that Act, continues to be covered by this Act if the obligation was incurred not more than 10 years prior to adoption of the 1981 Act and the statute of limitations is not tolled under Section 19(b). For example, if a State enacts this Act effective January 1, 1996 for property not previously presumed abandoned, the holder must report it if, as of January 1, 1986, it had been unclaimed for the abandonment period. A similar provision is found in Section 11(g) of the 1966 Act.

Paragraph (b) provides that if a State had an unclaimed property law prior to the adoption of this Act, a holder is not relieved of his duty to report and pay over the property abandoned under the Act then existing. Except as otherwise provided in Section 19(b), a holder who did not comply with the law in effect before the effective date of this Act is subject to the applicable provisions for enforcement and penalties which then existed and which are continued in effect for the purpose of this section.

SECTION 28. RULES. The administrator may adopt [pursuant to the Administrative Procedures Act] rules necessary to carry out this [Act].

SECTION 29. UNIFORMITY OF APPLICATION AND CONSTRUCTION. This [Act] shall be applied and construed to effectuate its general purpose to make uniform the law with respect to the subject of this [Act] among States enacting it.

SECTION 30. SHORT TITLE. This [Act] may be cited as the Uniform Unclaimed Property Act (1995).

SECTION 31. SEVERABILITY CLAUSE. If any provision of this [Act] or the application thereof to any person or circumstance is held invalid, the invalidity does not affect other provisions or applications of this [Act] which can be given effect without the invalid provision or application, and to this end the provisions of this [Act] are severable.

SECTION 32. EFFECTIVE DATE. This [Act] takes effect __________.

SECTION 33. REPEALS. The following acts and parts of acts are repealed:

(a)

(b)

(c)

Index

References are to paragraph (¶) numbers

S

T

U